An Addressable Community

Robert Allan Hill

WIPF & STOCK · Eugene, Oregon

AN ADDRESSABLE COMMUNITY

Copyright © 2016 Robert Allan Hill. All rights reserved. Except for brief quotations in critical publications or reviews, no part of this book may be reproduced in any manner without prior written permission from the publisher. Write: Permissions, Wipf and Stock Publishers, 199 W. 8th Ave., Suite 3, Eugene, OR 97401.

Wipf & Stock
An Imprint of Wipf and Stock Publishers
199 W. 8th Ave., Suite 3
Eugene, OR 97401

www.wipfandstock.com

PAPERBACK ISBN: 978-1-5326-8888-1
HARDCOVER ISBN: 978-1-5326-8889-8
EBOOK ISBN: 978-1-5326-8890-4

Manufactured in the U.S.A. JANUARY 28, 2020

Contents

Are We Lovers Anymore? | 1

Surprised by Joy | 9

Peace Like a River | 15

Road Work Tonight | 22

Age to Age | 30

Wrapping Wounds | 36

Generosity | 43

Taste and See that the Lord is Good | 53

Self-Control | 62

What Have We Learned? | 73

Where is Your Passion? | 78

What Are Our Patterns of Welcome? | 84

By What Authority? | 96

What Voice Do You Hear? | 104

Risk Management | 112

Mountainview | 119

Trust | 126

There's No Place Like Home | 134

Surviving Survival | 140

The Great Embankment | 150

A Summer Thanksgiving | 155

The Gifts of Summer | 158

Have a Good Summer | 163

Get Well Soon | 168

The Lamp of the Poor | 175

On Meeting Sin Again for the First Time | 181

Faith Handles Change | 189

For the Freedom We Have Received, Lord Make Us Truly Thankful | 195

A Tale of Two Persistent Women | 201

Family Ties | 209

Come Down Zaccheus! | 215

God at Night | 223

God at Dawn | 231

God at Noon | 243

God at Dusk | 249

Are We Lovers Anymore?
Rev. Robert Hill
September 12, 1999
Text: John 14: 18-26
1 John 4: 7-12

Longing

Fifteen years ago this autumn, I paid a call on one of the inactive members of an inactive church to which we had been assigned. I confess that my motives were not mixed and not entirely selfless. I was calling to see whether the lady of the house, an inactive member, would like to return to the fold, to drink from the living water, to swell the ranks of God's army, —you get the idea.

Quickly, as I sat with husband and wife over tea—it was a hauntingly lovely autumn day, befitting John Donne's line that in heaven it is always autumn—it became clear that she had, yes, taken a different journey, followed a different spirit, and, wonder of wonders, had married outside the faith of her ancestors. She no longer worshipped in the loving embrace of Wesley, Asbury, Erwin and Crossland, but, alas, had married—a Presbyterian. And, to make matters worse, she was attending, however happily I cannot say, a church of that other, aforementioned, religion.

So, unshackled from our earlier roles as potential parishioner and prospective pastor, we could simply talk, and enjoy each other, which we did. He sat silent as a tomb, starched, archly observant, looking somewhat rigid and looking, well, like a Presbyterian. She spoke in words that remain a part of my lifelong canon, my personal bible. We all have one. I wish I had recorded her song. She was remembering the church of her youth. Listen, for I think her portrait resembles a photograph of Asbury First today...

"I look back 20 years at that church. There were children in every nook and cranny growing up with God. The youth were loud and proud. Our Sunday school classes spilled out beyond any hope of fitting the already large building. My class met in the boiler room. I can still sing the songs, "I've got the love of Jesus down in my heart.." I can feel the hand of one older woman who sat next to us—she wore a hat with a bow—slipping candy into my pocket during the sermon. Once, in the winter, my parents and others slept outside in tents—I don't know why. I can

smell the greens at Christmas and the flowers at Easter. A boy from the north side came to my prom, and of course we were married at that altar. I have my 3rd grade Bible over here on the shelf, and here is a photo of my aunt, at the women's bazaar."
She stood up to bring more tea, and concluded: "I look back at that church and ... how can I put it?...there was so much LOVE there!"

As she went into the kitchen, her husband and I sat silent. Men don't talk, do they? If you heard her reverie, her retrospective, her memory, as *nostalgia*—and initially I did too—listen again. "There was so much LOVE there..."

Not nostalgia, but *longing* filled her voice. I can hear it now, after 15 years, after more experience and perspective. She voiced what we, down deep, deeply feel—a longing, a craving, a desire, a hunger, a yearning—for love.

Identity

You have so many disparate claims upon your soul. Your past takes a chunk. Your future takes a bite. Your work takes a cut. Your family takes a slice. Your friends take a part. Your church takes a tithe. You are pulled and prodded by so many, all more or less good, so many forces well beyond human control. And you have grown up, most of you, in America.

It is easy to picture Henry James, that difficult 19th century writer, walking around his Grammercy Park in lower Manhattan, strolling, outlining his plots, drawing his characters. It is also quite easy for us to hear the ringing, native truth, of his epigram, "The purpose of life is to learn something interesting and to do something useful." To learn and to do. School and work.

And what about love? With all our learning and doing, are we lovers anymore?

Spirit

It is a millennial question, perhaps *the* millennial question.

Hither and yon, today, you can hear various religious voices. Some apocalyptic...wars and earthquakes. Some theosophic...my karma ran over my dogma. Some moralistic...viva la culture war. All claiming a spiritual basis. There is a spiritual energy, one could say, afoot at the moment.

For the church of Jesus Christ, these spiritualisms are a mixed blessing. They can be a preparation for the Gospel, and they can be a perversion of the Gospel, and often they are both.

But the Gospel of John affirms the gift of the Spirit of Truth (Jn 14,15), the truth that sets free (Jn 8), that comes as a gift of God in the absence of Christ—another Counselor. It is this Spirit to whom we listen, especially, this autumn.

For the Gospel of John, a much later document than the other Gospels, replaces millennial hope with spiritual truth. Almost all the apocalyptic speculations of the Synpotics, of Paul, and of course of earlier Judaism—speculations on which everything from religious hokum to excessive Y2K anxiety are based—in the Gospel of John have receded into the background to make room for the real "millennial" guest, who is the Comforter, the Advocate, the Spirit, who will speak to us in truth, in Jesus' absence. Which would you rather have? The wild apocalyptic of Mark 13 or the brilliant, quiet beauty of John 14?

If nothing else, a calendrical interest in the new millenium, could at least give us a chance to affirm, and to enjoy the real presence, now, of the Spirit of Truth, which, according to the Christ of the Fourth Gospel, is pretty much all you get by way of apocalyptic thrill, at least until the very close of the age.

And what does this Spirit, of Truth, bring us as its gifts and fruit? The list for Paul and John, of course, begins with love.

The Great Commandment

And love is the heart of it all. "Love one another as I have loved you."(Jn 15).
        "Love your enemies..."
        "If you love those who love you, what reward have you..."
        "God so loved the world..."

Maybe a wisp of a murmur of a rumor of a reminder of such a vision of love is just what we need in our mission oriented age.

Oh, no one, from local church conference to the new and shiny intergalactic conference being designed by our church hierarchy, is more committed to mission than we: our mission is to develop disciples, in worship, education, and care. That is the great commission. In the words of a hymn many like, "Lord you give the great commission, 'heal the sick and preach the word', lest the church neglect its mission, and the Gospel go unheard." Mission is what we do. Good for us.

But it is vision that makes who we are! It is vision that sings to us! It is vision—something God packs into our rucksack along the trail, like manna or eucharist—that makes our hearts full and glad and ready to love!

As important as our mission, the great commission can be, it is nothing compared to the Great Commandment, God's vision of love. Rather, we should sing---

>Lord you give the Great Commandment,
>"love your neighbor as yourself."
>
>Lest the church neglect its vision
>And the Gospel lose its health.
>
>Help us to enjoy your presence
>With renewed humility.
>
>With the Spirit's gifts empower us
>For the love that sets us free.
>
>Lord you call us to your bosom
>"I have called you all my friends."
>
>That the world may see your beauty
>Joy abundant meant for each.
>
>Give us all new rest and leisure
>Closer in community.
>
>With the Spirit's gifts empower us
>For the love that sets us free.

I have to wonder whether some of difficulties we face in our denomination are due to the eclipse of vision by mission. We get so caught up in what we are doing that we lose sight of the great vision *God* has designed!

Are we lovers anymore?

When you bathe in the morning, remembering the water of your baptism, do you see in the mirror a learner and a doer, only? Or, behind that aging furrowed brow, is there something else God has given? Can you name yourself, first, a lover?

Try this, while shaving:

"Today, I am a lover. I have the vision of love God has given. I want to be loved and to love, for I am the beloved child of the living God and nothing short of true love is good enough for God or for me."

Can you sign the love card in the morning, and check your score in the evening?

Robert Frost

Or perhaps all this prattle about love seems too sentimental, too unreal. But love has grit. How surprised I was to hear our Poet laureate, Robert Pinsky, this summer recite a short poem, his favorite, by Robert Frost. A love poem—but tough, hard, true.

> Love at the lips was touch
> As sweet as I could bear
> And when at last that seemed too much
> I lived on air.
>
> That crossed me from sweet things,
> The flow of – was it musk
> From hidden grapevine springs
> Downhill at dusk?
>
> I had the swirl and ache
> From sprays of honeysuckle
> That when they're gathered shake
> Dew on the knuckle.

I craved strong sweets, but those
Seemed strong when I was young;
The petal of the rose
It was that stung.

Now no joy but lacks salt,
That is not dashed with pain
And weariness and fault
I crave the stain.

Of tears, the aftermark
Of almost too much love
The sweet of bitter bark
And burning clove.

When stiff and sore and scarred
I take away my hand
From leaning on it hard
In grass and sand.

The hurt is not enough
I long for weight and strength
To feel the earth as rough
To all my length.

No, love is powerful. Love is as strong as death and as hard as hell (SS6). Joseph loved his betraying brothers, from neither sentiment nor whim. Jeremiah and Job did so too, out of decisions to love. Hosea loved through infidelity and cantankerous selfishness.

Asbury First

Twenty years from now, someone who marries a Presbyterian may remember something about this church, at the turn of the millenium. Will she recall Spirit measured by love? Will she say, at the last, "there was so much love there?"

> *If we speak in the tongues of mortals and angels, but have not love, we are noisy gongs and clanging cymbals. Even if we have prophetic powers and understand all mysteries and all knowledge, and if we have faith so as to remove mountains, but have not love, we are nothing. If we give away all that we have*

and deliver our bodies to be burned, but have not love, we gain nothing.

Our vision is the fruit of the spirit called love. This is my experience:

> Asbury First is patient and kind.
> Asbury First is not jealous or boastful.
> Asbury First is not arrogant or rude.
> You do not insist on your own way.
> You are neither irritable nor resentful.
>
> Together, you bear all things, believe all things, hope.
> All things, endure all things.
> You have faith, hope and love, but the greatest is love.

I need that reminder. For there are administrative moments, opportunities, even in the church—surprise, surprise—that challenge us. I think of the scene in "Patton" where George C. Scott finds his whole army held up by one recalcitrant mule, and ten men trying to move it—he drives up, dismounts, pulls out his white handled revolver, shoots the animal, and the army marches on. That is efficiency, but not love.

And we are called to a vision of love.

Grover's Corners

Thornton Wilder knew it:

Now there are some things we all know, but we don't take'm out and look at 'm very often we all know that *something* is eternal. And it ain't houses and it ain't names and it ain't earth and it ain't even stars…everybody knows in their bones that something is eternal, and that something has to do with human beings…There's something way down deep that's eternal about every human being."

Are we lovers anymore?

Most everybody's asleep in Grover's Corners. There are a few lights on: Shorty Hawkins down at the depot, has just watched the Albany train go by. And at the livery stable, somebody's setting up late and talking— Yes, it's clearing up. There are the stars—doing their old, old crisscross journeys in the sky. Scholars haven't settled the matter yet, but they seem to think there are no living beings up there. Just chalk..and fire. Only this one is straining away, straining away all the time to make something of itself. The strain is so bad, that every sixteen hours everybody lies down and gets a rest...Hm...Eleven o'clock in Grover's Corners—You get a good rest, too.

One Day

For one day, in the fullness of time, Love will reign.

One day there will open space, luxurious freedom for all manner of difference, all kinds of kinds.
One day, the Old Testament says, the lion will lie down with the lamb.

One day, the New Testament says, there will be no crying anymore, nor grief anymore, nor tears, nor shall hurt any or destroy.

One day…and why not start here, and why not begin now?…there will be a real community of gracious love.

The darkness shall turn to the dawning and the dawning to noonday bright and Christ's great kingdom shall come on earth, the kingdom of love and light.

At the new millenium, let us be known that here, with us, it has got to be love all the way, love all the way, love all the way.

SURPRISED BY JOY
By Rev. Robert Hill
September 19, 1999
Text: Philippians 4: 4-7

Caves

Plato, 500 years before Christ, described the world as a great cave, in which dim reflections of an external light sent figures and shadows dancing upon the dank cavernous walls of life.

You do not have to be Greek or a philosopher or a Greek philosopher to appreciate his thought. We have our own spelunking experiences, our own caves. I think we come to church, Sunday, sometimes just hoping that somehow, someone will light a birchbark torch for us, to put a little more warmth and brightness into our cave.

Do you remember the end of *Tom Sawyer*, when Huck and Tom disappear into such a cave? A child of ours dies, a neighbor is raped, a friend falls ill, a job falls through, a limb gives way, a theological certainty cracks and crumbles, a relationship rolls downhill faster than a barrel over Niagara, and we sit among the stalagtites and stalagmites, listening to water drip below or behind, shivering in the near dark.

Not long ago I attended a meeting, in which people I knew well and loved deeply, for some reason became--not themselves, ghosts really of their real persons. They were reticent, somber, afraid, defensive, touchy. I cannot say why. As a newcomer to that circle, I wondered, though, whether there were memories long-toothed but not forgotten that returned with the rejoining of that meeting. Memories of past things—hurts, angers, betrayals—that still hung like mold and mildew on the wet walls of that cave. It felt like we had all gone down into the earth, into a cave.

My childhood friend's father ran a slaughterhouse. Though we didn't go when the cutting was done, you could feel and sense the past brutality there—it hung in the air, it flew through the spirit like a bat through a cave.
Life can become one long stint of hard time in the calaboose.

Prison

St. Paul is writing to the Philippians, and so to us, from a cave. He is to be heard today, from the heart of the Roman prison, where he evidently awaits execution. The Bible records loving, wise and faithful responses to pain, hurt and failure, to exile, and to execution. The Bible records loving, wise and faithful responses to pain, hurt and failure, to exile and to execution. Its remarkable trait is honesty about pain. Paul writes from inside a cave, Jonah in the belly of the provincial whale.

How stunning his word. Paul, in Philippians, writes largely about joy.

Spirit

All of the New Testament, but particularly the letters of Paul and especially the Gospel of John, bear witness to the earliest church's experience of Spirit. "Where the spirit of the Lord is, there is freedom", wrote Paul. And the Epistle of John, in a clear warning to those living in times like ours says, "test the spirits, to see whether they are of God." It is not enough to be full of spirit. Rather, the question is, which spirit? Which spirit?

Here again, the Scripture guides us. As we know people by their deeds, their fruits, so we are to recognize the footprints of the Spirit in the fruit she bestows, ripe in this spiritual season. The Spirit gives…joy.

Scripture

The good news of Jesus Christ, toward which we are summoned today, is throughout a glorious expression of joy. We trust the Bible as it records this open secret. Joy is truly native to God alone, and in God's word this joy enters our life.

Wise men from the east at last find a star and a child and they rejoice with great joy.

Common shepherds hear tidings of great joy, meant for all people, and are shaken to their boots.

Some seed falls on good ground and…you and you and you…receive the word with great joy.

A servant is faithful over a little, and is set over much, and enters…the joy of the master.

There is more joy in heaven over one who repents than over 99 who lack nothing.

Even the evening of his death, Jesus sings with joy his affection for his disciples.

And early women go to the tomb, and finding it empty are turned upside down and leave with fear and great, great joy.

Christ Jesus

Furthermore, in this passage, St. Paul reminds us that the Lord is at hand. Nearby. At hand but not in hand. Absent, yet close. It is the risen Lord whom we worship, in this and every age.

You are Christians, those for whom the pattern of struggle and rest, pain and glory known in Christ Jesus forms the basis of life. You are Christians, attentive to the Spirit who bestows such ripe fruit upon us. And we are in a season of spiritual harvest.

Where I run much of the summer there are apple trees. Most years, in summer, I have only been able to enjoy their sight. This summer, though, the fragrance of ripening fruit has been covering the dirt path along the lake for some weeks. The fruit is ripe, and surprisingly early. The fruit is ripe, and surprisingly ample.

The Spirit bears this fruit, of joy, into our common life, like a baby born into an expectant family. Yours is the family of Christ.

Which is, to put it less gently, to be reminded that we are Christians, not Jesusites. That is, we are Christians, not Jesusites. We worship Christ, the risen Lord, incarnate in Jesus of Nazareth. We are not enslaved, but freed. We are not Jesusites. We do not live in Palestine, nor do we feel we must. We do not wear robes and sandals (except at bedtime), nor do we feel inclined to do so. We do not travel by donkey or chariot. We do not, most of us, speak Aramaic. We do not read Hebrew. We are not in the synagogue on Saturday. We do not think that David wrote all of the Psalms, or that the world is flat, or that the Rock of Gibraltar is the end of civilization. And some of us are not celibate. We are not Jesusites.

The millennial question is not "What would Jesus do?" Rather, the question is "What does the Lord want me to do?" Where do I taste the fruit of the spirit? And blessed as we are with a mission to fulfill, it is the sun of vision, not the moon of mission that awakens us to real life. God is giving us a vision of joy!

Surprised by Joy

1. Worship

Sunday can bring joy. Yes, there is routine and there is attention required. Someone asked my son a couple of years ago about worship in Rochester and he said: "Church is church." Well, yes. Surprisingly, though, joy can overtake us here. In fact, this is an hour meant for joy. In prayer, or worship, or devotion of any real kind we enter the presence of what is given us and leave behind the cloying grasp of what we make. Joy finds us here—freedom in fellowship, through all our silliness and sanctimoniousness.

Do you remember David's dance? King David had won battles, slain foes, built a kingdom, defeated both Goliath and Saul (fightings without and fears within), yet, perhaps due to his many achievements, he could reckon with their limitation. In his older age he searched for joy. Way up north, in the hill country, he found an old ark, a box, mysterious and potent. Last fall, we heard about the ark and its landlord, Obededom the Gittite. The ark still brings joy! And when David found the ark—the Presence of the Holy—he danced! He made merry! He worshipped with song and lyre and harp and tambourine and castanet and cymbal, clad only in an ephod, which lies somewhere between a napkin and a handkerchief. Since God is present, joy is in the air. *Worship is the one time in the week when we don't have to celebrate ourselves.*

Remember the tides of the sea that swell up along the East Coast. And the twinkling stars that stand mute, seemingly motionless, light years away. The great brown fields of upstate New York. Another hand has given us our home and guided our history. Another heart speaks to yours in worship. We can say with Jeremiah, "O Lord, your word was unto me a joy!"

2. Judgment

The invasion of worship by joy is nowhere near as surprising as the next invasive step in joy's march. For after worship, according to Scripture, joy inhabits judgment. Down under the happy word of joy, caused by God, is the awareness that sometime we will need to give an account for our living. Christians have never questioned this. Scripture and Life, to sides of one truth, conspire to remind us. We have exactly one life to live, one string of days, one complex of history and hope, one chance. Sometime, someday we will give an account of how we have lived.

Paul's letter points to the day of Christ toward which we run, and not in vain. You can approach any and all accounting with joy. All that is good will have its just reward. Nothing is ever as good now as it will be later, and nothing is ever as bad now as it seems. Or as Barbara Brown Taylor said this summer, "The bad news is that we do not get what we deserve. And the good news is that we do not get what we deserve. God is more than just. God is gracious." We can approach the border, every border, with a joyful anticipation.

Let us be honest that we are all equally in the dark as we approach ultimate borders.

For some years I traveled across the northern border of our nation almost every weekday. I never lost completely a sense of anticipation and even dread at the border. One very cold morning, near 5 AM, down in the dark beyond Huntingdon Quebec, I stopped in the snow alongside a lost trucker. I lowered the window to catch his question "Ou est le frontiere?" When I had finally translated the simple sentence, "where is the border", I leaned back and haltingly replied in French, but before I could say anymore he caught my accent, or maybe it was my abysmal grammar. Sensing a common soul, and jumping for joy he said, "You speak English!" *There is a surprising joyful anticipation, in faith, as we approach the border. At the border, the same language we have used for a lifetime is in use, the language of grace.* We cross the same border with every confession of sin and every acceptance of pardon. We cross the same border with every awareness of idolatry and every word of forgiveness. We have crossed over before in the daylight, so that when night falls, we need not fear. We know what the Psalmist meant, we can hear it on the lips of Martin Luther King, Sr. at his son's burial, "Weeping may tarry for the night, but joy comes with the morning."

3. Persecution

More surprising still, even than joy's eruption in worship and judgment, is the presence of joy in the hearts of people persecuted. Joy abounds in the fellowship of worship, in the prospect of accounting and a s promise for the persecuted. Mt 5:11 "Blessed are you when men revile you and persecute you and utter all kinds of evil against you falsely on my account. Rejoice and be glad.

This seems at first a hard word for us, partly because we do not think we know much about persecution, and partly because we doubt it as an occasion of joy. We sense masochism and recoil.

Yet, I think some of you have known more persecution than you think. Some have learned the hard way that real virtue is not always rewarded on this earth. Some have paid dearly for speaking and living a less than popular truth. Some have seen the cost of accepting a calling in life: a life with purpose is not necessarily one free of pain. Some have been exposed to the difficulty of having to choose between home and work, between friendship and honesty, between the short term and the long haul. Look back. I bet you are heartened most by the running you did with unfairly added leg weights. In the long run, there is sweet, sweet joy in choosing the narrow gate and the straight path. The altar of this church and its cross are signs of promise that when persecution comes it will also carry a kind of joy. You can read about it in Philippians, or in C.S. Lewis' book, **Surprised by Joy**, or, probably, by getting to know well the person sitting next to you in the pew.

Vision

One day, in the fullness of time, Joy will reign.

One day, in the fullness of time, says the Old Testament, the joy of the Lord will be our strength.

One day, in the fullness of time, says the New Testament, they that sow in tears shall reap in joy.

One day—and why not begin here and why not start now?—we will count it all joy when various trials beset us.

I tell you truly—and base your struggles upon it---"weeping may tarry for the night, but joy comes with the morning!"

"Peace Like a River"
By Rev. Robert Hill
September 26, 1999
Text: John 14: 25-31

1. Be Reconciled

A man I know fairly well decided in the mid 1970's, after some struggle, to invest his work life in the working life of the church. As he was completing his college degree, he began to look for seminary programs, and also to consider their cost. A chaplain at his school apparently told him about the Rockefeller foundation, which for many years had provided full funding for at least one year of seminary education, especially meant for those who were struggling to find their way into the ministry.

After these months of heart wrenching deliberation and discernment—he knew that ordination constituted a kind of financial suicide—he was heartened to learn that some scholarship support might be available. He sent off the forms and waited. One day, an invitation came to interview for the Rockefeller grant. Eagerly, he drove to a nearby airport and met in a small hotel room with three people, a layman of color, a large female denominational executive, and a quiet Caucasian clergyman. The three reviewed his application, his Phi Beta Kappa award, his GRE scores and grades, his various achievements, and his personal statement. "You know, two years ago, you would have been an easy recipient of this award. For years, we have been looking for men like you. Your record, your statement and your interview have been fine. However, two years ago we made a decision to direct our funds mostly into hands of women and people of color who feel a calling to ministry. Since it is fairly late in the year, and you will have to make plans, we feel we need to be direct with you. We are sorry, but wish you well." And with a laugh, they added, "You just are not the right sex or color!"

My friend left the airport hotel ever so invisibly and ever so lastingly embittered. For years, he carried the mental photograph of the hotel room, Holiday Inn decor, the three New York foundation representatives, their wearied and joyless faces, their matter of fact rejection. Over the years, he saw them seated there, in the airport room. He saw them in seminary, late at night, when he worked a graveyard shift to pay for school. He saw them when others went downtown and he went to study. He saw them the night he barely got home from work in time to take his wife to the hospital, gravely ill in the 6th month of pregnancy. He saw them when one of the recipients came to him for help in Greek.

The scene haunted him over the years. He would bring it up with me at reunions, when we inspected what condition our condition was in. When Bishops were elected on the basis of skin color, he saw them. When appointments and superintendents were selected on the basis of gender, he saw them. When, across meeting rooms, it became clear that his voice, eyes, height, skin color, gender and orientation were working fully against him, he saw them. When colleagues welcomed him in spite of his sex and color, he saw them. When he lived for a decade under the watchful resentment of a supervisor, on the dark side of a dark moon, he saw them. When he paused to record the demise of the church during this same period of selective affirmative action toward others, he saw them. They sat perpetually in the hotel room memory, a kind of trinity for the tragic sense of life. And more than one ever could explain, they fed a kind of soul war, a dis--ease in work, ministry and life.

I had a chance to talk with him last year. With some fear and trembling, I asked him about the tragic trinity from the far off airport hotel.

"Well", he careful replied, "it is a privilege to live long enough to learn some things. Yes, I still see them and hear their laugh. But I see it all differently now. It was good for me to work nights. Whatever does not kill us makes us stronger! It was good for me to feel a little instance of what some feel every day, rain or shine—sheer prejudice. It was good to be forced to give up what otherwise I would have had to easily and perhaps not appreciated, and to see the open space provided for the talents of others. And I have now learned what good that enforced opening has done. I feel ashamed that so much feeling over so many years was attached to that one episode, when life is so teemingly full of good, of God. About a year ago, I saw the tragic trinity for the last time, and realized that I had no feeling when their mental image appeared. I have peace, like a river, flowing round about me there. Somehow God has given me that peace. In fact, I believe that God was trying for some time to give it to me, and to fix my heart, but I didn't want it. I guess I rather enjoyed my self-righteous bitterness. I was so busy with my mission that I lost the sight of God's vision of peace. What a gift is peace!"

2. I Love You

Several years ago, a young man grew up in the North woods, saying little, like his neighbors. In fact, he found that he was frightfully shy, especially around members of the other gender. But since he did show some academic ability, and twice answered questions out loud in 12th grade history class, he was recommended for border guard duty. He passed the exam in the summer after graduation, and for the next 35 years drove out to the river crossing, took up his post, and used the only English he ever needed, in four questions: "What is your name? Where are you from? How long will you be here? Do you have anything to declare?" These four interrogatives formed his whole volubility, his whole working life. He lived with his parents in Massena, and then when they died, he lived alone, until he retired.

Then he was seized after retirement with a profound desire. He could not name it, but he felt it just as well.

He traveled 30 miles east, and bought a plot of land looking down over the St. Lawrence. On the land, he built with his own hands a fine log cabin, with a porch facing northwest to catch both the river view and the sunset. He covered the house with a bright orange roof, like many he had seen down in Cornwall, on border guard training trips. He marked off a garden, and planted it full. He beamed with pride when the young pastor would bike by and say, " 'Love that orange roof."

One Saturday morning, as he finished breakfast on Route 11 at the Cherry Knoll restaurant, he found across him in the booth a two month old copy of *Guns and Ammo* magazine. Over coffee he leafed through it, absentmindedly, until he came to the back pages, where he discovered an advertisement—women from Asia were looking for American husbands! They were willing to risk marrying! Even someone whom they didn't know! Was he interested?! If he was, would he write to PO BOX 400 Vancouver, BC?! He was! He did!

Several months later, in the week of the January thaw, when the temperature swung up all the way above zero at noon some days, a knock came at the door of his orange roofed cabin. Putting on his shirt, he went and opened the door. There stood a middle aged, medium height, medium build woman, from China. She carried a single suitcase, and a purse. "Hello" he said. "Yes", she answered.

From that day forward, they lived and worked together like Adam and Eve. They kept the finest house. They produced the finest garden. On market days they wore the broadest smiles. Sitting silently in church they held hands, at a minimum. They were so evidently happy and so clearly enraptured, that they incited a certain amount of jealousy. She in particular was vilified in the neighborhood gossip, in which there was speculation about the rapturous nature of their love. But they cared not at all. They tilled their garden and trimmed their hedges and lived in love.

They never spoke. He wouldn't speak. She couldn't speak. So, they never spoke. They simply worked together and watched each other. At night, they would fry their eggs, side by each, and cook the Canadian bacon real tough, and pop open two cans of Labatts Blue. He would read National Geographic, and she would read her only book, a dog-eared copy of the Tao Te Ching. But as the sun set out to the west, trimming the frozen river with orange and red, they would stop, and look at each other, and then recite their evening litany, each to the other, before they silently slipped, on tiptoe, upstairs.

He: "What is your name"

She: "Yes."

He: "Where are you from?"

She: "Yes"

He: "How long will you be here?"

She: "Yes"

He: "Do you have anything to declare?"

She: "Yes. I LOVE YOU."

Then she would ask and he would answer...yes...yes...yes... "Do you have anything to declare? "Yes. I LOVE YOU." At night in dark he would think, "Now I am at peace. Looking back, I guess God was always trying to give me peace, but I wasn't ready to receive it." What a gift the Spirit makes in peace!

3. Endowment

Setta Moe had been a member of her own church, like many of those we honor today at our church, for over 50 years. In her youth, the church had grown to a great expanse, supporting the construction of a spanking new facility, and the advancement of the cause of Christ--as she liked to put it: "a combination of deep personal faith and active social involvement."

In those years, especially for some reason once the new building was finished, Setta's church ran into troubles, troubles. One day in church she looked into the stained glass windows beside her, and uttered a little prayer of grief. For some reason, her church had been saddled with pastoral problems. The various episodes came to her mind. One involved a painful personality conflict which threatened to divide the church. She prayed, "Lord why did that happen?" Another involved sheer sloth, end of ministry laziness by the church's leader. "Lord, why did you let that happen?" One involved real bad misbehavior by a minister, someone she had come to love and respect. "Lord, why did that have to happen here?" Another involved a marital shipwreck, painful to endure and equally painful to observe. "Lord, why did that happen?"

Setta laid all these hurts before God and looked across the sanctuary as the sermon rolled on. She could see her beloved sisters and brothers in Christ. They were listening. They were learning. And they even had grown to love their leaders, all the earlier betrayals to the contrary notwithstanding. Setta prayed again, "Lord, help us to listen and to learn and to love more. But Lord, I pray, Lord, help us also to *trust*, to trust our leadership."

Setta was quiet again. A thought jarred her. She looked up again at the stained glass, and remembered all that her parents and others had sacrificed, before the troubled years, to build the church. What gifts they made! It occurred to her that, just as her parents had endowed the congregation with a great building, she also might build trust and future ministry by endowing the expense of the minister's salary. She mused, "I wonder what it would cost to permanently endow, permanently cover the cost of one of the minister's positions? That would open a new day for ministry here—in part by the trust it would express in leadership for the future."

The sermon that day escaped Setta's attention. But her heart was full and her mind was resolved as she left worship. What peace, after so many painful years, so many hard hurts, what peace filled her heart! She reflected, "I guess God was trying for some time to give me such peace, but I wasn't ready to receive it. What an invasive gift of the Spirit is peace!"

4. Vision

I need to ask you a question that may be life and death, heaven and hell in the balance: Is God trying to give you peace? Are you listening?

One day, in the fullness of time, Peace like a river will reign.

One day, in the fullness of time, the Old Testament says, "of the increase of his government and of peace there shall be no end" (Isaiah 9).

One day, in the fullness of time, the New Testament says, in that great watershed verse of Romans 5:1, "Therefore, since we are justified by faith, we have peace with God through our Lord Jesus Christ."

One day, in fullness of time—and why not start this fall and why not begin in the bosom of Asbury First?—Peace like a river will attend our way.

One day, from the least to the greatest, all will know the peace of God—drowning past bitterness, embracing arms for embracing, building trust for future good—which, finally, passes all understanding.

The fruit of the spirit is peace.

"ROAD WORK TONIGHT"
By Rev. Robert Hill
October 17, 1999
Text: Job 19: 1-12, 23-29

An Adversary

Suffering is the single greatest obstacle to faith for many good people today. The wiser and more sensitive the soul, the more potent is suffering, especially unearned and innocent suffering, as an adversary to faith. I assume that every Sunday at least one of us is on the brink of despair, on the edge of fragmentation, on account of suffering. Says Job, "He has kindled his wrath against me and counts me as his adversary...my hope he has pulled up like a tree."

Neither the shame of sin nor the fear of death has such power. The poison arrow in life's quiver is unearned suffering, the tragic dimension of life. Ever since Adam donned his fig leaf and Cain slew his brother and giants walked the land, this great Adversary to faith has been striding the earth, like a colossus.

Why should the innocent suffer?

Who can answer Job's complaint?

How can I believe in a God of love, when around me I hear the cries of the hurt? I hear Elie Wiesel, in the death camps, saying that God is swinging on the rope in the face of the hung child. I hear Arthur Ashe, dying of Aids, saying that the experience of racism is far worse than his illness. I hear Werner Klemperer bear witness to the slowly tightening noose around his Jewish neck in the Germany of the 1930's. I hear the report that surgical abortion is being used widely today for gender selection. I hear Frank McCourt tell about licking greasy newspaper to survive childhood in Ireland. I hear Agate Nasal tell of unspeakable horrors inflicted on defenseless women on the eastern front in the 1940's. And these all bear witness to hurt in history-with another list needed for hurricane and earthquake and tornado and plague, nature's own force against us.

And then there is your night, your illness, your entrapment, your hunger, your hell. You never know when it will strike. On a sunny warm day, I drive along the highway, carefree, and see the prophetic signboard—"Caution: Road Work Tonight". And I remember a drive this summer, from midnight to 7am, down through the heart of Pennsylvania, in the pitch black, with occasional spotlights and blowtorches and melting tar and 100° heat, and a few forlorn souls driving south, into the heart of darkness, while all along the way, the citizens are comfortably asleep.

Here is where faith flounders.

The Question: Why does God permit suffering?

If this were a philosophical problem mainly or only, we would not need a pulpit, for we could turn to the sages, from Socrates to the New Age, and find a range of teaching. But suffering is a very personal matter.

An incurable illness, of unknown origin.

An untimely death, and with it generations of lingering difficulty.

Sickness that with hope deferred sickens the heart.

You are not spared suffering, nor given inside information with which to comprehend it.

Says Job, "I call aloud, but there is no justice."

God permits suffering. God's world east of Eden includes, alongside radical human freedom, the real, the surreal dimension of tragic hurt, the dark night of the soul.

As William Sloane Coffin said, at his son's funeral, a son who died along some New England roadside at night: "God gives us minimum protection, but maximum support."

When you see your own children harmed, or worse, when you are driving down the endless highway, amid the terror of night road work, you have little to say. And standing just to the side of the road, watching and smiling, there stands a figure in a grey flannel suit, satanic in demeanor, smiling and composed, whispering, "You'll never understand this, never."

The Response: Patience empowers us to withstand even when we cannot understand.

Jesus Christ may enter your life, at this point, along this night road crowded with terror. So utterly gracious is He that you may not notice without at least a homiletical whisper of introduction.

He makes no philosophical response. To Plato he leaves the thought that really, suffering is illusory, unreal. To Aeschylus he leaves the proposition that suffering produces wisdom. To Boethius he leaves the idea that suffering is instructive, since we need truth more than we need comfort. To Freud he leaves the deep insight that all life, all creativity springs forth from some birth-pangs of suffering. He makes no philosophical response.

Jesus meets us inside our suffering.

He meets us when we ask to withstand even when we cannot understand. He is reliable and you can trust Him to guide you through all the night road work of your journey. You will be aroused by his presence when your heart is touched by the spirit of patience.

We find Jesus in the longsuffering of our people.

In Jacob who worked for 7 years for Leah and another 7 for Rachel.

In the Old Testament teaching about the utter patience of divine love—throughout the exodus (Exodus 34), in the heart of the wilderness (Numbers 14), in psalms of lament (Psalm 86), in prophetic pain (Jeremiah 15).

Can't you hear Jeremiah crying out: "O Lord, thou knowest: remember me and visit me and take vengeance upon my persecutors. In thy patience, take me not away, now that for thy sake I bear reproach."?

And here he comes, prefigured in Job.

In Hosea, patient with adultery.

In Isaiah, awaiting resurrection.

In John the Baptist, patient before death.

In Paul, and Peter, and John of Patmos.

You know, we can get so immersed in our own mission—and how important a clear mission is—that we lose sight of the vision. We can attend so fully as a church to developing disciples in worship, education and care, that we no longer are ready and open to receive and taste the fruit of the spirit, which falls to us like a ripe apple in autumn---Patience.

Sometimes, when we miss Jesus amid all our activity, we may find him again, or rather be found again by him, entering the hurt of his people…standing with the ill, ministering with the aging, incarnate to the lonely, showering himself on the pains of this life, present as the charismatic fullness of real life—patience, patience, patience.

I heard Alice Walker say recently that she has decided to slow down a little in life so that whatever is waiting to catch up with her will have a little easier time of it.

Contrary to the worn epigram, patience is not a virtue, for that would make it merely a human trait. Patience is a gift, the fruit of the Holy Spirit, to be consumed not controlled, enjoyed not enjoined.

We sing:

> *Rescue the perishing*
> *Care for the dying*
> *Snatch them in pity*
> *From sin and the grave.*

We might better sing:

> *Visit the perishing*
> *Sit with the dying*
> *Near them taste patience*
> *That outlasts the grave.*

Jesus Christ empowers us to withstand suffering, even when, honestly, we have no way to understand it. He reminds us that we can't always get what we want, but if we try sometimes we just might find that we get what we need—manna, word, eucharist, and, yes, spirit.

We have this treasure in earthen vessels, to show that the transcendent power belongs to God and not to us. We are afflicted in every way but not crushed; perplexed but not driven to despair; persecuted not forsaken; struck down but not destroyed; always carrying in the body the death of Jesus, so that the life of Jesus may also be manifest in our bodies.

For this slight momentary affliction is preparing for us an eternal weight of glory beyond all comparison, because we look not to the things that are seen, but to the things that are unseen; for the things that are seen are transient, but the things that are unseen are eternal.

Suffering, patience, endurance, hope.

Here is Jesus Christ, publicly portrayed for you as crucified, who, unlike any merely religious representation of God, invades the depth, the troubled night road of life, to claim that darkness is as light for Him and for his own.

This is why I carry around a few sentences that Paul Scherer wrote in a much more patient era:

"I know the things that happen: the loss and the loneliness and the pain...But there is a mark on it now: as if Someone who knew that way himself, because he had traveled it, had gone on before and left his sign; and all of it begins to make a little sense at last—gathered up, laughter and tears, into the life of God, with His arms around it!"

The challenge: Feasting daily on the fruit of the spirit called patience.

May we feast together on Patience, the very fruit of the very Spirit of the very living God. You might call this the patience of Job, though your meaning would invert the conventional wisdom.

For Job's patience meant rebuke of suffering, as he howls along through 28 chapters.

For Job's patience meant bearing witness to what his experience had taught him, all along for 28 chapters.

For Job's patience meant putting God on trial, or trying to, for 28 chapters.

For Job's patience meant a brutal authenticity about the silence of God in much of life, though for him it was, always, *GOD'S* silence.

Road Work Tonight

Look: up ahead. Do you see it? The sign for this quadrant of the twilight zone carries a prophecy: "Road work tonight." You are invited to prepare for the journey and to stuff your rucksack with fruit, falling today like manna from heaven. Patience....Patience....Patience....Love suffereth long and is kind...

May Job's patience fill our hearts, our homes, our church, our denomination, and, one day, our world.

May our hearts burn with a worry killing patience.

May our homes teem with a frenzy killing patience.

May our church, Asbury First, overflow with an anxiety killing patience.

May our denomination brim with a war drowning patience, abounding in the fine arts of ecclesiastical diplomacy.

May our world, one day, find space enough and time enough and courage enough to wander, in ecstasy, through the meadow of Patience.

One Day

For one day, in the fullness of time, Patience will reign.

One day there will emerge a people filled with a passion for compassion.

One day, as the Old Testament says, in the heart of difficulty with Job we will "sing songs in the night". And, "they that wait upon the Lord shall renew their strength. They shall mount up with wings as eagles. They shall run and not be weary. They shall walk and not faint."

One day, as the New Testament says, the "longsuffering" grace of God will prevail. Suffering will produce patience, and patience endurance, and endurance hope, and hope shall not disappoint us, because of the love of God made manifest in Jesus Christ.

One day…and why not start here, and why not begin now?…there will be a real community setting a patient beat, a cadence of quiet endurance.

One day, in the fullness of time, Patience will reign.

> *O Day of God draw nigh*
> *In beauty and in power*
> *Come with thy timeless judgments now*
> *To match our present hour.*
>
> *Bring to our troubled minds*
> *Uncertain and afraid*
> *The quiet of a steadfast faith*
> *Calm of a call obeyed.*

"AGE TO AGE"
By Rev. Robert A. Hill
October 24, 1999

Beloved, Sisters and Brothers in Christ, our children bring us so much week by week. We also recognize that the parade in which they have been involved is one into which we are folded, day by day and especially week by week. As they are processing down the center aisle we too find our places in a parade of God's faithful, God's covenant people through many years and many places and at many times.

This is the parade of Abraham, and of Isaac and of Jacob. This is the parade of Deborah and of Ruth and of Esther. This is the parade of Peter and James and John and this is the parade of the people of God at Asbury First in the year of our Lord 1999.

We are invited by the scripture read today to remember ourselves as part of God's people in the world. "I am the vine and you are the branches" and through God's fruitful presence among us God's spirit is giving life to the fruit of God's spirit in love, joy and peace and kindness and goodness, especially today in faith and in gentleness and in self—control.

Yes, we are the people of God and we have joined together in this moving, on-going parade of faith through time.

Because the Bible speaks directly to us and we honor its place in our common life today, we have asked four lay witnesses to raise their voices and personally to bear witnesses to the fruit of the spirit, the gift of faith and I'm so happy to introduce to you first of all, Barbara Steen.

"AGE TO AGE"
By Barbara Steen
Test: I Corinthians 13: 13

The scripture I have chosen for this morning is I Corinthians 13th Chapter, 13th Verse (J.B. Phillips Translation) ,"In this life, we have three great lasting qualities-faith, hope and love-but the greatest of them is love."

As some of you know, Tom, my late husband and I lost out two children-Susie and Tom. The greatest gift we have is God's love-the essence of the spiritual life is love-that's really our only security-everything else can be snatched away. The things that have helped me are my deep faith, my love of God, my prayer life and all the love and support I receive from my friends everywhere.

I always remember Tom saying to me and to his congregations: "Our children are loaned to us, that we might learn from them-they have much to teach us. In life we have to learn attachment and detachment, for we only keep what we give away."

God is very real to me-I believe in the Holy Spirit-and I do feel His presence continually at my side. I am grateful to Him for still have a zest for life! That doesn't mean I don't have sad moments and lonesome days-of course I do-but God is the One I depend on.

I have learned many things regarding my spiritual journey. I need to make sure that my inner life and outer life are going in the same direction. Gordon Cosby, a dear friend, said, "One of the great weakness of our lives today is that, while we have talked about the inward journey, I doubt if any of us has actually worked with the inner life in the depth that is crucial." I feel strongly that this church, Asbury First, has this as one of its top priorities. Right, Bob?

I will close with these thoughts that have great meaning for me, and that ties into the scripture I have chosen for this morning. Tom said at Susies memorial service:

> *"The love God gave today,*
> *Must be spent today,*
> *Not tomorrow, or the next day,*
> *But today.*
>
> *You can't store up love,*
> *Love has to be experienced day by day.*
> *God only comes alive, as you spend*
> *That which He gives you each day.*
> *It is not given to hoard,*
> *You have to love and serve God each day."*

And you know what? That's where the blessing is! AMEN.

REV. ROBERT HILL

These Beloved are the voices of the people of God, for one and all. Love is given and spent day by day. We receive God's grace like Manna in the wilderness, like euchrist morning and evening. Like the fruit of the spirit that is to be enjoyed, not enjoined. That is to be consumed not controlled. That is to be received, not achieved.

You are the people of God, your hallmark, your watchword is not I must, I shall, it is rather I may, I can. The world is full of potential. For freedom, Christ has set us free, and the Holy Scripture at 66 books together is a library about freedom. The bible is a book about freedom. So the pulpit is about freedom, and the church is the defense of the voice of freedom and the book of freedom.

We are celebrating today the glorious liberty of the children of God, and so from Age to Age we hear the voices of faith, faith is a gift we receive. Today we also have the honor of our high pulpit, fifteen feet above contradiction. A voice of the future to Jessica Dutcher who speaks to us about a boat and a storm and a Lord. (Jessica Dutcher speaks)

"FROM AGE TO AGE"
By Jessica Scott-Dutcher
Text: Mark 4: 35-41

This scripture I chose was Mark 4: 35-41, where Jesus stills a storm. On that day when everyone had come he said to them, "Let us go across to the other side" and leaving the crowd behind they took him with them in the boat, just as he was. Other boats were with him. A great wind storm arose, and the waves beat the wind to the boat. So the boat was already beginning to be swamped, but he was in the stern, asleep in the cushion. And they woke him up and said to him, "Teacher do you not care that we are perishing? He woke up and rebuked the wind and said to the sea, Peace, be still", and then the wind ceased and there was a dead calm. He said to them, "Why are you afraid? Have you still no faith?" and they were filled with great awe and then they said to one another, "Who is this that did this? Even the wind and the sea obey him.

I've always liked this story, ever since my mom read it to me when I was little. In the book, "The Mouse's Story", the mouse lives on the fishing boat Jesus took out to sea that day. I can just imagine being the mouse on the ship, with the storm crashing and banging, and Jesus just sleeping.

I like this story because it reminds me that in the middle of our troubles, like the storm, Jesus can calm us down.

REV. ROBERT HILL

In the midst of the storms of life Jesus can always calm us down by bringing to us the fruit of the spirit in this season of spiritual harvest. You are a people on a journey. You're a part of the parade of God's covenant folk. You also know at your heart, in the marrow of life that freedom is our great birthright, our living sense of God's presence.

But God also in the scripture gives witness to your life as a part of a community. The scripture is a communal book. It has a history, it doesn't fall from heaven without any intervening hand, it is human as well as divine it requires interpretation and so as the people of God we invest carefully and heavily in the interpretation of scripture. In the building and maintenance of a beautiful nave, in the setting of a high pulpit, in the support of clergy and other interpreters, the job of the interpreter, the main job is to be an advocate for that which is interpreted.

And so today we are a part of a community in which we know freedom, through which we parade in time. One among us, Robert Payne is going to speak to us about a parable and about a sower, I believe. Bob. (Bob Payne speaks).

"FROM AGE TO AGE HARVEST TIME"
By Bob Payne
Text: John 15: 1-12

In Mark 4:26-29 Jesus is explaining the kingdom of God to his disciples through the parable of the growing seed: He also said, "This is what the kingdom of God is like. A man scatters seed on the ground. Night and day, whether he sleeps or gets up, the seed sprouts and grows, though he does not know how. All by itself the soil produces grain-first the stalk, then the head, then the full kernel in the head. As soon as the grain is ripe, he puts the sickle to it, because the harvest has come." Earlier in

Mark 4, Jesus referred to the seeds that had fallen on the good soil as multiplying thirty, sixty, or even a hundred times.

As I was growing up, my parents had introduced me to this story, and as I look back, it seems that there was a lot of reinforcement of it throughout the years. Things like the part of the Lord's Prayer about being led not into temptation, things like the golden rule, and even a lecture by Stephen Covey about valuing personal integrity above personal gain. Some of you have heard me mention a little prayer about asking for direction amid some of life's trying situations. As I pass through middle age, I start to see evidence of the value of adhering to this guidance. But the harvest I am reaping isn't material. The real harvest is the overwhelming feeling of support around me in all of my activities and responsibilities, whether it is at work, during family time, or as part f the Stephen Ministry. Sure, some seeds will not ripen, but consistent sowing of the good seeds will eventually be rewarded.

And speaking of seeds, as the chairperson of our Stewardship Work Area, I have also planted some in the form of pledge cards in the ritual of friendship tablets, so that any among us who might need a little reminder about our current pledge campaign could help Asbury plan its ministries for the coming year. In an earlier announcement, I referred to opportunities facing Asbury that are dependent upon additional funding, and asked if we could all consider taking a step in increasing our pledge. One way that some could do this is to continue pledging at the level which included the roof campaign, even after the conclusion of the roof project mid-next-hear.

Keep planting! Share the joy of harvest!

REV. ROBERT HILL

Thank you Bob. What a picture of the divine Bob has shared with us. Did you see it? A sower went out to sow.

God is not worried. God does not fret. God does not have a furrowed brow. What a picture of optimism! Sisters and Brothers in Christ, we worship Jesus Christ, crucified and risen. The scripture is the story of the people of God, born for freedom. On parade in history, known in the person and work of Jesus Christ, Lord and Savior.

We meet today at the intersection. At the dawn of the east, with the twilight of the west, of the cool of the north, and the calm of the south, of the transcendence, presence and love of God with the imminent, humble, earthly Christ, of male and female, black and white, rich and poor, one and all here at ground zero.

The scripture reminds us of our identity, our names, our baptismal covenant in Christ Jesus. So today we hear two voices that are a little older than I currently am and two voices that are a little younger and our final lay witness is Mr. Jessie Welch who loves the scripture from Ephesians about the whole armor of God. Jessie has received his Bible today, let us give ear to this word.

"AGE TO AGE"
by Jessie Welch
Text: Ephesians 6: 13-17

Therefore, take a whole armor of God that you may be able to withstand in the evil day, and having done all, to stand. Stand therefore, having girded your loins with truth, and having put on the breastplate of righteousness, and having shod your feet with the equipment of the gospel of peace; faith, with which you can quench all the flaming darts of the evil. And take the helmet of salvation, and the sword of the Spirit, which is the word of God.

REV. ROBERT HILL

Thank you Jessie.

And are we not on parade, and are we not freed by God's grace and do we not receive the gift of the spirit of God known in faith, are we not bound together in community do we not find our name in that name that that is above every name? Beloved let love be genuine, hate what is evil, hold fast what is good, love one another with mutual affection, outdo one another in showing honor, never lag in zeal, be ardent in spirit, serve the Lord, rejoice in your hope, be patient in tribulation, be constant in prayer, contribute to the needs of the saints. Practice hospitality. Amen.

"WRAPPING WOUNDS"
By Rev. Susan S. Shafer
October 31, 1999
Text: II Corinthians 1:1-7

Rachel Naomi Remen, M.D. has contributed a nourishing collection of poignant, healing stories in her book KITCHEN TABLE WISDOM. A story entitled "In Flight" is a place to begin this day in listening to our Scriptural Word. She tells the story of boarding a flight to San Francisco, sinking in her seat with relief and belting herself in. Seated in the bulkhead on the aisle, she noticed an elegant gentleman next to her in the seat by the window. She took out a murder mystery and began reading. When lunch was served an hour later, she was deeply engrossed in her book. She was given a salad, a bagel, and a pint container of yogurt. (Times have changed.)

"Continuing to read, I tucked into my plate until my seatmate gasped in dismay. Turning my head slightly, I saw that he had upset his full container of yogurt onto the floor, spilling it on his shoes, the rug, and part of his overnight bag. He was looking out the window. I waited for him to take some action, but nothing happened. Looking down again, I saw that he was slowly drawing back his right foot, the shoe covered with yogurt, until it was almost hidden under the seat. I could not see his left foot clearly. His ankle was swollen and a metal brace emerged from his shoe. His left leg was paralyzed."

"The seat belt sign was on. I reached up and rang for the flight crew. No one responded. Some time later when the drink cart arrived, I indicated to the floor and asked the stewardess for a wet towel. Before I could say anything more, she went ballistic: 'There are four hundred and fifty-two people on this plane' she snapped. 'I'm doing the best I can; you'll just have to wait.' Her defensiveness baffled me. We looked at each other in silence. Then I realized that it had simply not occurred to her that I was a participant. 'If you bring me a wet towel, I will be able to get that up,' I said quietly. She hesitated and I wondered if she had heard. Then she raised her eyebrows, turned on her heel, and brought a towel. After the cart had passed us, I looked again at my seatmate. He continued to look fixedly out the window, his left foot motionless, his right hidden under the seat."

"I used to love to fly but I find it difficult now," I said, and I told him that in the past few years I have had trouble seeing. Still looking out the window, he told me that eight months ago he had suffered a stroke and now had no feeling in either of his arms from his fingertips to his elbows. Yet, he had flown halfway across the country to spend some time with his son. He was speaking almost in a whisper and I leaned toward him to hear. 'Since my stroke I am incontinent,' he said, 'I have to wear a diaper.' I nodded, marveling at the choreography of this chance seating arrangement. 'I have an ileostomy,' I said. (He turned to look at me and asked what that was, and I explained that my large intestine had been surgically removed and I wear a plastic appliance attached to the side of my abdomen to collect my partly digested food. I added, 'Even after thirty years, I am concerned that it may leak. Especially on a plane.') After a moment, we smiled at each other. Then he looked at the towel I was holding and I looked down at his feet. As we talked he had brought his right foot out from under the seat. 'May I?' I asked, motioning with the towel. Kneeling, I began to wipe his shoes. As I was doing this, he leaned forward and told me, 'I used to play the violin...'

"When I returned the towel to the galley, two flight attendants thanked me profusely. Later, another, who was serving me a coke thanked me again. Nothing further was said but when I left the plane, the pilot was standing in the doorway. I smiled and nodded as always but he stopped me. 'Thanks,' he said, and pressed something into my hand. Halfway up the jetway, I looked at it. It was the little gift that the airlines often give to children after a flight, a pin in the shape of a pair of wings."

"A flight crew deals with hundreds of thousands of Americans every year. Their surprised reaction to a simple act of kindness is chilling. Perhaps we are no longer a kind people. More and more, we seem to have become numb to the suffering of others and ashamed of our own suffering. Yet suffering is one of the universal conditions of being alive. We all suffer. We have become terribly vulnerable, not because we suffer but because we have separated ourselves from each other."

How often is it that we try to ignore suffering, our own and other peoples' because we want to be happy? Yet, becoming numb to suffering will not make us happy. The part in us that feels suffering is the same part that feels joy.

Remen knows what we are reminded through Christ. To be human is to be wounded, and more than that, our Scripture would tell us to enter into another's woundedness and our own. To wrap another's wounds and our own is truly to know life, its meaning and its beauty. In our own woundedness we can become a source of life for others, the presence of Christ.

Emboldened by the sacred listening of another to my own woundedness and by prayerfully listening to the woundedness of others, I have an unfolding awareness that brings me into the crucible where creation's pain and God's healing meet and mingle. My understanding of this healing ministry is undergirded by an understanding and experience of the complexities of life and the paradoxes of God's healing.

I do not seek so much today to fathom the mystery of suffering as to touch the mystery of faith responding to suffering.

> God does not send us suffering, and yet…suffering is deeply drenched with the palpable Presence of God and the possibility of splendor…..
> God, as we see through Jesus, passionately longs to heal all wounds, and yet…so many wounds are not healed the way in which we would want….
> God calls us to be healers, and yet…within the healing stance we experience our own woundedness…
> God asks us to share our hearts as living bread, and yet…not to let the breaking and sharing to become self-shredding…
> God asks us to reverence the mystery of suffering and yet…this reverence can be distorted into tragic, complacent blocking of Christ's passion to heal.
> God invites us into the mystery of the Cross, and yet….God promises to overcome and resurrect us from that Cross.
> God saves by stepping into the fray of human life and disrupting the course of all the raging waters that can sweep us into seeming oblivion.

Trained by the discerning eye of faith, we begin to recognize that Light, Christ's Presence, which the darkness of human suffering cannot overcome. And as this vision grows stronger, we can affirm with the confidence of the psalmist: "I know that I shall see goodness of the Lord in the land of the living." (Psalm 27:13, GRAIL).

Henri Nouwen was one of that great company of witnesses who remind us that a spiritually formed life is a life of deepening participation in the saving work of God in Christ. Like Jesus, and in his company, we are called to be "wounded healers," to wrap the wounds of ourselves and others.

There is an old legend told in the Talmud and resurrected by Henri Nouwen:

> "Rabbi Yoshua Ben Levi came upon Elijah the prophet ....
> He asked Elijah, "When will the Messiah come?"
> Elijah replied,
> "Go and ask him yourself."
> "Where is he?"
> "Sitting at the gates of the city."
> "How shall I know him?"
> "He is sitting among the poor covered with wounds.
> The others unbind all their wounds at the same time
> And then bind them up again.
> But he unbinds one at a time and binds it up again,
> saying to himself,
> 'Perhaps I shall be needed: If so
> I must always be ready so as not to delay for a moment.'"

WRAPPING ANOTHER'S WOUNDS...

Author and spiritual guide, Parker Palmer, speaks so beautifully about what it is to wrap another's wounds and his own. Parker suffered from a depression that took him as he says, "All the way down". He says there were some people who came to give him advice and blessedly others who had the courage to stand with him in a simple and healing way. One of them was a man who, having asked his permission to do so, "stopped by late every afternoon, sat me down in a chair, knelt in front of me, removed my shoes and socks, and for half an hour simply massaged my feet. He found the one place in my body where I could still experience bodily feeling - and feel connected with the human race."

"He rarely spoke a word, and when he did, he never gave advice but simply mirrored my condition. He would say, 'I can sense your struggle today,' or, 'it feels like you are getting stronger.' I could not always respond, but these words were deeply helpful: they reassured me that I could still be seen by at least one person, life-giving knowledge in the midst of an experience that makes one feel annihilated and invisible. It is almost impossible to put into words what my friend's ministry meant to me. Perhaps it is enough to say that I now understand the Biblical stories of Jesus and his foot washings at new depth."

This is the kind of love that neither avoids nor invades the soul's suffering. It is a love in which we can represent God's presence to a suffering person, a God who does not "fix" us but gives us strength by suffering with us. By standing respectfully and faithfully at the borders of another's solitude, we may mediate the love of God to a person who needs something deeper than any human being can give.

WRAPPING ANOTHER'S WOUNDS

The Sunday October 10 issue of THE NEW YORK TIMES gave a story written by Roger Cohen of a polish Roman Catholic priest who is pictured outside the Nazis' Majdanek camp. Romuald-Jakub Weksler-Waszkinel is his name. The story tells the complicated and amazing story of a man who would like to say to the Israelis staring at him, "I suffer in the same way you are suffering." Romuald-Jakub is a priest and teacher at Lublin's Catholic University who discovered late in life, HE is a Jew. Having pieced the fragments of his life into a semblance of truth, he now believes that his mother, whom he never knew, was murdered at Majdanek in 1943. He calls the ashes near the crematory 'the tomb of my mother." Romuald-Jakub was the son of good Polish Catholics., his father a metal worker...his mother, of the doting type. These were the long unquestioned facts of his upbringing. One day at seminary, his mother came into the chapel and wept profusely, in a way that was hard for Romuald-Jakub, a way he had never seen before. A few weeks later his father died of a heart attack. At one point before he was ordained to the priesthood there was some question as to whether he had ever been baptized. He was outraged and called the questioning an insult to his parents. He came to his mother whom he now calls his Polish mother and said that he sensed a secret. He noted that when he read to her about the Jews (she was illiterate) she often had tears in her eyes. When he would ask why she cried she would answer, "Don't I love you enough?" As he relates this, he has tears in his eyes, still shaken, it seems, by the long deception that was also his salvation.

Finally in 1978 while his mother was ill he told her that the time had come for her to tell him the secret that he had always sensed. She told her son that his true parents had been wonderful people who loved him. She told him they had been Jews and they had been murdered. She said she had only wanted to save him from a similar death.

The other part of the story then emerged. He had been born in 1943 to a Jewish couple in the town in Poland that is now in Lithuania. He had an older brother. His father was a well-known tailor. His mother, trapped in the ghetto, made contact with Emilia and begged her to take the infant and save him. Emilia hesitated. But then the priest's Jewish mother said something decisive and eerily prescient that his Polish mother would never forget:

"You are a devout Catholic. You believe in Jesus, who was a Jew. So try to save this Jewish baby for the Jew in whom you believe. And one day he will grow up to be a priest."

Hearing this, Father Weksler-Waszkinel was tremulous, for he had fulfilled the prophecy of his mother, a woman he had never known. 'You must love your mother for she was very wise,' Emilia told him. "Those words she spoke were the words that saved your life because they convinced us to take you in." The priest decided to tell nobody, except Pope John Paul II. An enormously supportive letter came back from the recently elected Polish pontiff, addressed to "My Beloved Brother." It said the priest's pain was part of the pain of the cross, a sign of love. It urged him to persevere. Father Weksler-Waszkinel said: 'I know that while there are people calling themselves Christians capable of putting a mother and a child in a gas chamber, there is also a Polish Catholic woman who could risk her life to save me.'

The Priest carries on a chain an emblem that has become the symbol of his life: a Star of David with a cross in the middle of it. 'I am the Star of David with the cross inserted.' He said. 'That is my life as I see it. The cross is love. Without love, it is the Roman gallows. Jesus is not responsible for the wrongs perpetrated in His name, and I would like to resemble him, if only a little.' His predicament makes him laugh. "You know, I can be a Jew in Poland, but as a priest, I cannot be a Jew in Israel." But beneath the mirth, pain lingers. (He wonders still about a brother of his mother who left for America early in the century. He worries because he recently found a pamphlet called "The Myth of the Holocaust." "It is good to see all the Israeli students a Majdanek." He said. "But I wish they went around in the company of Polish kids.) 'In Israel, wrong things are said about Poland. And here, the stupidities about Jews persist. I am in the middle and I know that what is needed is contact, understanding and Love.'" An amazing story!!!!

We are invited each day within the furnace of the world's pain, to make those small but cosmic free decisions to hear the pain of the other, to see the pain of the other, to reach out our hand to touch the pain of the other, experiencing the wound in our own hand, but never without the encompassing presence of God. To be a wounded healer, to wrap another's wounds whose life is mingled with and empowered by the Christ is to become the truly who we are created to be.

God in Christ, gives to all, the promise that the hands of all of us wounded and wounding healers, held in God's heart, are forgiven, restored and transformed. With our hands within that God's heart, when we touch another in healing love and comfort, the hand and heart of Christ surrounds and encompasses our own hands. When we become aware that we do not have to escape our pains, but that we can mobilize them into a common search for life, those very pains are transformed from expressions of despair into signs of hope. May we live in the hope wrapping our wounds and one another's.

There is an important conclusion to the story of the Rabbi's question to Elijah.

> "Peace unto you, my master and teacher."
> The Messiah answered, "Peace unto you, son of Levi."
> He asked, "When is the master coming?"
> "Today," he answered.
> Rabbi Yoshua returned to Elijah, who asked,
> "What did he tell you?"
> "He indeed has deceived me, for he said
> "Today I am coming and he has not come,"
> Elijah said, "This is what He told you,
> 'Today if you would listen to His voice.'"

"The master is coming, not tomorrow, but today, not next year, but this year, not after all our misery is passed, but in the middle of it, not in another place but right here where we are standing, wrapping one another's wounds...

> May we witness to the living truth that the wound,
> which causes us or another to suffer now, will be
> revealed to us later as the place where God
> intimated his new creation.

Generosity
By Rev. Robert Hill
November 7, 1999
Text: I John: 1-3

Prayer: O Lord, give us an appetite for the fruit of your Spirit, we pray. We ask today, especially, for a taste of Generosity—surprising, spacious, seductive Generosity. Amen.

Stewardship Sunday Morning…

"But I don't want to go…"
"You have to go. Come on. Get out of bed, and get dressed."
"I don't want to go to church today…"
"You have to go. Get dressed. Come downstairs. Polish your shoes."
"Do I have to go every week?"
"This is Sunday and Sunday is church. You are going to be late, hurry up and eat your eggs, they're getting cold."
"My friends aren't going today—I know they're going on a trip.
"But you have to go. Come on, out the door."
"Why do I have to go?
"Because. You're the preacher!"

So one can feel, especially in the first year or two of ministry. No seminary prepares any preacher for Stewardship Sunday. (Some people who teach in seminaries do so precisely in order to avoid Stewardship Sundays!) You have to learn, if you do learn, on the job. And what do you learn?

Over time, you learn to love this day, almost more than any other. We savor, today, what the Scripture names as the Spirit's fruit—goodness, or, perhaps better rendered, "generosity", goodness that does some good, generative goodness, AGATHOSUNE, generosity.

This is the day, either literally or figuratively, in which the material world is invaded, assaulted, attacked, by Another Reality. The beachhead of this invasion is unmistakable, as real and sacrificial and human and costly -- and victorious-- as Normandy.

Tom Brokaw has written about the Greatest Generation. Tom Hanks has starred in Saving Private Ryan. But that kind of beachhead, won against frightful gunfire and destructive opposition, is also visible every November even in the lowliest church and even in the poorest parish. It goes simply by the name of generosity, and generosity is a surprising interloper, a fruit of God's Spirit, a visitation from Another Reality. With the enemy fire raining down, Generosity marches on.

Into the teeth of congenital selfishness, cultural stinginess, communal exclusiveness, and congregational sanctimoniousness, Generosity marches on.

Into the terror of rational question, too, Generosity advances. "You can't give like that now, you're just getting started. You shouldn't do that, you have little mouths to feed. Now is not the time, you are paying a mortgage. How can you give with kids in college? Better save now, your hair is receding and so is your bank balance. Your teeth are decaying and so is your portfolio. Your stomach is growing and so is your debt. Your eyesight is fading and so are your options. You'll need resources as you get older." Against all that, Generosity moves forward, into the teeth of the gale, the fierce enemy fire from hidden outposts.

But what is the character of the fruit of the spirit known as Generosity? How shall we know its taste in this season of spiritual harvest?

An Apocalyptic Moment

Last month I did have a Sunday off—what a luxury. We were in Phoenix, with sunshine and 100 degrees. I got up late, skipped breakfast, went to a church service someone else had prepared, ate lunch, and then headed out to see if I could get into a major league football game—Cardinals and Giants. I have followed the Giants since YA Tittle and Del Shoefner and Frank Gifford, but never have seen them live. So I got to the stadium, worried about a ticket. Scalpers had some--$100 dollars. No thank you. At last, the ticket booth, with a little crowd gathered. I stood and waited in line. Suddenly a Phoenix fan appeared, dressed in Cardinals hat, Cardinals shirt, Cardinals socks, Cardinals Buttons. He was a burly bloke, and not overly tidy in his attire. He also was quite a large person. He wore a beverage Container on his back that had a tube running to his mouth. His Cardinal hat was shaped like a bird, and had wings that moved up and down "in flight" as he walked. He wore size 13 Converse sneakers. He stood in the ticket area and said, "I have two

$50 tickets that I want to give away. I don't want them sold, I want to give them away."

No one moved. No one spoke.

"I have free tickets here. Two of them. They're on the 30-yard line, 18 rows up. I want to give them away."

I don't know why, exactly, but no one moved or spoke. We couldn't believe it. "There must be something wrong—a catch."

Finally, exasperated, Mr. Cardinal slammed his tickets on the counter, and said to the taker—you give them away, at which point yours truly, not born yesterday, said, "Well, I appreciate your generosity-thanks for the tickets. May the best team win as long as its New York."

But we don't really appreciate generosity. We don't expect it so we don't see it. It stomps up to us and bites us and we still don't see it.

I was given a place at the table, a seat at the banquet, a ticket to the game—space, entrance, inclusion.

So armed, I walked to the turnstile and realized I had two tickets but only needed one. So, I walked over to a group nearby and said, "Listen, I have a free ticket here. I don't want it scalped. Who would like it?"

Guess what? Dead silence. "Hey. This is legitimate. This was given to me-it's yours for free." Nothing.

I turned to leave, when an older man said "OK, OK, I don't know what your angle is, buddy, but hand it over." Which I did.

So on a 100 degree Sunday off in the southwest I was given a free ticket, and also, as the game progressed, and my mind wandered, an apocalyptic insight into the nature of the fruit of the spirit known as goodness, generosity, in three particulars.

Generosity surprises us. Generosity makes space for others, especially for the stranger, the outsider, the other. Generosity seduces us, at last, into offering our own generous gifts.

A. Generosity Surprises Us
For Instance…

An elderly couple who met at Depauw University in 1926, but who never graduated, decided to leave that school their whole life savings, $128 million dollars. 75 students a year will attend that school with full scholarships.

Surprising generosity. A person visits our office and late that week mails in a check for $3,000 to be used "as you see fit". Surprising generosity.

A woman who does not attend our church is inspired by the work of the Dining Center and leaves that ministry a quarter of a million dollars. Surprising generosity. May her tribe increase.

A family needs a place to stay for a summer trip and, hearing the need, a brother in Christ provides a home for the visit. Surprising generosity.

A president is defeated at the polls after only one term, but goes on to live a faith both public and private, the Carter center thrives. Surprising generosity.

Someone is saved from psychic hell through the pastoral care of their church, and chooses to endow the expense of pastoral ministry. Surprising future generosity.

It is in the nature of the spirit to take us somewhat by surprise, and nourish us generously. So the Scripture teaches us.

Psalm 33: The earth is full of the HESED (generous goodness) of the Lord.

Romans 15: You also are full of generosity.

Galatians 6:10: Let us be generous to all, especially to those of the household of faith.

Colossians 1:10: Be fruitful in every good work

2 Cor 9: "The Lord loves a cheerful giver."

Romans 12: "Let love be genuine."

Matthew 6: "If anyone asks for your coat, give him your cloak as well. If he asks you to go one mile, go a second too."

Galatians 6: "Bear one another's burdens and so fulfill the law of Christ."

Or think of Jesus' parables of sowing and reaping, of mustard seeds exploding from tiny to great, of talents used and underused, of dishonest but generous stewards and of that haunting and joyous refrain, may it reach our ears at heaven's door! "Well done though generous and faithful servant, you have been faithful over a little, we will set you over much. Enter into the joy of the master." How frightful, daunting, awesome, profound is our charge in this life to minister to one another so that we are ready to hear such a sentence pronounced: "...well done, thou generous and faithful servant.."

If we have savored generous surprise, then we may also sense that this form of the Spirit's fruit makes space for others.

B. Generosity Makes Space for Others

Look at Asbury First, flourishing because of the surprising generosity of hundreds of faithful people, who want the world to be a better place, who believe in the Lord Jesus Christ, who understand that as the seedbed for wonder, morality, and future generosity, the church has a prior claim on our giving.

Let me push you a little here. I know it is appealing to give to many particular causes and special projects. But it is Another Reality, the fruit of God's own spirit known as goodness, which ultimately feeds all giving, and to which the church alone bears full witness. I think we run the risk of taking our church for granted. It will prevail into the new millenium only to the degree that another generation of young adults learns and chooses to reflect divine generosity with some of the human variety.

One day a veteran faithful member of our church commented to me about our ministry. In conclusion she said, and the words carried a depth of meaning perhaps even beyond her intention, "e don't want anyone left behind."

But that's it! No one is to be left behind, left out, left off the list, left outside. Not at least for those of us who worship the Jesus Christ of the manger, the wilderness, the borrowed upper room, the cross, and the empty tomb! Jesus lived and died "outside", to remind us on the religious inside of those still outside. So that all might have space, have a seat, have a place at the table. You and I have had seven courses of faith, when others lack even the appetizer. "We don't want anyone left behind."

Asbury First's current growth and future health are fed by Generosity, goodness that does good. Generosity makes space, in this church, for those who are not yet inside. Why? Why more? Why grow? Because God is generous, and we believe in God. Because the need of the county is great, and we care about that need. Because the future health of this congregation depends on our becoming, over a decade, welcoming, inviting and generous, and we love this church. Because when our own generosity is quickened, faith is less a dull habit and more an acute fever.

Amid surprise and extra space, the Spirit can seduce you, even on a Stewardship Sunday.

C. Generosity Seduces Us

For we learn over time. Sometimes the best gift you can give somebody is the opportunity for them to give themselves. That is what this sermon is about. We are trying today, in this season of spiritual harvest, to feast upon the fruit of the spirit known as Generosity. And the best gift you can receive is the chance to give of yourself.

A while ago friends were going on a trip and needed someone to watch their children. I heard the request and did what you would have done. I referred the idea to the spiritual leader of our home. Jan said sure. I wondered a little about it, but the day came and all of a sudden, we had again multiple teenage voices in our home. And what a treat they were, what a joyful presence, what a gift!

But if our friends had not had the courage and taken the risk of asking, of giving us the real gift of a chance to give, we would have missed a little bit of heaven.

So in that vein I am going to ask you to give today. This church can prosper if you will generously support it. It's entirely up to you. I invite you to give, to pledge, to pledge strongly and to tithe. I am aware that this is a very personal decision. And not everyone likes to hear, let alone preach a stewardship sermon. One wag said, "It's not that he preaches so badly about money, it's that he preaches about it at all!"

But the world is not going to be healed by token pledges and convenient giving. This is a giving church. It needs to become a generous one. That is your opportunity today. "Ask not what your church can do for you. Ask what you can do for your church."

Remember your forebears. These are the people of whom Diognetus wrote in the year 130ad:

They display to us their wonderful and paradoxical way of life.

> They dwell in their own countries, but merely as sojourners.
> Every foreign land is to them their native country.
> And yet their land of birth is a land of strangers.
> They marry and beget children, but they do not destroy their offspring.
> They have a common table, but not a common bed.
> They are in the flesh, but they do not live after the flesh.
> They pass their days on earth, but they are citizens of heaven.
> When reviled, they bless.
> When insulted, they show honor.
> When punished, they rejoice.
> What the soul is to the body, they are to the world.
> What salt is to earth and light is to world, are you to this country, to this region.

The church stays open for people on whom almost all other doors have closed. For the poor. For the irascible. For the loony. For the difficult. You are sitting in the most open, and generously vulnerable public space in this county.

As Lorraine Hansberry wrote,

"When do think is the time to love somebody most? When they done good and made things easy for everybody? Well then, you ain't through learning, because that ain't the time at all. It's when he's at his lowest and can't believe in himself 'cause the world done whipped him so".

The mission may be the bit and bridle, but the great steed, the real horseflesh of life is found in vision, a vision of a healed and loving world, where there is space, real quality space, for all. We dare not let the moon of mission eclipse the sun of vision.

Now we sing:

> *Take my life and let it be*
> *Consecrated Lord to thee*

We might better sing:

> *Take my life and let it be*
> *Shaped by Generosity.*

Jane Addams' Warning

In closing, maybe we need to remember the young woman from Rockford Illinois, Jane Addams. She grew up 130 years ago, in a time and place unfriendly, even hostile, to the leadership that women might provide. But somehow she discovered her mission in life. And with determination she traveled to the windy city and set up Hull House, the most far-reaching experiment in social reform that American cities had ever seen. Hull House was born out of a social vision, and nurtured through the generosity of one determined woman. Addams believed fervently that we are responsible for what happens in the world. So Hull House, a place of feminine community and exciting spiritual energy, was born. Addams organized female labor unions. She lobbied for a state office to inspect factories for safety. She built public playgrounds and staged concerts and cared for immigrants. She became politically active and gained a national following on the lecture circuit. She is perhaps the most passionate and most effective advocate for the poor that our country has ever seen.

Addams wrote: "The blessings which we associate with a life of refinement and cultivation must be made universal if they are to be permanent. The good we secure for ourselves is precarious and uncertain, is floating in midair, until it is secured for all of us and incorporated into our common life."

Yet it was a Rochesterian who, for me, explained once the puzzle of Jane Addams' fruitful generosity. This was the historian Christopher Lasch. Several times in the 1980's I thought of driving over here to visit him. But I never took the time, and as you know, he died seven years ago. Lasch said of Addams, "Like so many reformers before her, she had discovered some part of herself which, released, freed the rest."

Is there a part of your soul ready today to be released, that then will free the rest of you?

I wonder, frankly, whether for some of us that part is our stewardship life, our financial generosity.

Is that part of you, the wallet area part, ready to be released today, and in so doing, to free up the rest?

I think with real happiness over the years of men who have, just for example, taken up the practice of tithing, and in so releasing themselves, have found the rest of their lives unleashed for God.

Is there, as there was for Jane Addams, some small part of your soul ready to be released today, which then will free up the rest of you?

Deep, real life change comes from apocalyptic insight and cataclysmic experience. "All who enter the kingdom of heaven enter it violently".

A sensual experience can reorient a life (Pablo Picasso). A religious experience can reorient a life (Ignatius of Loyola). A patriotic experience can reorient a life (John McCain). A near death experience can reorient a life (Christopher Reeves).

Sex, religion, nation, death all can produce such a cataclysmic release. All sticks of existential dynamite. Money is another. And today is Stewardship Sunday. "...oh we keep the rest for another day, yet knowing how way leads onto way..." I wonder about the verve and youthful zest of your lower wallet area? I wonder what condition your condition is in?

Is there a part of your soul which, once released, would free up the rest? A catalytic experience or moment? Is it possible, that such an experience is waiting for you, metaphorically speaking, in the lobby outside your bank? Not in sex, or religion or nation or peril, but in...generosity?

Meryl Streep is reminding us that music brings structure, focus and discipline to life. So does tithing, and moreso.

Maybe we can know, in the surpise of Generosity, in the space provided by Generosity, in the seductive attraction of Generosity, what made a man of God out of John Wesley, and helped him to live on a mere 60lbs sterling year by year for his whole adult life, and in the process build a cross continental movement for good, of which we are heirs and debtors. Go, tithers and future tithers, and live his motto:

> *Do all the good you can*
> *At all the times you can*
> *In all the ways you can*
> *In all the places you can*
> *To all the people you can*
> *As long as ever you can*

TASTE AND SEE THAT THE LORD IS GOOD
By Rev. Robert Hill
November 14, 1999
Text: Galatians 5:22

El Aqueducto

Have you tasted the kindness of the Lord? To acquire such a taste for kindness, especially in 1999, especially for you, will mean a rejection of lesser tastes, and willingness forever to leave behind the little treats that mean-spiritedness does afford. A taste for life means a distaste for death.

The middle of one ancient Spanish town, Segovia, is parted by the hundred foot high remains of an ancient acqueduct. The Romans built the duct before the birth of Christ, and it channeled water through barren Castille until 1914. It stands now, parting the village and attracting tourists, its many stately roman arches raised like hands into the sky.

Beneath the acqueduct, at the corner of the town square, you find a small restaurant, "Los Alamos", which has little space, little atmosphere, little distinction. On Sundays they serve a roast lamb, a local specialty, tasty and rich. Some years ago a young American writer frequented "Los Alamos", writing in the afternoons on the broad pine tables, then sharing the town's evening paseo and conversation from the restaurant's porch. A writer's life is necessarily a lonely life, a constant and draining scrap with his craft. This writer found the evening comraderie, underneath the silent acqueduct, just the elixir his mind required, and in "Los Alamos" he wrote a great novel.

At the same time, as the novel progressed, he quit smoking. Writers and nurses seem to smoke more than anyone else, and quit less often. Underneath the two thousand year old Roman arches and carried along by a kindly people, the writer wrote his masterpiece and at the same time gave up tobacco.

Years later, Ernest Hemingway stood on the porch of "Los Alamos", just beneath the Segovian acqueduct, and remembered the writing and the fun, the tables and talks, and his newfound break from addiction. He was asked about the year he spent there, writing <u>For Whom the Bell Tolls</u>. "I remember at last having the will power to stop smoking. The local people were so kind. The local wines were so fine. The book was going so well. I realized one day that to live well and to write well and to be able to taste the wine as it deserved tasting, I would have to give up smoking."

A Torrent of Kindness

A native of Rocky Mount, NC, and a victim of Hurricane Floyd, wrote this fall about seeing his hometown underwater: traffic lights blinking red and green underwater; furniture and unearthed coffins floating underwater; homes full of childhood memories underwater. He wrote for the NY Times (10/2/99) though under the theme, "a torrent of kindness": "We Southerners invented the phrase 'the kindness of strangers'. But nobody ever talks about— the strangeness of kindness. I mean the curious intuition that lets one person imagine what might, right this second, help others the very most. When those jeopardized are our friends and neighbors, whatever class or color, when we see them stranded screaming in treetops, and if we happily own a boat that hasn't left our garage for eight months, and if there is gas sloshing in its outboard, we still know, not why this happened, but what to sort of do. In our millennial paranoia, we suspect that the Book of Revelation's last days are now quaking up among us, fault-finding. If you're scared the world is ending in fire, reconsider. May we, the waders of North Carolina (all these snakes) half-reassure your? It'll probably be water. But even in this catastrophe's toxic wake, we're inching toward the high ground of a glum communal hope. Some 19th century willingness to act is yet there, if called upon. People are still imagining each other so they can rescue each other. A strange, radical thing, kindness."

The Taste of New Wine

Have you tasted the kindness of the Lord? You have no doubt

acquired some habits along the way. The spiritual nicotines that we confront. Looking out for number one. Some secret pleasures. A lazy willingness to take the short view. A nursed and venemous grudge. Television. Delight in the downfalls of others. A willingness to minimize the good in others. Savoring gossip. A trained and rancourous irreverence for reverence. The arrogance high. We have our spiritual nicotines, which offer a present excitement at the expense of corruption to come. They make it hard to taste the fine wine of love. Your lips and tongue and psyche get so coarse that the good taste no longer differs from the bad. Mean words and thoughts, conversation and daydreams, cause us to lose over time a taste for God.

Have you tasted the kindness of the Lord? Without such a taste you are dead, or nearly so, even now. With this taste alone, you come alive to real life. You can rejoice when you should and weep when you should and be patient, patient, patient with all your circumstances.

Have you tasted the kindness of the Lord?

Kindness and Scripture

The Bible says that God is kind. The Bible is our measure for words about God, being itself the word of God. Hence our interest in the Bible, weekday and Sunday. A love for Christ and a love for Scripture go always together, siamese twins. A person who scorns the Bible scorns also Christ Whom Scripture attests. Said John Wesley, "Let me be a man of one book!" The Bible says that God is kind.

Have you tasted the kindness of the Lord? You may be a member of the church, and yet not really turned on to kindness. You may be teaching children, and yet not convinced by kindness. You may be in the choir, a lover of the muses, and yet skulk daily in meanness. You may be a clergyman, and yet in all an unkind whited sepulchre. You may be new to the church, and waiting to test the church's kindness. You may be a hearer of sermons and a clever religionist, and yet still addicted to the nicotine of vicious spirits.

God is kind, says the Scripture. God is good, so sing to his name, for he is gracious (Psalm 135). He is a Mighty King, a lover of kindness and justice (Psalm 99:4). He is A God ready to forgive, gracious and merciful, slow to anger and abounding in steadfast love (Nehemiah 9). With everlasting love God will be kind to us (Isaiah 54). God is kind and merciful (Joel 2).

Jesus looks us in the eye from the pages of Luke and says, "Be sons of the Most High, for He is kind to the ungrateful and the selfish."(Luke 6:39)

Have you tasted the kindness of the Lord? I wonder.

Kindness in our Time

I wonder how deeply we trust that God is kind. I look out at the great sea of life and see much harshness, and of course this harshness washes over you, day by day. It is a rough and tumble world we are building. In our construction business, we are all to some degree in the world construction business, do we trust that God is kind? Is this kind of construction what pleases a God of kindness? Harsh realities surround us. Abducted children. Rancorous marriages. Abortion for sex selection. Child abuse and neglect. Racial misunderstandings and hatreds. All in the shadow of a nuclear arsenal that still could make this world silent and dark, darker than a hundred midnights down in a cypress swamp.

It is no wonder then that on this harsh cultural sea, the religious sailing ships of our time have a harshness to them as well. These past ten years have seen the rise of harsh religion, the success of unkind religion. Violence in worship that parallels musical and political violence. We have grown gradually accustomed to religious talons and fangs, expecting such meanness as a price for success in the religious market. So, American Protestantism with Methodism its largest denomination, seems slightly antiquated in the new age. So much so that some, across our church, seem ready to discard the diplomatic arts of kindness in favor a more warlike approach to difference.

God is kind, yes. But have you really tasted his kindness? Isaiah had his lips tinged with holy fire when at last he saw the kindness of the Holy One. How about you? Are your lips seared?

Have you become convinced that no matter what else, at home or at work, your life is saved for the Master Jesus, and not meant for meanness? Paul says, "Be kind to one another, tenderhearted, forgiving one another as also God in Christ has forgiven you." (Ephesians 4). God is kind to the ungrateful and the selfish.

How will I know if I have tasted the kindness of the Lord? Ah, here the Scripture answers with gusto. When at last this taste for the fine wine of loving kindness overtakes you, you will fall to repent, and so you will know. It is a shock, a mortal blow, to realize how terribly kind God has been to you. When it comes, then you know for you want to repent, leave off the nicotine, in favor of another finer taste. Paul says, "Do you think lightly of the riches of God's kindness? The kindness of God is meant to lead you to repentance." The kindness of Almighty God is meant to lead you to a kindly life.

Vision and Mission

We can become so invested in our own activity that we lose a taste for the New Wine of God's love. The moon of human mission can temporarily eclipsed the bright Sun of divine vision, the fruit of the spirit, today named kindness.

Every so often we sing:

> *Like a mighty army moves the church of God*
> *Brothers we are treading where his feet have trod*

We might better sing:

> *Like a festive party moves the church of God*

Filled with royal kindness, all have tasted God

Student

A while ago we had lunch with a college student who was struggling through a conflict. A teacher with whom she studied was causing her grief. It was humbling to listen to her careful step through the reasons why, as far as she could tell, she could not manage to work well for this one professor.

"It's not just the willfulness, nor do I mind the rigor and demand, and it isn't even the aloofness. I guess what really bothers me is that there is no kindness, no kindness. I was raised with kindness, so I guess I expect to find it in others."

Dear John

John took pretty rough treatment growing up in his small town. People discounted him, and much worse, because they knew his parentage. It scarred him for life, these silent taunts, and much worse, and he grew up and left. His bright red hair and good looks took him quickly through education and into the work world where he made good. But the hurts of grammar school linger. Take heed you who watch out for young children. John developed a quick tongue to go with his congenital quick temper and he used it like a sword whenever he felt the slightest taunt coming his way. Over time the verbal sparring became second nature to him, and he took some energy and pleasure from it. Once, though, in a soft-ball game, something happened. The young pitcher for the other team was mowing down John's side, and mocking John to boot. John stood at the plate and glared at what looked like a younger version of himself. In baseball and in conversation, John liked to swing away, swing for the fence. And in baseball and in conversation he hit some homeruns. He also struck out alot at the plate and in his judgments. The third strike was just called when John threw down his bat and yelled at the young pitcher, "Go back to where you came from you no-good." He saw the boy redden and then turn away. John heard some murmuring and a little laughter from the opposing team's fans.

And he recognized, keenly, that he had said more than he meant. This boy was growing up with the same harsh words he had known, and now John was himself delivering the blows!

Driving home, alone, John was overtaken. For some reason, in that one verbal strikeout, he became aware of all the meanspirited living he had ever done. What a thing to say! I of all people should know better! He began to think back a week. To a cute, hurting jest in the office. Back a month. To a play on words at another's expense. Back a year, to a full swing sentence that laid his cousin down in agony. John cried. Hard. The tears of someone that hasn't cried in ten years. He pulled the car over and wept at the wheel. "My Lord, all this time spent in parsimonious and niggardly talking. My Lord. How kind all this while you have been to me, as I, unkindly, have hurt others. I know better. I'm sorry."

Do you presume on the riches of God's kindness? It is meant to lead you to repentance. John left off the nicotine of verbal agility for a finer taste, the taste of kindness.

Have you tasted the kindness of the Lord?

The fruit of his spirit is present by grace in persons and churches and nations. Kindness, in the Bible, is just this: It's that great experience of <u>God's love</u>, which is revealed in Christ and shed abroad in the hearts of his people by the spirit (Romans 5:6), and it works itself out in life and the church as <u>kindness</u> toward one another.

Deliver De Letter De Sooner De Better

The fruit of the spirit called kindness is found in people. Joe bears kindness. Joe is a mailman. At age 59, though, he has been a lot more than a mailman to his neighbors. They know his kindness:

"When my son was wounded in Vietnam he waited on the porch for me to get home to give me the news himself. He didn't have to do that."

"I was out at age 69 knocking down icicles. I lay on the walk for almost an hour. Then Joe came by. He saw me and ran to me and put me over his shoulder and carried me into my house. He called the doctor, too."

"I was in college and asked if there were any pretty girls on the route. Joe said yes, he set me up on a blind date. We were married two years later. Joe was at the wedding."

"As a little girl I would walk part of his route with him. Joe was my favorite. I swore that when I grew up I would be a mailman too. And I am!"

The fruit of the spirit is kindness. In people like Joe Corbin, walking his route in upstate N.Y. for 36 years. They call him "Joe". We call it kindness, God's spirit bearing fruit.

Have you tasted the kindness of the Lord?

Even in Church

Kindness grows in churches, too. There is no kinder, gentler group of people than those in our own U.M.W. As pastor, I am an honorary U.M.W. member, and proud, very proud, to be so. At Christmas lavish baskets go out to the needy and shut-ins. On Sundays, flowers travel in kindness to hospitals and nursing homes. There is a monthly report made of the number of visits by each circle. But kindness is not just in deeds, it is a spirit, dwelling in kind hearts. Let's get busy and bear some fruit!

Have you tasted the kindness of the Lord?

Opposition

Is there not, though, a "kindness that kills"? An unwillingness to speak the truth, when only brutal honesty will do? An avoidance, for the sake of ease or safety, of the sterner virtues, in the name of this fruit, kindness? A reluctance, even to a dangerous degree, to ruffle feathers, let alone pluck those that need plucking? A distaste for pruning that finally leaves the garden overrun? Is there not a kindness that kills?

Yes, it is so. Odd, though, how we tend to raise this point in the first inning, when it is a ninth inning question.

Nationwide

But kindness is found in nations, too. You have to look a little harder, maybe, and discern a little more carefully. History shows us kindness in nations. Since we began in Spain, maybe we can end there, not far from that same porch and aqueduct, in old Castille, out in the hills north of Segovia. The year is 1938, and war tears the land apart. The Spanish Civil War was as cruel and brutal a war as the world has known, mainly because it combined internecine civil strife with 20th century weaponry. It was Bull Run with bazookas instead of bayonettes. And yet. In that utter darkness, the light of a spirit of kindness yet lived. Hemingway captured a look at such kindness in the figure of Robert Jordan, a teacher from Montana, who joined the Lincoln Brigade and went to Spain to fight Hitler. There he too was entranced with kindly people caught in the whirl of war. And there, in <u>For Whom the Bell Tolls</u>, Robert Jordan died, giving his life as a sacrifice of American kindness, against the mean spirit of Hitler's Germany. (Quote ending?)

How about you? Is it time?

Are you ready to leave the spiritual addictions behind and taste at last the fine wine of Love?

Have you tasted the kindness of the Lord?

As Socrates meant to say, "The unkind life is not worth living."

SELF-CONTROL
By Rev. Robert Hill
December 5, 1999
Text: John 1: 6-8, 19-28

Advent Anticipation

We come today to the end of the single verse which has occupied our attention since September, Galatians 5:22. With loving patience, and joyful good humor, and a kindly, gentle peace, you have faithfully endured a whole season of preaching dedicated to just one line.

Now, however, the time has come. The streetlights have been lit and the summer evening is ended. The whistle has blown and the train is headed out. The housemother rings the bell or flicks the lights and the date is over. The hour is coming (and now is!) John the Baptist is banging on the door, and it is time to move on, to Advent, to Christmas, to the Millenium, into God's open future.

And really, the whole of Scripture, is replete with last words. Joseph hears Jacob's last word and final breath. A last word. Deborah celebrates the end of a military victory. A last word. Moses, aging and toothless on Mt Nebo, gives his blessing to another generation—Joshua. A last word. Think of Elijah and Eliesha walking through every blessed Palestinian town until the heavenly chariot came down. A last word. Jeremiah, crippled, and on his death bed, taking the longer view. A last prophetic word.

And our Gospel today, St. John, is largely presented on the night of Jesus' betrayal. In fact, all Jesus says in John, with little remainder, he says on the last night, the night of betrayal. A dominical last word.

Just one word remains of our Fruit of the Spirit. It is, in fact, a word that John the Baptist, dressed in camel's hair and feasting on locusts and wild honey, would truly have appreciated. You know, John the Baptist has to be faced, and heard, every year before we can walk on to Bethlehem. Every year, on this Sunday, we brace ourselves to hear his wintry voice, his prophet's call, his voice that bears into our psyche what we may not want to hear but usually need to hear. One year, the theme is tithing. Another year, we wrestle with abortion. Still another Advent, we celebrate "precursors" like the Baptist in all of life. Last year, we heard about evangelism. So it goes, down by the river's edge, outside the city, in the cold dark, as night falls.

I picture him every year. He has such endurance, standing as he does just outside the city limits. John the Baptist waits down by the subliminal river, down outside the bright lights and big city, down in the riverside thicket of the subconscious, down in the dream world that sets the beat, far more than we ever care to acknowledge, for our waking, official life. Have you had a dream lately? Then you know his voice.

The voice of one crying in the wilderness.

It is fortuitous that he waits for us today. He would appreciate our struggle to understand this last mark of Spirit named by the great apostle to the gentiles, enkratea, "self-control", especially here at the end, at least from one accounting, of the millenium.

Y2K

Perhaps the most striking feature of much millennial discussion this year, one could argue, is its familiarity, its bland predictability.

What is the great bogeyman of the month? Y2K? The possibility of technological failure. I honestly expect nothing unusual to occur January 1. But what is striking is that what some others fear, even if it happened, would be...NOTHING UNUSUAL. Do you see, to paraphrase Ecclessiastes, technological breakdown? Ah—it has been before. Your network has never gone down? Your computer has never blanked? Your car has never stalled? Your dentist has never made a slight error? Your preacher has never given a dull sermon? Failure? Human and mechanized?...

NOTHING UNUSUAL. "To err is human", wrote Alexander Pope 300 years ago.

So we have a kind of millenial angst. We sing, "Have a holly, jolly Christmas.."

We might better sing,

> *Have an anxious, edgy Advent*
> *To end the millenial year*
> *The cold wind blows*
> *With heavy snows*
> *The nights are touched with fear*
>
> *Have an anxious, edgy Advent*
> *The darkest month of the year*
> *O By Golly*
> *Have an anxious, edgy Advent, this year.*

Listen: If your fear is that Y2K will mess up your checking account, take it from one whose checking account has been in disarray since ordination—it's nothing unusual.

But our Y2K ennui goes deeper than a January hesitation, a January hiccup.

Listen, and you will hear it, abroad...

Why is our Poet laureate speaking to packed houses today, when he recites Frost and Auden, and asks people to read and write their own poems? Is it out of a longing, a yearning, a hunger—the new problem with no name—for meaning? Paul said freedom, in Galatians, but meaning will do.

There is a longing, a craving, a hunger abroad for a new creation.

Why is Arthur Miller's **Death of a Salesman** playing with such force, 50 years after its writing? Is it because the consumption culture finally does not feed us? Or, as Paul wrote in Galatians, "if you bite and devour one another, take care that you are not consumed by one another." Yes Willi, yes Mr. Lowman, attention must be paid.

There is longing, a craving, a hunger here for a new creation.

Why did Kevin Spacey choose to star in *American Beauty*, a millennial film about suburban emptiness and marital hell? Is it because we have in face, as Paul wrote in Galatians, been set free in Christ, and over time, down deep, we begin to recognize cages however gilded, as cages nonetheless.

There is hunger, a longing, a craving here, for a new creation.

Why did Bill Clinton's perjury and infidelity so rivet our attention and illumine our national landscape, with such costly, indelible, and pervasive consequences? Is it because, at last, a whole generation is waking up to the ironically confining, and paradoxically enslaving power of unmitigated self-indulgence? This is what Paul—however quaint and dated and sexist and heterosexist his earnest words now sound—was trying to convey to the Thessalonians, "that each of you learn to take a wife for himself in holiness and honor".

There is a hunger, a longing, a craving here for a new creation.

Spirit and Flesh and Law

Our human expectation is fear not hope, and usual not unusual.

All of this—Y2K, Willi Loman, Kevin Spacey, Bill Clinton—and what shall we make of the heavily masculine angst here?—is what Paul called "flesh", and the effects of the flesh.

It is this human penchant for competition, for pride and envy, this human tendency toward the impulsive desire, this human banality, finally, which is under attack today, according to St Paul and St John. Paul calls this "flesh".

Watch carefully. The Fruit of God's invasive Spirit is the antidote to "flesh", not the Law. It is the Spirit that gives life, not the law. It is Spirit, not religion, not compulsion, not athleticism, not achievement, not LAW.

Blake had it close to right:

> *When Satan firs the Black Bow Bent*
> *And the Moral Law from the Gospel Rent*
> *He Forg'd the Law into a Sword*
> *And the Spill'd the Blood of Mercy's Lord*

It needs to be said: Much American religion today resembles that of Paul's opponents in Galatia—biblical, traditional, ethical, disciplined, castrative, and above all, reverent before religion law. But Paul warns them and us—it is not law that will free you from flesh. It is not religious observance or self-discipline or harsh order that will free from flesh!

What must Paul have meant, then, by including in his description of Spirit—an actual, real, historical force—*enkratea*? What is this strange presence?

Self-control here means something other than what we think of as self-discipline. After all, for Paul these are fruit of the spirit, not merely human virtues. These are the gifts of the Gift of the living God! More than jogging, more than fasting, more than frugality, more than self-discipline is at stake here.

Nor are the many and helpful current lists of helpful habits what Paul has in mind. *Enkratea* means more than

> *Being proactive*
> *Beginning with the end in mind*
> *Putting first things first*

Thinking win/win
Seeking first to understand then to be understood
Synergizing
Sharpening in the Saw

More than habits of highly effective mortal units is at stake here. As practical as Steven Covey's list is, Paul has bigger fish to fry.

Vision and Mission

You know, we can get so enmeshed in our own activity, our own mission in life, that the illuminating, enlivening power of God—the vision and purpose and meaning of life—can be obscured. The moon of human mission, even of very pious and very important and very religious and very churchly mission, can eclipse, for a time, the bright sunlight of Christ, in which we are warmed and healed and made right. But it is the Spirit that gives life! The flesh is of no avail. It is the fruit of the Spirit on which we are meant to feast as we face the open future.

We are living in a season of spiritual harvest! God has stepped onto the human scene and is waging war against all that enslaves the human being. And we are enlisted—you and you and you—in the army of liberation. God's Spirit is feeding us, if we will but taste and enjoy, and sending us forth into the new creation.

And to this part of the army of liberation, God has given a map of the new territory meant for us. You can take the bulletin home today, with the nine fruit listed, and use it as a map for your spiritual journey. Every pastor who goes to a new town quickly acquires a map of the county, which she reads and uses with care. Often, too, he just calls back to the office for directions. But the map serves to mark out the new territory. The City of Rochester. The County of Monroe. The Village of Pittsford. The Town of Brighton. Webster. Hilton. Spencerport.

In the fruit of the spirit, the Scripture gives us such a map, to mark out our real home, the place we were meant to live, for which we were made, the new creation set free in Christ. See—the city of love. Look—the county of joy. Watch—the village of peace. There—the town of patience. Over there—the suburbs of kindness, goodness, faith, gentleness.

AND SELF-CONTROL IS MEANT AS OUR COMPASS. PAUL MEANS WITH THIS WORD SIMPLY TO FOCUS US ON THE REAL MAP OF THE REAL WORLD—NOT TO BE CONFUSED WITH THE ACTUAL WORLD—FOR WHICH CHRIST DIED.

Self-control simply keeps you pointed in the right direction.

A New Creation

This is the staggering news of Jesus Christ whose advent we await, whose Spirit feeds us like a wet nurse. Not religion, not law, not technological excellence, but a new creation, a totally new creation, is in our future.

> Our heaven is too low, today.
> Your heaven is not high enough, today.
> Our heaven is too low, today.

We await a little larger return on our investment, when the Spirit of God is making us soldiers who are landing on the beachhead of a new world.

The fruit of the spirit are locations within a new creational community. The works of the flesh are anathema, not because they show individual weakness, but because they harm community, the new creation. You may go through the list yourself in Galatians 5. Paul warns about the works of the flesh, not out of some hidebound killjoy religiosity, but because they keep us from our real native land, which is a wholly new creation.

Racism delays the new creation. Alcoholism delays the new creation. Self-indulgence delays the new creation.

"God does not want a new religiosity, but a renewed creation under the cosmocrator God." (Kasemann)

This is why the list of nine ends with *enkratea*, self control. The Spirit gives us the gift of freedom, which is "the gift to be obedient to God in God's presence." (Martyn)

So, the antidote to impulsive sensuality is not more self-discipline (law), but a new creation of love.

So, the antidote to wreckless consumption is not more frugality (law), but a new creation of joy.

So, the antidote to destructive competition is not more values clarification (law), but a new creation of peace.

It is a whole new creation that awaits us—in every direction. I believe that our church is a part of God's beachhead into the world of flesh. Here we can receive hands and lips with which to touch and taste the fruit of the spirit.

Endnote: Pear Trees from Augustine to Today

My grandmother Coons, a graduate of Smith college, born 28 years before women's suffrage, Sunday school teacher, homemaker, communion steward, and cook, was also a sometime gardener. In her little backyard she had a pear tree (like the one from which St Augustine stole in 370ad?), somehow planted and tended and guarded in our harsh climate. She kept a long handled pear picker in the garage, and once or twice a year we would come and take the pears, now ripe, and let them fall into the hoisted bag. You know, there are some moments that last forever, they just linger. Out behind her modest city home—very like our Rochester house in fact--I stand with the pear picker to take the fruit. I feel the sun of an autumn day. I hear the last of the insects buzzing. I see the gold and green of the pears. I hear the rustling in the nearby kitchen, a meal cooked to precede the newly picked dessert. I watch—there is no ending for such a moment—once the little picking chores are done, and a table is spread with linen and china and silver. Ruddy hands are carrying the serving plates, with potato and chicken and gravy. And there is the ripeness of the fruit, its scent and heft and color. And there is the family together at table, its care and intimacy and warmth. So I place the pears in a white bowl, and start toward the house. (Was it in such a garden and such a day that Augustine, at last, received the Spirit, take and read? Was it from such fruit that he received the gift, at last, of self control?) Hands are washed, and heads are bowed, and a prayer is offered and the meal stands ready. There, you see, in the middle of the table is the bowl, with nine good empire state pears. *Love, joy, peace, patience, kindness, goodness, faithfulness, gentleness, self-control.*

After my grandmother died, on All Saints Day, 1987, I was asked what from the house I would like, and, who knows why, I mentioned the pear picker.

It is our prayer that these sermons, all too human, will help you to pick the Fruit of the Spirit out of the tree of life, and so nourish you as soldiers of the new creational struggle, that God's day, in you, will come a step closer.

It is our prayer that the ministry of this church, all too human, will provide you with a spiritual pearpicker or two, in worship, education, care, spirituality, membership, stewardship, and communication.

So now you have the map. And now you hold the compass. And there is the New Creation. Happy hiking.

"What Have We Learned?"
Text: Matthew 18: 15-20
Sermon preached Rev. Dr. Robert A. Hill
Asbury First United Methodist Church
September 8, 2002

My friend mentioned that this had been a splendid summer, hot and sunny, warm and exciting, splendid, with one exception. Exception? It ended.

We go home in the summer. Home to past associations, home to tangled relations, home to memories, home. I spend some of each summer walking along a village green, attended by ghosts. We talk. It makes for some confusion among the ordinary population. The ghost of Marilyn Loop greeted me. There must have been some trouble there, I thought. In the fifth grade, she asked the teacher, Mrs. Klingensmith: "If God created everything, who created God?" A long pause. A pregnant silence. The clearing of the throat. "I guess we will have to ask the minister about that". I have been waiting 40 years for the answer, with none apparent, and now I AM THE MINISTER. Hurt makes us ask things.

We deposited our last financial dependent at college. In the morning he met a classmate who had been in the same school for second grade. What brought Dad to Syracuse in 1988? I went that fall to work with the study abroad program. Oh, oh, oh my goodness. Yes, I still write to the families for my own sake. I agree. The Chancellor never recovered. There are so many questions about Lockerbie, about life. Hurt makes us ask.

Jan and I had dinner with Elie Wiesel in 1978, before he was famous. He spent 10 years silent after Buchenwald, and then wrote his *Night*. He tells about a few of the deaths in the camps, out of millions. I tried to copy in his scene about the boy's death, but somehow the words would not stick to the page of the sermon. You will remember the scene anyway, the hanging of a young boy. Tragic, evil, wrong. And how it ends: "Behind me I heard the same man asking: Where is God?" Hurt makes us ask.

And now Lockerbie has become 9/11 and the Syracuse 200 plus the New York 200plus. What have we learned?

1.   Have we learned to revere freedom?

In the past twelve months we have recovered a deeper respect for the temporal freedoms we have inherited in this great land, as citizens here: freedom from the tyranny of kings, from the bondage of slavery, from the threat of dictatorship, from the despotism of ideology, from the fear of terrorism. We continue to have before us our President's fine phrase, "We shall meet violence with patient justice."

In the past twelve months we have also recovered a deeper respect for the spiritual freedoms of our faith: freedom from the tyranny of religion, from the bondage of flesh, from the threat of judgment, from the despotism of defeat, from the fear of the future. In W. Crossland's verse, we are free to do "the best things in the worst times and to hope them in the most calamitous".

In the past twelve months we have also recovered a finer sense of the divine gift of freedom, from God who loves us into love and frees us into freedom. Desmond Tutu: "God must surely love freedom, for God will allow us freely to go straight to Hell if we so choose."

2.   Have we learned to recognize sin?

Sin may be out of our lexicons, but it is not out of our lives. The bitter biblical truth is clearer to us: there is something radically wrong with a world in which young mothers from Rockaway Beach and Union City go to work on time and plummet to their deaths. We get lost. It is our nature, east of Eden. We get lost in sex without love: lust. We get lost in consumption without nourishment: gluttony. We get lost in accumulation without investment: avarice. We get lost in rest without weariness, in happiness without struggle: sloth. We get lost in righteousness without restraint: anger.

We get lost in desire without ration or respect: envy. And most regularly, we get lost in integrity without humility: pride. If you have never known lust, gluttony, avarice, sloth, anger, envy or pride you are not a sinner, you are outside the cloud of sin, and you need no repentance.

But sin is not only personal. Sin is pervasive. Sin has a corporate, expansive, even institutional reality. We mistake its power, if we see only, say, several dozen individuals acting to destroy property and life in lower Manhattan. That of course is real, and true. But sin is the power of death, throughout life. Sin is the condition of life under which such treachery takes place. Sin is the absence of God. Sin is an orb of confusion in the world. Sin is the advance or retreat of a great thunderstorm, a frontal advance, though theological not meteorological. Sin is like a city blacked out, a power far beyond any individual lamp turned down, any individual light switch hit. Sin is a shadow, the one great shadow. Whatever is not of faith, is sin.

3. *Have we learned to regard suffering?*

Wiesel's scene in the camps, following the question, about divine absence, ends with the retort: "Where is He, Here He is- He is hanging here on this gallows." Jewish theologians - Fackenheim, Greenberg, others, have known for a generation that any real talk about God, after Auschwitz, centers on silence and suffering. They have long ago been driven to second Isaiah, to Lamentations, to Job. Now we too, in the Christian communion, will walk more readily toward the passages in Scripture that speak of divine passion. Can one speak of God after profound suffering? Where was God? Hurt makes us ask. If we are to speak truly to another generation we shall have to be brutally honest about God's absence and presence. Where was God? By God's choice, present in the broken hurt of the dying. By human choice, absent in the violence that begets more violence.

There is much of Good Friday in this world on every day, and those of us who worship before a cross find God not in redemptive violence but in redemptive suffering.

The real question, we could add, for every preventable catastrophe, is not Where was God, but where were we?

- Where was love? Buried in hatred.
- Where was joy? Underneath the rubble of pride.
- Where was peace? Awash in desire.
- Where was patience? Forgotten in the race to vengeance.
- Where was kindness? Given up for power and wealth.
- Where was goodness? Transfigured into willpower.
- Where was faith? Replaced by a faith in redemptive violence.
- Where was gentleness? Where indeed.
- Where was self-control? Lost in ideology.

God has chosen the way of the cross to bring love and freedom. In stark terms, that means that there is no divine goalie out there to stop the slap shot of nuclear misjudgment. We shall have to work out our own earthly nuclear salvation in fear and trembling. We have no time to waste.

4. *Have we learned to hold out hope?*

The Gospel of Matthew, which we shall follow this year, and beginning with today's lesson, holds out a great, high hope for human life, especially expressed in the life of the church. The gift to us of God, in Christ, is expressly this wondrous gift of the church. The very existence of the church, including this church, is a sign of divine confidence in what yet may be, divine confidence in our human capacity to untangle relationships and restore justice, divine confidence in an open and promising future.

We think of Ernest Freemont Tittle, who more than most in his generation fifty years ago, saw the contours of the future. Tittle:
...We of this generation are confronted with the revelation of divine purpose given in a human interrelatedness and interdependence that justifies the term "one world"...We find ourselves in a situation where no one nation can prosper unless all prosper, no one people can dwell secure unless security is assured to all ...we have got to act with due consideration for the rest of mankind if we ourselves are to prosper and dwell secure... Something beyond us, a superhuman purpose and power, is working in history, bringing about the increasing interdependence of men and nations, so that our sheer survival becomes ever more contingent upon the establishment of justice and fair play in all our relations to one another."

Unlike the terrorists of 9/11, our hope is for the reign of God on earth as it is in heaven. Our children just offered that same prayer.

For us. One Day

The wolf shall live with the lamb
The leopard shall lie down with the kid
The calf and the lion and the fatling together
And a little child shall lead them.

The cow and the bear will graze
Their young shall lie down together
The lion shall eat straw like the ox
The nursing child shall play over the hole of the asp
And the weaned child shall put its hand on the adder's den.

They will not hurt or destroy on all my holy mountain
For the earth will be full of the knowledge of the Lord
As the waters cover the sea.

"Where is Your Passion?"
Text: Matthew 18: 21-35
Asbury First United Methodist Church
Rochester, New York 14607
September 15, 2002
Sermon preached by Rev. Dr. Robert A. Hill

1. *Jim's Passion*

Thirty years ago I was *invited.*

I was that morning invited out of a European History class into an adventure called the future. I met that day a college admissions recruiter. With our best, all our heart and mind, we all represent something. In breath, in mind, in body, today, you represent something, someone. Who? What?

Jim was perhaps 25, blond and tanned, dressed by the prep school model of the day, happy and easy, and he spoke quietly to me about college.

What, he asked, was my interest? He asked, straight, as later I will ask you, straight, about your passion. Where was I interested in going? Tufts - academic strength. Air Force Academy - western and different. Syracuse - Methodist (sort of). He listened, and then quickly, joyfully, happily explained how I could have them all, on a full scholarship, at a small Methodist college in Ohio. He neither pressed, nor pushed, nor persuaded. But he did make an invitation: "Why not come to Ohio Wesleyan?" A small private, academically strong, midwesternly awake, and Methodistically straight. (As my friend's daughter says, "A small Methodist school for small Methodists"). Kindly, honestly, with a real and cool passion for his mission, he invited and welcomed me. In a simple 30-minute talk, my life changed for the better, and that of my family for the better, and that of my children for the better.

No one I knew had ever been there, none of my relatives were OWU graduates, nor any of my friends. But when the letter came, a month later, with the promised scholarship, and a note in red ink at the bottom, "Bob, I loved your essay - come to Ohio Wesleyan" - I just sent the card back in a moment, and accepted, in fact - see how nonchalant we were back then before the search for a college became the quest for the holy graille - I accepted though I had not even seen the place, or heard any other voice but Jim's.

I asked Jim that day if the school had a sailing club. O yes, he said, I am the advisor. You know a sailing club in mid-Ohio, where there are no lakes and very little water, is like a snow skiing club in Alabama or a mountain climbing troop in Iowa. Yet, for a month, until I found another sport, I paddled around with Jim and others in the brown mud of the Oletangy. At Thanksgiving, headed for Connecticut, Jim offered a ride and dumped me out at the Carrier Circle.

Even then, somewhere down under, I knew I had been given a gift. And later my sister, now a lawyer, came too. And later my sister, now a mid-wife, came too. And later my daughter and son and son came too. All out of a cool passion and one simple invitation. And now with three children in Delaware, Ohio Jan and I should probably buy a house there and rent an apartment here.

And a month ago, 30 years within weeks of my talk with Jim, our daughter took a new job, doing something for which she has real passion. Oh, I wish I could say that she has Jim's desk, office, route, territory and sailing club duties. She hasn't, much as that would have helped the sermon, which always needs as much help as we, in love, can give it. But she has something of his. She has his passion. And this week she will sit with high schoolers in Cleveland and Chicago, and with a cool passion she will ask about theirs, as I will today ask you one thing about yours. In just a moment. While I believe this word for you, plural, to be a divine word, that belief is not based on my so-called insight, imagination, experience or wisdom (Of which there is plenty to be sure!!!). The divine invitation to your passion emanates from this year's evangelist, St. Matthew, from the long history of his Gospel in the church, and from your life today, potential though rather than kinetic. That is, this invitation to you plural, to you as a congregation, excitedly to unwrap the divine gift of a new passion, comes from text, from tradition, from today.

2. *The Passion of St. Matthew in the Text of the Gospel*

St. Matthew's fiercest passion, hidden from you in this sermon for a moment in order to build some interest and suspense, wells up out of the scripture for these weeks in September. Matthew holds a very high view of the church, far higher than we expect, far higher than yours and mine, I could add. In waxing religion today, the church is largely an expedient - to be used, often for good causes, but to be used to be sure, and then, if there is time, to be loved. If the horse is dead, dismount, says one. In waning religion, the church is often also an expedient - though here for causes more progressive than traditional, interests more mental than physical - to be used, often for good causes, but to be used to be sure, and then perhaps loved. This the fundamentalists and radicals have in common. What did Augustine say? We use what we should love and we love what we should use. Yet for Matthew, the church is empowered: with the means of lasting forgiveness (emphasized in today's harsh parable), with a mind for sound ethics, and especially with the real presence of Christ: did we really hear the word last Sunday, "wherever two or three are gathered together in my name, there I am in the midst of them"?

Matthew trusts this risen Christ and this voice of the risen Christ to free him to follow his bliss, to succumb to his passion. And what is Matthew's passion? What passion pulses through the parchment of this popular gospel? What force of energy is on the "kiviev" on the lookout, on the wing, hanging ten, parachuting in, ready to climax here today? It is the passion of an evangelist who finds every blessed possible way to connect a Jewish Jesus with a Greek world. It's the passion of an evangelist who enlists an old missionary teaching tract ("Q") to spread inspiration, truth, and joy. It is the passion of an evangelist who portrays your Savior among pagans, amid harlots, appended to the cross, about the resurrection work of compassion. It is the passion of an evangelist who sums up his Gospel this way: "Go make of all disciples". Here is this year's Gospel: the point of St Matthew the blessed evangelist is that he is an evangelist. *The whole point of the gospel of St Matthew the evangelist is that he is an evangelist.* He it is, not me, he it is, not we, who points you, Asbury First, to a new passion, one you plural have not intimately known. Matthew's passion? Seeking the lost! Churching the unchurched! Expanding the communion of saints, the only real circle of divine love!

3. *This Passion in Tradition*

So Matthew has been read, now and then. I turn the historians among you to the poetry of Dionysius the Aeropagite, the archaeological preservations of St.Helena, the mystic fervor of St. Theresa of Avila, the fecundity of Susanna Wesley, the marvelous zeal of Sojourner Truth, the compassion of Jane Addams, the alacrity of Berta Holden, the diligence of Margaret Wilcox, the voluminous voice of Violet Fisher. Some men helped along the way too.

This same passion moved Wesley from the Anglican Tree, shipped Asbury out from Brittany, placed the Gospel in a far country, and saved the souls of you and me.

One outstanding fact: by far and very far, Matthew is the most frequently quoted gospel in the first three centuries of the church's life.

4. *Your New Passion*

I know the taste - I have savored it before. I can recall the landscape -I have seen it before. I want you to come with me. It is a long way from here and many days journey, some at night, and some in the rain. There are mountains to ascend and rivers to ford. Some grasshoppers will look, for a time, like giants. It may take up to 40 years. You will feel like you are in a wilderness. I cannot do it for you and I will not do it to you. But I can do it with you. You will have to follow, because as a church you have not been there before. You have been in many great lands - we have been in them together. The land of fine music, passionately played. The mountain range of excellent preaching, passionately presented. The high sea of fervent learning, passionately engaged. The broad river of mercy, in soup and socks, passionately provided. The stately garden of architectural splendor, passionately defended. The broad plain of investment, passionately guarded. The principality of excellence of care, passionately promulgated. The sphere of citizenship, passionately prepared. Yes, you are a great church, God's chosen people.

But have you forgotten the love you had at first? Have you begun with the Spirit to end with the flesh? Hear the Gospel! St. Matthew the evangelist, all this fall, will invite you to succumb to another passion, one you have not yet fully known. Not in the guilded age of progress? Not in the poetic artistry of Cushman? Not in the grand style of Crossland? Not in the programmatic varieties of the eighties? Not in the steady though stodgy growth of the last few years? No.

There is a divine disappointment and, embedded there, a divine invitation to us, here today at Asbury First: Come to the land of milk and honey, the milk of compassion and the honey of welcome. Discover, careful now as you unwrap the gift, the pure joy of a passion for compassion, a desire, of the first water, to welcome the stranger.

5. *An Invitation*

Where is your passion?

Here is a divine gift, Matthew's evangel. Come to church having looked all week for a chance to invite another along. Come to prayer having prayed through the week for someone alone. Come sing having recruited another singer and having sung the praise of Christ. Come to enjoy those happy in God by making someone else happy too. You talk too much to people already well known to you and Jesus. Here: invite, invite, invite, invite, invite. You only truly have what you possess well enough to give away. You only truly know what you have the desire to share.

This church is a rocket ready to take off. What is a rocket for? To polish and protect? To admire and praise? To dust off and inspect? To consider and critique? A rocket is meant for flight, and there is hardly anything in life more fun than the feeling of the rocket launched and sailing, on a saving trajectory, and we are on the edge, the cusp, the shoreline of such a launching! Houston, we are ready for the ignition that comes, and will come to this poised church rocket, when you risk with cool passion, an invitation to another. Let us agree, across the board, not to come to church again until we have invited someone else to come, too.

"What Are Our Patterns of Welcome?"
Asbury First United Methodist Church
September 22, 2002
Text: Matthew 20: 1-16
The Rev. Dr. Robert A. Hill

A. The Generosity of Divine Welcome

It is the generosity of the divine welcome that has placed us here this morning. The whole lesson today, and in fact much of the Gospel for everyday, can be stated as St. Matthew, at the end of this parable which he alone records, so states: "Do you begrudge me my generosity? Are you envious because I am generous?"

Only a sense of pure excitement, biblical or personal, will do to announce the outset and onslaught of this autumn, this year, this high moment in which, for the first time in its nearly 200 years of life, Asbury First may become, by God's grace, a welcoming community.

A welcoming community is ready to receive divine joy, eager to accept divine help, hungry to be addressed by divine truth, prepared to accept divine discipline. A welcoming community is honestly committed to engage in divine service. We are boldly set to go where none has gone before.

I feel sorry for those who sit, but not in church; who hear music, but not of this choir; who receive news, but not Good News. On Sunday I feel what Sondheim placed on the lips of Bernstein's Maria (before he had gone down the dark paths of Sunset Boulevard): "I pity any girl who isn't me tonight!"

The Gospel according to Matthew, *The Evangelist*, by which we shall tour the Gospel this year, while not the earliest gospel (said honor belonging to Mark), and not the kindest gospel (said honor belonging to Luke), and not the oddest gospel (said honor belonging to two dozen documents which the church rightly left out of the Bible), and not the most spiritual gospel (said honor belonging to John), Matthew was the most popular Gospel. Hence its place first in the canon, its obvious presence in the earliest Christian writings, and its place of honor in church history. Matthew exudes confidence in divine grace: open, lively, and embracing.

God is generous. Liberally so. Or so this parable teaches. Agathos is the word - generous, giving, good, loving. God is generous, even past the point of our grudging, reluctant belief.

The churches use little bits of Bible, lectionary passages, like the one read earlier, on Sunday morning. There is much to commend this practice, which for a second year we are using too. But it has been the death of Methodist preaching, to some degree, because it focuses on the mouse and not the elephant in the room. So these weeks I have been interpreting Matthew, and his lectionary bits, from the bird's eye view.

The main point is that Matthew has a passion: invitation. He invites you to share the divine generosity.

The main point is that Matthew is opening a gift wrapped package for this church, the relatively undiscovered passion for compassion, for sharing good news.

The main point is that Matthew, in this parable as in virtually all, celebrates the generosity of the divine welcome. So, this parable is about that generous welcome, made in the teeth of economic justice: But aren't they all, all the parables, really about this same announcement? God is like a man who goes out and sows bushels of seed. God is like a fisherman who casts out a net, wide and open, and catches the kingdom of heaven. God is like a patient king who forgives. God is like pearl giving, treasure finding hunter. God is like a boss who appreciates talents. God is like a shepherd hunting for a lost sheep. All these in Matthew! And when we add a prodigal son, a good samaritan, a lost coin - a Lukan parable set to match, it is the same astounding word: generous, generous, generous to a fault is the gospel of divine welcome. If we read Matthew right, in the large, he would rather learn from one bird how to sing, than to teach 10,000 stars how not to dance.

Methodism is at a crossroad. What is our passion, our reigning desire? We were born out of two proverbs: "the world is my parish", and "go on to perfection". Breadth and depth. Wesley said them both. They both have biblical merit, and traditional root, and reasonable appeal. But, in shove and push, which matters more? Breadth or depth? We have many deep passions: history, liturgy, architecture, music, education, service, through which are going on to wholeness, that rounded wholeness that is a sign of the holy, the perfect. Is this the love we had at first? Is this the spirit that conquers flesh? Is this the work of which Wesley said: spend and be spent in it?

I asked Jane Amey, whose mother carted her around the creation of the unified Methodist Church in the 1930's. Which is it Jane, which is the more important? World or perfection? She thought a minute and, blessedly, said: ""the world is my parish" is the more important, if you have that you may get the other." So right, so good, so true.

B. *The Promise of Human Welcome*

1. *Welcome Space*

Therefore, we do believe in God whose gracious love is open, lively, and embracing. Hence we want to become a welcoming community, and to take the next step toward making our church home as fully welcoming as possible - welcome space, gathering space, youth space, family space.

Let me pause to relate a short, possibly humorous story. Last winter an older man, a first time visitor, talked with a greeter and a pastor in the cloister. "Can you direct me to the rest room?" he asked. We started excitedly to speak to him about some future possibilities, including the hope that a new rest room might be located between where we stood and the parking lot. We began to describe the other welcoming characteristics of this new space:

greeting area, places for coats, washrooms, space for fellowship and coffee, a library table, a movable altar for informal services, places for meeting and intimate conversation. He offered an elfin grin, complimented the plans, and said: "That sounds great. I'm impressed. *But I really can't wait that long - where is the men's room?"* To welcome the stranger is as central a joy, task, and calling as there is in the Christian life.

We have experienced God's lavish, uncritical, personal love for us, in the passion and presence of Jesus Christ, and we want to share that love as regularly and warmly as possible. The church leaders who have been assigned to address space issues for the future think that the time may have come to prepare our campus for the 21st century, especially in accessible welcoming, gathering, youth and fellowship space. In other words, it may be time for Asbury First United Methodist Church to add a welcoming area, a "family room" to our church home. Our house already has a "formal parlor" (sanctuary), a "dining room and kitchen" (Fellowship Hall) and "bedrooms" for individual groups (adult classes, Sunday School, choirs, campus based ministries, staff, denominational offices). We lack what is essential for welcoming, fellowship and family life: ample, gracious, open, lively, embracing space in which to welcome the stranger.

People come to church with many needs and questions. Two are regular and primary. 1. "Can you help me find meaning in life?" 2. "Can you help me raise my kids?"

Regarding our current plans, it seems to me that the welcoming space addresses the first of the above questions, and the youth space addresses the second.

The gathering or welcoming area, in particular, allows the church space to "be", to live together, to discover meaning in the simple and direct way of sharing one another's life journey's and life stories. Guided by the Holy Spirit and focused on the Lord Jesus Christ, we can help one another find meaning in life: in fellowship time on Sundays, in gatherings after and before services, in receptions occasioned by particular life moments, in smaller group sessions, in some devotional moments, in the interstitial connections that occur coming and going as a church, in enjoyment of art work, in the powerful experiencing of meeting another soul in the confines of a beautiful space. The new welcoming space would meet these needs.

2. Gathering Space

Our mission at AFUMC is to develop disciples through worship, education and care. This plan is designed squarely to address that mission as so stated. In ***worship,*** for instance, potential advances in the Sunday morning experience of worship as it is intertwined with fellowship are addressed in this plan: simply put, we would not build a church today without connecting the sanctuary with ample gathering space, so that vertical expression of God's transcendence and horizontal trust in God's immanence are both affirmed. Whether or not this plan meets that dual need, the congregation will need to say. Whether the need so met is worth the price, the congregation will also have to say. But the plan is directly aimed at the <u>*mission*</u> of the church at this worship/fellowship point. Likewise ***education,*** particularly youth discipleship, is addressed here, downstairs. Likewise ***care***, especially in the full use of accessible spaces, certainly the gathering space for funerals, weddings, meals, small groups, is addressed here. In short, the whole plan was consciously and systematically created around the clearly stated mission of the church. Said one leader, "I think the basic issue is whether as a church family we want to add a family room or not. The last two places we have lived, as a family, one parsonage, and one our own house, we have done so. We have been glad we did, though we would not have ever gone into debt to add them."

Some general, further thoughts about our campus master plan (most of this most have heard before, or many times before):

   a. The building serves the mission of the church (see above), and supports the ministry of the congregation. We want a ministry centered building, not a building centered ministry. "A mighty fortress is our God", not "our God is this mighty fortress". Hence, any physical property issue is always a level B issue, not a level A issue.

b. Our first priority is people: their health, nurture, safety, forgiveness, growth, discipleship, salvation, and eternal rest. *Within this, our first priority is new people, those who are starting their course in faith, and beginning their walk as disciples.*

c. Further, as this plan comes forward, it is clear that we "could" do this. The question is, when and how does the needle move toward, "we should do this". It is not a must. It is a may. When does it become a should?

d. This plan is a high B. It touches the heels of level A issues like generosity, stewardship, welcoming, fellowship, evangelism. To enact it, we would have to become a tithing church. This is good. To desire it, would have to become an inviting church. This is good. To construct it, we would have to become a united church. This is good. All good, and all hard.

e. On stewardship. For this plan to work well into the future discipleship of AFUMC, we would need to model good stewardship: no debt, every home committed, carefully planned, 50% of the money in hand before the full appeal to the congregation. At a minimum, this plan would cost the average giver 6 times the gift made for the roof.

f. Then we could live the dream: We would walk in peace and joy along the *Village Green* of life. Here, take a lantern. It is nightime. We leave the sanctuary. We walk through the spacious, open welcome area. Then (for this is only a start), we tour the expanded grounds of our ministry. At every turn, in this dream, there is a lamp lit. Look: just here is a new United Methodist conference office, for a combined upstate conference. Look: just here is a pastoral counseling center which specializes in the needs of women, created and guided by a retired pastor. Look: just here you find a lamp lit on the porch of an Urban Retreat Center, spiritually led by a spirited minister committed to this cause. *(And each of these projects tithes from their own budget back to the mother church that created them, thus providing the possibility of further growth. They learned to do so, over time, from the Storehouse, Dining Center, Nursery School, Daycare and others)* Look: just here there is the lamp of the porch of the county wide Wesley Foundation, a center for student ministry. Look: just here a lamp is lit over the door of a Hemispheric Hispanic ministry Center, from Emmanuel to Amor Fe y Vida. Our lamp leads us further: just here you find a religious drama center, K-12, and an elder care program, and.....Behold Asbury First United Methodist Church, The Lamp of the Poor!

3. Youth Space

There is no one who appreciates and needs welcome and welcoming space more than a new teenager. Listen to the following testimony from one of our former youth group members:

"Good Morning. Hopefully you have noticed so far that the theme of this service is the concept of a journey. If you haven't, I'm telling you now. A journey can take on many forms: A journey is taking a trip, or finishing a novel. A journey is running in a cross-country race. For any of you that have run cross-country, you know that it is physically painful, and emotionally straining. Similarly, a journey is staying awake through an entire sermon on an early Sunday morning. Everyone encounters opportunity to journey every day. In thinking about this topic, I came to the conclusion that my life is basically a series: some good, some not so good, but all with something to offer. I want you all to look back about four years to the summer of 95. Ben Hill as a pre-freshman 14-year old. It may astonish some of you to know that I was not the robust man you see before you. I was about 5 feet tall with big glasses and a baseball cap. It was at the beginning of that summer that my parents told me that I was to go on a mission trip with 25 of the youth from our soon to be new church. Now, it's not to say I wasn't grateful for the invitation, but the idea of spending a week with 25 kids, mostly older than me that I had never met before, was not exactly appealing. Nonetheless, my parents insisted, and comforted me by saying "Everything will turn out all right". Well I was glad that they believed that, because I sure didn't. I remember arriving, and having an awkward conversation with Chris Zimbelman, who is now a close friend, while carrying boxes that I thought were pretty heavy, down to the youth room. I remember being embraced by one of the parents of a youth on the trip. For the sake of confidentiality, we will call her R. Barrett. The week that followed was one of the most interesting weeks of my life. For me it was like going to summer camp for a week, except that everyone else there had known each other for years. I couldn't tell you who the first friend I made was on that trip, I don't remember. It was as if I had been absorbed into the group through osmosis. I cannot begin to describe to you the importance of that journey. It increased my comfort in a new place, and allowed me to know someone in the hallway at school. When I look back, I can't think about my start in Rochester, without thinking about that trip." (For the sake of confidentiality, we will call the author Ben Hill)

4. Family Space

It may be that the time has come for Asbury First United Methodist Church to add a family room to our church home. As we said earlier, our house already has a "formal parlor" (sanctuary), a "dining room and kitchen" (Fellowship Hall) and "bedrooms" for individual groups (adult classes, Sunday School, choirs, campus based ministries, staff, denominational offices). We lack what is essential for fellowship and family life: gracious, open space, welcoming and inviting space, a space to meet and greet and watch our children grow, a place where men younger and older, women newer and more veteran, people single and married, children and grandchildren and great grandchildren can get to know each other, and where, before and after and outside worship, the people of God can justly welcome newcomers. Is it time to add on a welcoming, family room?

5. Supporting Advantages of the Project

1. The project advances our mission of developing disciples through worship, education and care. Our worship of the transcendent God can occur in tandem with devoted intimacy with one another. Our education of youth can receive needed new space. Our care of one another finds a place where we can, as a full congregation, "watch over one another in love".
2. The project enhances our vision of becoming a spiritual village green, the religious epicenter of the county.
3. The project teaches good stewardship to another generation by encouraging tithing, rejecting debt, requiring 100% involvement, and perhaps using up to 10% for missions or for a missions endowment.
4. The project is unifying for a broad and diverse congregation that needs more unity.
5. The project helps us continue to grow, as churches across the country testify.
6. The project expands our youth space.
7. The project is difficult, and will cause us to stretch and use new muscles, and to get in good shape.
8. The project builds on the care and maintenance of the last 7 years (new roofs, parking lot paved twice, Campus Care Coordinator hired, new sidewalks, Teak Room, new porch 1050, improved entrances to 1010 and 1050, upgrades in education wing, Dining/Caring Center expansion, refurbishment of 1010 and 1050 interiors, computer network installation and upgrades, 1010 apartment rehab, sound system twice, organ enhancements, carillon replacement, landscaping work, youth room improvement, etc.).
9. The project meets three primary needs as identified by the congregation: accessibility, expanded youth area, and welcoming space.
10. The project provides for a gathering space envisioned in the 1950's, approached in the 1980's and imagined again in the later 1990's to be used for: welcoming newcomers on Sunday morning, deepening fellowship across generations,

interests, and groups on Sunday and during the week, settings for informal fellowship weekend and weekday, place for alternative worship space for non-Sunday services, and in general open space like that provided by a village green in a small town.
11. The project comes at a time of significant growth in worship attendance, membership, and ministry.
12. The project honors and enhances the architecture of the past while addressing the emerging needs of the future.
13. The four primary risks of the project are debt, discord, deflection, and decay. Debt can be avoided by raising the money before spending it. Discord can be avoided through laborious, careful and lengthy processes of discourse. Deflection from our mission can avoided by keeping the project in perspective. Decay in our future ministry will be avoided depending on the kind of leadership, primarily clergy leadership, in the next generation, which this kind of forward thinking project may rightly inspire.

6. Thoughts on the Process Moving Forward

1. As a subcommittee of the Board of Trustees, who corporately bear responsibility for our physical plant and invested funds, the proposed plan from the Master Plan Implementation Committee (MPIC) goes first to them for their consideration, rejection, approval, or emendation. It goes without saying that they may do what they want, as and when they want, with our work. I believe they both need and deserve to take ample time to analyze this plan that is fifty years in coming and will have 50 years of effect. (Completed 2001)
2. Ad Cab next needs to see whatever report, in any shape they desire, that the Trustees would like to provide. Ad Cab too, from a broader programmatic and ministerial perspective, will want and need time to pray and think through the plan, as proposed to them. (Completed 2001).
3. At the direction of the Ad Cab, an Advisory Council meeting could then perhaps be convened, for full church advice and counsel. Such a meeting could either initiate or

culminate a traveling presentation of the plan, for consideration, comment and alteration, throughout the adult classes and group life of the church. The full leadership staff would provide one of these settings. (Completed 2002)

4. At this point, a time of prayer, personal and congregational, well-developed and well-practiced, is crucial. Perhaps our Spiritual Life Committee could help guide us here. I have in mind a congregational letter, seasonal prayer vigils, and active work by the Intercessory Prayer Group, so that the whole process will continue to be immersed in serious prayer. The 'MPIC' devotions, so well crafted over these months, might at this point be compiled, printed and distributed for fuller use. (Informally addressed)

5. If consensus seems to be building after steps 1-4, then a feasibility study (approximately 2 months, and $8,000) would be appropriate to test what real, measurable financial support, from the inside the existing congregation, is present and has developed. For a campaign of this size, scope and moment, I would not personally choose to proceed without a professional, experienced, autonomous feasibility study (a kind of 'future audit'). The recent Sunday reading from Luke 14, on counting the costs and resources for projects, seemed to be oddly appropriate for us. (In process, Autumn 2002)

6. Our District Committee, and the District Superintendent and Bishop, would need to review and approve, modify or reject the plan (assuming the cost of the work exceeds 10% of the current property value). I do not see this as a lengthy or difficult step, but it is an important one to keep in mind. (tbd)

7. If at this point, the questions of "if", "what", "when", and "how" have responses that carry solid consensual congregational support, then a plan, including a plan for funding, and a plan for building, would rightly come before a Church/Charge Conference, heavily communicated, and perhaps further prepared by another Advisory Council meeting, and other smaller group sessions. Such a conference would be at the request of the Pastor-in-Charge,

and at the direction or discretion of the District Superintendent. There may be still other process issues (Preservation Board, etc), and some of these suggestions noted above may prove to be inappropriate, once we are underway. (tbd)
8. In the end, whatever we do or do not do, may those looking back from 2010 or 2020 on our process marvel together: "See how they loved one another through it all, and see how the project further enhanced the church's growth".

7. A Personal Word

I believe that our plans, to the best of our ability to judge this sort of matter, are the right thing in the right way, and close to the right time. I support, personal and pastorally and publicly, the plan to add this welcoming space. Now it may take us a while to get finished. After all, in some sense this plan has been on the map for 60 years. So we shall have to gauge the time as we go. But let us make our start. As you well know, I cannot do this for you and I will not do it to you. Here is what I mean. I can think of a church that built a great building, but relied on their pastor to raise the money. He did. He did it for them. They missed the chance to learn to tithe, and went forward with generations of weakened stewardship. It will not help to do it for you. I also can think of a church whose minister made peremptory choices about symbols, choices that may have been right. He did. He did it to them. They continued for generations to harbor a resentment about and a distrust of pastoral leadership. It will not do to do it to you. But I am eager, and I believe we are eager, to do it with you. We can do it. We should do it. So let us begin. Let us this week, individually and in our groups, set apart times for discerning prayer about this question: "What are our patterns of welcome?"

"BY WHAT AUTHORITY?"
Text: Matthew 21: 23-32
Asbury First United Methodist Church
September 29, 2002
The Rev. Dr. Robert A. Hill

A Biblical Question...

The other day I stopped at the Seven Eleven for a paper. Three of us waited while a new cashier, perhaps from India or Pakistan, grappled with the mysteries of her computerized register. Her customer was not pleased. He had asked for a pack of cigarettes, which she haltingly produced. The computer did not cooperate. She apologized. He fumed. At last the register registered his bill. He did not have, or could not locate easily in his jeans, enough money. Angry, nettled, embarrassed, he hurled the cigarettes back, scooped up what money he had, and raged on out. The pick-up truck squealed as he shouted and gestured a form of valediction. Our service provider returned to her struggles. The day *inched* forward. Somewhere, though, the question lingered about our angry white male customer: who died and left him boss? By what authority does one hurl judgement at another? And what one of us has not done so?

The Gospel of Matthew, we understand, was composed, part by part, to meet the needs and answer the questions of the third generation church. Now Jesus has gone. Now Paul has died. Now those whom Jesus gathered have gone. Now those whom Paul inspired have died. Tell us, Matthew, the good news in truth about living together as a church. Tell us about your passion for compassion. And tell us, too, about children and their place in life; about marriage and divorce; about money and its ills and blessings; about heaven; about leadership; and, so today, about authority. What Jesus has said Matthew has noted in ways that are helpful to his church.

At the end of the first century, when this Gospel was written, the still new Christian church, spread out across the Mediterranean, needed answers to big questions. Is the gospel meant for some or all? How shall we determine the truth about this and other issues? Where can we locate the authentic words of Christ? Who will have authority in the church and of what kind will that authority be? Matthew teaches about authority a dozen times in the course of his gospel. Today we traverse the path of one point in his teaching.

A Personal Question…

After the Seven Eleven paper debacle, I was reluctant to enter another store. Shopping, in any case, for me is stepping into the forecourt of hell. I need little excuse to avoid it. In any case, I had a sermon to imagine. I had agreed, though, to pick up some more paint. We are painting our empty nest. It is good therapy in an odd season. For the first time in twenty years I can get a good night's sleep on Saturday night. You would think the sermons would improve. Entering Sherman Williams, I paused to let another fellow, clearly a professional and experienced painter, or at least an energetic and swashbuckling painter, in any case, one self-painted from head to toe, pass by as we headed for the counter. I needed two gallons of the interior latex paint on sale for $18.00. I knew this coming in. It was my only planned and only needed purchase. A two minute deal. One attendant greeted us. Who is first, his eyes asked. I deferred, to my contestant, in the way you do when you know that both of you know that you were there first. Of course though out of courtesy, you are giving way you know and the other knows that you were first and he will of course readily say so and demur, deferring back. He did not. I waited as 5 different gallons of specially mixed, exotic paints were prepared over many minutes. I fumed. I paced. I glared. I looked up and outside, and there, working in the hot tar and paving the parking lot, was the disappointed cigarette purchaser, and colorful valedictorian, of the Seven Eleven. Now he was outside, calm, pouring tar, and I was inside, pacing, nettled. 25 minutes later my contestant, the professional painter, paid the bill, still looking down, not sheepishly, or at least not sheepishly enough. Somewhere amid brushes and drop cloths and rollers, though, a question lingered. Who died and left him first? By what authority? By what authority, too, did I silently hurl judgment upon him? Who made me judge and jury?

The lectionary harms us again this week. Following from the two parables read September 16 and September 23 comes this dark tale of unresolved authority. With only our public reading of the gospel, you would never know that St. Matthew has just a moment ago, in Chapter 20, delivered a remarkable sermon about authority. It bears frequent repetition. It might well happily, that is, have been included in the lectionary. But no. We shall have to cut and paste.

You remember that in Matthew 20 the mother of the sons of Zebedee asks that they be given special position, when Jesus brings the kingdom. But Jesus takes aside James and John to say that it is to be different among his people. They are not to lord it over one another. They are not to find authority in power, but power in authority, not authenticity in power, but power in authenticity. They are to watch over one another in love, but to remember that responsibility shared easily becomes responsibility shirked. Everyone's business is no one's. As Paul told the Galatians in verse 2 of his last chapter, "love one another and so fulfill the law of Christ"; or, as he then interpreted himself in verse 6: "each man must bear his own load". They are to define authority by hardworking service, by responsible self-giving. Who would be greatest, must be servant of all - slave of all, with a little self-awareness thrown in. As T. S. Eliot wrote: "who would serve the greater cause may make the cause serve him". Authority raises a personal question.

A Religious Question...

My Saturday continued, unaware that its unsuspecting contours would later be fitted to the flow of a narrative sermon. Using the historic present: I park for a moment to be inspired again by the spire of this church. I wonder if the congregation will take the preacher at his word the next day and invite someone to come along, whether or not the invitation is accepted. 24 hours later I am to be jubilantly impressed at how many have done so. It is good exercise. Asbury First is like Bermuda, an enchanting combination of physical visual beauty, and personal verbal courtesy, the best of nature and architecture and culture and posture. An oasis, of sorts.

There is a rising tide of discourtesy flowing over us, to be sure. But it is what comes out of a man, said Jesus earlier in Matthew, that defiles him. I suppose I am too sensitive to this question about authority. In the well nigh radical sphere of freedom that is the open expanse called church, there are hourly authority issues. By what authority? A firmly and rightly posed question. The Protestant churches have hundreds of years of experience trying to balance the needs for order on the one hand and the inevitable corrupting influence of ordering power on the other. So Luther split the church in twain, over authority. So Calvin retranslated and reinterpreted the Scripture, over authority. So Wesley ordained Coke and Asbury, to work in this country, over authority (telling them never to call themselves bishops). So in our time, the endless struggles over theology and order devolve so often into contests over authority. We rightly, from the perspective of the tradition of this church, delicately weigh all assertions about authority.

Otherwise we fall victim to a form of religious blindness. See: like the lectionary, the Pharisees have missed the whole point. Jesus knows they are trying to trap him, to see if he will commit blasphemy. Jesus here falls in behind John, as he did in their births to Elizabeth and Mary, as he did later along the Jordan river at the outset of baptism, as he did in the prophetic preaching of the 1st century in recollection of the prophets of old, as he did in avoiding the charge of madness ("he has a demon—behold a glutton and a drunkard"), as he did at last in death, the baptist beheaded well before the crucifixion.

But the church for which these words were meat and drink, Matthew's church, and the many others who used his collection, did not miss the point. Jesus had something to say to them about authority. He had known and dodged the dangerous challenges of political and religious authorities. He slips out, slips by, at least for now. It would not be hard to imagine how encouraging and inspiring the scene might have been, remembered in the year 90ad.

If nothing else, as practical help this week, let us with Matthew and his church admire and smile and chortle at the creativity, imagination and enterpreneurial cunning with which Jesus evades the cops. The middle gospels, Luke and Matthew, are written near and during the reign of Domitian, a Caesar who sent out an empire wide persecution of atheists, that is of Christians, and of others who did not worship the Roman Gods. They also were dodging and weaving in the face of civil and not so civil authority. Some were perhaps being taken, and some dying.

Here is how our gospels came to life:

Faced with the care of widows and orphans, Matthew remembered Jesus' teaching about the poor and the young.

Faced with the need to raise another generation with discipline and compassion, Matthew remembered Jesus' teaching about a house built upon the rock.

Faced with inevitable dilemmas related to money and resources, Matthew remembered Jesus' parables and sayings about God and mammon.

Faced with the desire to share his own fierce passion - saving the lost, reaching the outsider, welcoming the stranger, churching the unchurched—Matthew remembered Jesus' own parables and manners and patterns of welcome.

Faced with the vital questions of how to arrange and manage the affairs of a nascent organism, a church body, Matthew remembered that Jesus had something to say as well about authority, and that Jesus had run his own risks in the face of authority. Authority raises a religious question.

A Political Question...

Meanwhile, along the roads in Rochester, my shopping duties done, I had finally meandered into the office. Coffee on, e-mail dispatched, desk cleared, ah, a moment to meditate and to write.

Writing and visiting, two joys that keep me in the ministry. Another of the real joys of ministry with you is the thrill of anticipating our gathering on Sunday. From the layer beneath the skin, in the old bone structure of this church, there is a physical mind that is ever alert, ready to sense, beneath all our pageantry, a full sacrament of love. A Presence. All of the symbols of our common life, even in the great and beautiful space of this sanctuary, are symbols of servant authority. A pulpit: filled by a servant of the Word. An altar: prepared for the eucharistic sacrifice of praise and thanksgiving. A robe and stole: worn to signify the yoke of Christ, a burden and light. A cross, a cross, a cross....GONG! My reverie was suddenly interrupted. The Saturday doorbell rings, and in comes an unknown neighbor to comment on the playing of the chimes—*is there something wrong with your bells?* No. Apparently we were playing some unfamiliar hymns. (Like our sermon hymn today.) We would love to see you in church. *Oh, I am distant from religion.* Even so, he listens, and stops to question the ringing authority that somewhere, somehow means something to him. He leaves, and in the quiet of a Saturday I am again left alone to murmur and ponder the people of God in worship, to see the faces uplifted in hymn and affirmation, to sense the hidden struggles, to admire the silent courage under duress, to be humbled again by the individual acts of kindness and goodness embodied on the Lord's day. Here you are. You are beautiful.

I lollygag. The paper bought at the outset of the day and the onslaught of this narrative episodic sermon lies unread. I flip - now a habit—to the op-ed page. I skim - now a habit - the last two paragraphs of each editorial. A Yale teacher is wondering about authority. Can one nation act alone and unilaterally? Now, paper before me and a sermon for eight days hence to consider, I can see and overhear an anxious concern in the hearts of our people. It is related to the question of authority. In August our staff committee met and I listed three concerns I could see on the horizon for the fall: staff development, building issues, war and peace.

War and peace. Ah, yes. Coffee brewed, radio tuned, here is what I wrote last Saturday. Over time, I would covet your responses: *In most of our churches, people of faith have usually assumed one of* two traditional positions in the face of armed conflict, or as is often the case, a kind of wisened situational combination of the two: pacifism or just war. Often, too, the chief job of the pastor in such a time is to help the congregation think clearly, and also to maintain space for a variety of views within one body. There is much space here at Asbury First. Think of it as an expansive village green. The pacifist position depends upon Matthew, in verses like Chapter 5: 38: *You have heard that it was said, "An eye for an eye, a tooth for a tooth". But I say to you, do not resist one who is evil. But if anyone strikes you on the right cheek, turn to him the other also."* The activist position does too, in verses like Matthew 10: 34, *"Do not think that I have come to bring peace on earth; I have not come to bring peace, but a sword...he who does not take his cross and follow me is not worthy of me."* How shall we think about this?

I know, given the stature and venerability of this pulpit, that many of you have heard these points rehearsed many times, and engaged wisely and sensitively in the past. Perhaps there is little that I can add. You remember that there have been five basic criteria, from Augustine to Aquinas to us, in the so-called just war theory: just cause in response to serious evil; just intention for restoration of peace with justice, not self-enrichment or devastation of another; last resort; have legitimate authority; have a reasonable hope of success, given the necessary constraints of discrimination and proportionality. I am indebted to my friend Phil Amerson for this summary in a recent Oxford paper, available in our church office. These are difficult times and serious questions. Shakespeare: *"Who the sword of heaven will bear must be as holy as severe."*

Response...Restoration...Last...Authority...What has caught me, at least, unprepared this fall, is that it seems that our current course as a country moves in a third way, apart from both the pacifist and activist positions in the history of Christian thought. It seems, at least, that some of our moral debate has now taken leave of the history of Christian ethics altogether, leaving behind both the pacifist and the activist, both the non-retaliatory and the just war positions. What Congress now debates, and is apparently ready to approve, is not a response but a preemption; not a restoration but *a dislocation; not a last but an initial resort; not an act based on a communal authority, but a nearly unilateral act. We are told that this is a new age, that patience must be balanced with realism about the threat at large, that in due time we shall be shown the proof for the need of this new doctrine. But let us be clear: preemption, destruction, initiation, usurpation—these have little basis or foothold in the history of Christian thought, to this point. None, in fact, that I can locate, though am eager to learn from you and others. (No proof more profound can be found to show that truly we live in a post-Christian age). We are left, as disciples of Jesus Christ, either to redefine the expanse of Christian ethics developed over 2000 years, or to reconsider our current debate. Let me ask us in the coming week to assess what we think is true by the mysterious measure of today's scripture: "By what authority?"*

And So...

The rest of this one day in the Day of God was consumed in the act of painting, together, across the quieter expanse of a now empty home. I had no illusions about the authority under which I was set to work. Like the children of Israel I labored a bitter yoke, struggling to accomplish what had been ordered. Mercifully the day ended as we had been invited to two social dinners, both by adult classes of our church and in our church. In the fellowship of this autumn evening we were again connected to our roots in faith. The welcome of a happy gathering, a good meal, a thoughtful program, a generous greeting, a confident service - all these greeted the end of this day. Particularly charming were the clear evidences, in both classes, of active and effective welcoming to newcomers, strangers, new friends. There is a form of authority that is not authoritarian at all. It is the authority of service, to which we are drawn as to our truest home. "Whoever would be great among you must be your servant...Even as the Son of man came not to be served but to serve."

The servant welcome of the adult classes came to mind again in our men's group as it studied Service Tuesday early in the morning (ex libris Dallas Willard), "service":

"What Voice Do You Hear?"
Text: Matthew 22: 1-10
Asbury First United Methodist Church
October 13, 2002
Rev. Dr. Robert A. Hill

Presence in an ordered service of divine worship, your presence here today for instance, is one sign of trust that in this life we are being addressed from beyond. Your presence this morning is an indication, a witness if you will, to your intimation or confidence or something in between, that you are hearing voices, that you are called, spoken to, addressed. What voice do you hear? What characterizes the voice you sense from beyond the bounds of time and space?

By the way, this sensibility created Methodism. Our movement was given voice in this question. Wesley put it a little differently: "Do you know God to be a pardoning God?" What voice do you hear in the reading today? The parable of the wedding banquet, retold in Matthew from a kinder Lukan version, rests on this conviction of a divine beckoning and calling. Here the call is part invitation, part warning, and part summons.

Invitation

Do you hear a voice of invitation?

I think we seldom recognize what a powerful thing an invitation can be. In composing this point I had to stop for a while to let the flood of memory subside along the riverbank of understanding.

In late 1978 we were beginning to adjust to the thought of a first child on the way. Some of you are adjusting to that thought today. Later that winter Jan fell ill and was hospitalized at six months. Surgery was required to remove an ovarian cyst. We were very frightened - at such invasive action, at the prospect of a child lost, at the possibility of even greater danger. We relied on families and friends and young faith. We prayed like you do when you have nothing else. In the time that followed, in the weeks of recuperation, I had a call from an old friend, Bill Swales. He had been thinking about our condition. He called to invite us to take a church in Ithaca. "You can finish school long distance. Forest Home is not much of a church, but it is open. And we want you to come home." On the strength of that invitation, carried along the veteran voice of trusted superintendent, we changed our plans, and 25 years later the formative power of that humble human beckoning looms very large indeed.

We know the power of an invitation when we hungrily receive one heartily desired. Nothing in all the world ever happened between persons without invitations. Every sermon is in some way an invitation to decision for Christian discipleship.

You receive today, again, a personal invitation. The invitation is meant for you, sent to you, an event for you. You are invited to attend the wedding of heaven and earth, to lead a godly life, to lead a life worthy of God, to live in faith and by a conviction, which is a trust, faith is a personal commitment to an unverifiable truth, if we had all proof we want we would not have all the faith we need. Will you come to the banquet?

The voice of invitation is an enticement, a coaxing, a luring, a courting. The board is spread, the meat and drink are prepared. All is well in the house. This open invitation is the mark of Christianity at its best. This invitation is a sign of respect for the diversity of the creation, lived out in tolerance of differences. And what is tolerance but to listen, listen, listen? This church, for all our faults, exemplifies such an openness and tolerance of difference. All too often a church is made up of "moral people who have not time for Jesus, and little interest in the joyful news of the kingdom of God." This invitation is not only open and far-flung; the invitation also goes out with a note attached: "the food will be tasty". In this kingdom there is concern for quality as well as for quantity. There is something satisfying to be had at this meal. We are not always fully awake to what is available within the tender web of human relations.

You remember that St. Matthew, the Evangelist, has a passion. It is evangelism. The point of the Gospel of Mathew the Evangelist is that he is an evangelist. This is his love. His first love. To seek the lost, gather the dispersed, church the unchurched. And it is a passionate love. I can see your passions in the red cheeks, changed breathing, throbbing temples, scowls and sighs, angers and fears and hopes and dreams that attend them. Music, architecture, history, homily, mission, symbol, country, group - these inspire passion. Mostly good. Matthew offers the gift, divinely wrapped, of another, different passion: sharing a first encounter with Christ with those who do not know a single verse, cannot recite a single psalm, cannot describe baptism and communion, do not have a favorite hymn, and have no experience of church committee meetings. This is the great joy of faith, to share it. We only have what we can give away.

The fun of teaching knots is to show the tenderfoot the square knot. Everything else is derivative. The joy of coaching swimming is to help someone learn to float. All the rest is a corallary. The excitement of instruction in a language is the alphabet and the first declension and the initial vocabulary. All the rest is subordinate.

Matthew's passion, offered to Asbury First as a new gift this autumn, is invitation. This is the gift that truly keeps on giving. Find the joy of a treasure in a field, a lost coin found, a prodigal fed, a seed planted, a mustard seed nurtured, and a wedding feast celebrated, and you have found St. Matthew's passion.

The capacity to offer a genuine invitation depends on the measure of verbal kindness, and so personal trust, within a community. Let me ask you to pause for a moment and think about the way we speak.

- What words are on our lips in worship?
- What goes into our conversation at the dinner table?
- What do we say to each other over morning coffee?
- What do we tell our children as we tuck them in at night?

- What news do we share during commercials?
- What is the quality of our discourse?

We are invited to feast with one another. We are invited somehow to communicate to one another that the joy of the Lord is our strength.

You know that Jan and I spend much of the summer on a lake in Central New York. I have overburdened you in the past with reminiscence about a lovely college town nearby. There are other towns too. One is the little hamlet of Morrisville, whose banners carry the slogan, 'One step ahead...' I mentally add, "..of the sheriff". Visually Morrisville offers little. It is a town that never really found itself. Like many lives we can name. You will notice there the sagging roofs, old buildings, gas stations and pizza shops and bars, and a struggling two-year college. It is nothing to look at. But I must bear witness also to what I hear in this visually vacuous village.

In the course of one hot afternoon, I am addressed with kindness. In the car shop: "the tires need rotating". Neither greed nor pride, but honest concern. In the grocery, over bottles returned: "How are you doing without him?" Neither perseverating grasp nor idle curiosity, but genuine concern. In the hardware, "Did you hear about Bill's wife?" Neither gossip nor chit chat but heartfelt worry. In the Town Hall, "It's Rev. Hill". Neither flattery nor false humility but genuine concern. For all its visual vacuity, one hears there a verbal beauty that is cultural prelude to the gospel. Those who have cultural ears to hear, may yet hear.

How many of us, by contrast, live lives that are visually beautiful but verbally vacuous? Maybe that is why Luke, in his telling of this parable, has the invitation go out to the poor, the maimed, the blind and the lame. To begin to invite, let us begin by attending to the character of our conversation as a community.

Warning

But the master's call, as Matthew's darkening tale reveals, is not heeded. The invitation is "taken lightly", or as Matthew puts it, "they made light of it, and went off, one to his farm, another to his business, while the rest seized his servants and treated them shamefully." As they had, we are meant to interpret, the prophets of old.

The divine calling does not stop, but we now hear a second dimension of it. Here the call is not so much an invitation as it is a warning. One of the most startling points in the study of the parables is to notice the difference between Luke's account of the story in Luke 14, and today's reading. Matthew is angry. Here a man has become a king, those who refuse are not forgotten but violently killed, those who miss their chance are not worthy, and many are called but few are chosen. It is hard for me not to overhear some bitter church experience here, perhaps related to the persecution under the Emperor Domitian in the last decade of the first century.

While we may chafe at Matthew's intensity, we can readily appreciate this new voice, a voice of warning. Jesus exists for us at some points as a warning. A warning that there does come a time when it is too late. All the parables have this element in them. The mercy of God is eternal, never ending, all pervading. But the time to accept the invitation is passing; the time to accept is the eternal now. There comes a time when it is too late. When we are sensitive, we hear this same warning all around us.

Here is a business leader, Charles Willie, warning of emptiness: "Those who would master the institutions of our society-a company, a community, or any other collectivity-must decide here and now to give themselves over fully to that which they wish to fully control. By so doing they also will forfeit some of their freedom and flexibility. Is mastery worth the outcome of an imprisoned personality that is efficient, well-organized, but constrained and unspontaneous?"

Here is a scientist, Charles Darwin, of whom a new biography was published recently, naming him the greatest Englishman of his age: "My mind seems to have become a kind of machine for grinding general laws out of a large collection of facts...the loss...is a loss of happiness, and may possibly be injurious to the intellect and more probably to the moral character."

Here is a philosopher, Soren Kierkegaard, warning about motives: "The greatest evil comes not from selfishness but from selflessness in the service of a great cause".

Here is a Methodist Bishop, Sharon Christopher, writing for all our Bishops this week: "A preemptive war by the United States against a nation like Iraq goes against the very grain of our understanding of the gospel, our church's teaching, and our conscience. Preemptive strike does not reflect restraint and does not allow for the adequate pursuit of peaceful means for resolving conflict".

Here is our Bishop, Violet Fisher, warning us about our present peril: "I ask us to turn over to God for healing the anger and the fear and the desire for dominance that would lead us to harm another human being or to acquiesce in harm done to another".

Here are the sermons offered from this pulpit two years ago, along a village green, in which all the predicament of our present perils were forewarned.

There does come a time when it is too late. The parables shout this warning. We cannot play forever with life-threatening nuclear weapons. We cannot supply the world with arms and expect them never to be used. We cannot applaud forever a narrow nationalism ill suited to a global village. There does come a time when it is too late. The parables gracefully warn us of that time. Those of us laden with much property, much knowledge, much position may have a harder time hearing this than we would otherwise.

(The sad story which Matthew alone knows about the poor bloke who has no wedding robe apparently is a warning, either moral or spiritual. If moral, it is a warning that grace is free but not cheap. If spiritual, it is a warning that those invited to a daily feast should appreciate and celebrate.)

Summons

The call to the banquet is an invitation and warning, but in the end it is a summons. "Go therefore to the thoroughfares, and invite to the marriage feast as many as you find…and those servants went out into the streets and gathered all whom they found, both good and bad; so the wedding hall was filled with guests." Gather them all! Good and bad together! Such is the kingdom of heaven. For the corporate community lives by its ability to make distinctions, this blending of good and bad is anathema. For a community that lives on its ability to produce excellence, this common mixture is anathema. "We cook for the common people" said even Origen.

An open, general summons goes out.

Last week, during the sermon before communion, we were invited to think about meals from our time growing up. I recalled in one of our churches long ago the memory of an elderly man, thinking of the summons of a school bell. Every morning he would prepare to go off into the cold, at age 6. For the winter he would cover himself from head to toe in layers of clothing. Then his mother would take a huge pancake from the griddle and put one in each mitten to keep his hands warm. The summons came. The bell rang. He dressed, prepared, and went.

I sat at the traffic light the other day and wondered whether we have the space to receive such a voice. I watched a woman across the traffic light.

Perhaps she is on the run from dawn to dusk. While the coffee is brewing, she throws in a load of wash. While the wash runs, she pours the kids breakfast cereal. While they eat she combs her hair and puts on the day's war paint. Dressed for success, she drives to work, listening to the news and planning comments for the morning meetings. She remembers a football game 12 years earlier. While she types, she reviews the winter wardrobes (son needs boots, daughter a coat). Over lunch she writes a note to her mother: "thinking of you". While mailing the note she realizes her high school's 20-year reunion is next year. On the way home she stops to buy the groceries and gas. While fixing dinner, she calls a friend. A fleeting image of a happy day in the summer puts a catch in her throat. While on the phone, she mops up a spilled glass of milk. While serving dessert, she thinks about the evening meeting, remembering that she agreed to do the devotions. This produces a moment of terror. While the sitter bathes the kids, she heads for the meeting, realizing that the bottles need to be returned. Maybe tomorrow. While the meeting drones on, she plans tomorrow's dinner. At home, she drifts off to sleep, wondering if the kids have clothes for the next day.

For her, for me, for you, this summons is delivered: work is not meant to drive out love. No, nor are any other penultimate passions meant to take the place of God, the God of love in our lives.

I am convinced that in Jesus Christ, light came into a world of darkness. In him we are called - invited, warned, summoned---into the kingdom of heaven. This call is not an abstract, universal bellow. It is a whispering that touches and knocks at the door of every human heart. Jesus teaches of a pardoning God, who is quick to forgive. Jesus tells us of a gathering God, who gathers good and bad together. In him has the light shown in the darkness.

> What voice do you hear?

> How will you respond?

"Risk Management"
Text: Matthew 25: 14-30
Asbury First United Methodist Church
November 17, 2002
The Rev. Dr. Robert A. Hill

Divine Silence

If a sermon is about God and about 20 minutes, a parable, like this one on risk management, is a divine 2 minutes. What does this familiar autumn story tell us? Can we learn something here about divine silence, divine confidence, and divine generosity?

It may be that our ears turn particularly sensitive, today, at the mention of risk. How will we ever manage risk? We are swimming in a green pea soup of anxiety, certainly for the last couple of autumns, and theologically since the moment of another departure and another silence, during the walk out of the Garden of Eden. It is stunning, to some measure, that we have the energy to get here at all, Come Sunday. The church doors open, someone throws on the lights, and in troop young and old, naturally carrying heavy yokes. Perhaps our own job has not been removed, but a neighbor or coworker is on our minds in the invocation. Perhaps we have no illness trailing us, but there is a relative or friend whose face we imagine in the hymn. Perhaps today we do not attend weightily to Osama Bin Laden, but there are other days and other nights when worry takes the upper hand, and maybe, in the Scripture, we meditate on wailing and gnashing of teeth. Perhaps just this moment we are not anxious or fretful or fearful or worried. Perhaps not. The worship service has got the better of us for a moment. Good. Still, we know about fear. Silence and absence are the seedbeds of fear. And this season, at the opening of the 21st century is a season of fear.

Do you remember the autumn of 1999? Another autumn, and another range of worries. Eliot wrote that man is "fear in a handful of dust". Roosevelt asserted, " the only thing we have to fear is fear itself". In 1999, we prepared for Y2K. A woman preparing to preach last week in a workshop in Buffalo recalled that season. She had been a bank teller in December of 1999. She remembered the anxiety of very normal people. "Not just the crazies", she remembered, but all of us, to some degree. Not to get to personal, but, think for a moment. Perhaps you didn't take out any extra money that week - $500 or $5000 "just in case". Perhaps you didn't put a little extra gasoline in the tanks "just in case". Perhaps you didn't fill some extra jugs with water "just in case". Or did you? I remember that at the last minute Jan and I decided not to take a quick trip to N.Y.C. on December 30th to see a play, "Wit", that meant a great deal to me. We decided to stay home, "just in case". A college student in Syracuse remembered that she was then 15, living with her grandmother, who had all her siblings sleep in the basement that night, surrounded, as she colorfully reported, by spam and canned corn. Number 10 cans. When the night passed, they went upstairs, until Dec 31st of the next year. Gramma thought maybe the traditional calendar was right and Y2K was really to start on 1/1/01. So they slept with spam and corn, one can of which had exploded in the cold sometime in the intervening 12 months. And in what exotic city did all this occur? Webster, NY. As Mark Twain said, "I have faced many dangers and troubles in life, most of which never happened".

Y2K is probably as emotionally close as we will ever get in our time to the religious setting of this parable in the life of Jesus and the preaching of the church. The story comes out of a time of apocalyptic expectation. One verse from this era may stand for volumes: "the pitcher is near to the well, the ship to the harbor, the caravan to the city, and life to its conclusion". As in all times, personal or collective, of all fear, so in Matthew's church as in our culture, people swam in a green pea soup of anxiety. They feared an unknown future and sensed divine silence, even divine absence. We are not the first generation to know daily, edgy, fear.

This parable, on the lips of Jesus and in the teaching of Matthew, begins with utter realism. It is as if a man were going on a journey. It is as if the Master were to go away. It is as if the Master has gone away, off to a far country. It is as if a divine, thunderous silence were ours to face. The parable faces divine silence, and encourages us to do the same. So we will begin to manage risk if we begin to risk management. The story emboldens us to name our fears, to admit our sense of ennui, to confess our apprehension. I believe there is a great and healthy good simply to naming, in prayer, morning by morning, what we fear. Otherwise, we may just allow our fears to overcome us. Going to worship, to be present in the divine silence of church, is one way weekly to overcome our fears. We can be honest about divine silence. No one has ever seen God. And would we have it otherwise? Would we truly want a God as plain as the nose on your face, a blasting search light of omnipresence, like a hovering mother unable to cut the umbilical cord, a shouting presence filling every space? In that there is no freedom, neither divine nor human. Thank goodness for the Biblical admission of divine silence.

Divine Confidence

The divine silence carries another gift. For fearful folks such as we, the measures of divine confidence narrated today should be truly encouraging. It is a tremendous vote of confidence in human capacity for good that lies at the heart of the mysterious universal Silence. Has this confidence been bruised and abused? The era of Dresden, Hiroshima, Auschwitz, Tet, Lockerbie, and 9/11 may seem to make such confidence seem ill-placed. Still, the confidence, conveyed in the wide range of human freedoms, remains. For all the possibilities for evil and ill that lie before men and women, nations and states, there are more possibilities for good. Einstein could look relativity and quantum mechanics and their shrouded interplay straight in the eye, and still affirm, "God does not play at dice". He may not fully have internalized the randomness of life. Maybe no one does. Yet his often-cited affirmation is a reflection of divine confidence in the human being, free to love and free for love. The Master of this story goes away. Before leaving, though, he commits Himself to the welfare of his servants. He leaves things in their hands, confident that they will manage risk by learning to risk management. He gives no instructions. He provides no direction. He includes no briefing, no game plan. There is no briefing from the heavenly White House. He takes his leave, confident. Those who will learn to manage risk will learn to risk management. There is only one way to live with freedom. Freely. As confident as a bridegroom leaving his chamber, ready to run his course with joy. This is the confidence of the sun coming up bright and golden on the morning horizon and saying, ray by ray, "Day is breaking. Light is shining. Life is good, and what is good is what lives." Maybe the silence of the divine in our time is the clearest speech possible to declaim the eternal confidence in what human beings can become. Maybe the divine absence of our time is the fullest presence possible to embody the eternal confidence in what human beings can become. I admit the audacious risk.

There is fear and risk aplenty today. I know the fear of a 401K becoming a 201K, and the risk of searching for peace in a nuclear jungle. But look east. Dawn is breaking. A great orange sun. Spectacular. The sun will rise upon whatever we do, just as God's creative power will continue. The rays of this orb will travel to us whatever we do, just as Christ's forgiving grace will continue. The sweet touch of this SON LIGHT upon our cheeks, winter and summer, will continue whatever we do, just as the Holy Spirit cannot stop loving you. Behold the divine confidence, entrusting this global village to human hands.

Colin Williams, an English Methodist, ran the Yale Divinity School a generation ago. Here is his view of Sunday morning: *"THE ESSENTIAL WORK OF PREACHING IS TO GIVE PEOPLE A BASIC SENSE OF SECURITY FROM WHICH THEY ARE FREE TO CREATE CHANGE AND TO WORK IN THE WORLD."*

We are burying a generation of saints who learned this and taught it and knew it in their bones. They have a confidence that has not curdled into certainty. This reflects the divine confidence acclaimed in the talents parable. One of our recently deceased Christian Gentlemen, Forrest Witmeyer, as a young man was a close friend of Norman Vincent Peale, while Norman preached in Syracuse, and just before he met Ruth Stapleton, a young co-ed at SU. Here is a lifetime, 95 years, of preaching summed up in Peale's 7 words: "You can if you think you can."

The divine confidence is meant to wash out all that prideful pseudo-humility we somewhere pick up, in moving to adulthood. Better, far better, especially in earshot of Matthew 25, better to hear the admonition attributed to Nelson Mandela: "Our deepest fear is not that we are inadequate. Our deepest fear is that we are powerful beyond measure. It is our light, not our darkness that most frightens us. We ask ourselves, Who am I to be brilliant, gorgeous, talented, fabulous? Actually, who are you not to be? You are a child of God. Your playing small does not serve the world. There is nothing enlightened about shrinking so that other people won't feel insecure around you. We are all meant to shine, as children do. We were born to make manifest the glory of God that is within us. It is not in just some of us; it is in everyone. And as we let our own light shine, we unconsciously give other people permission to do the same. As we are liberated from our own fear, our presence automatically liberates others."

Divine Generosity

To this moment the divine silence and divine confidence do not come empty handed. A talent, as you have often heard, is a year's salary. A talent is a lot of money. And five? And two? The point of tale is clear: there is no divine parsimony at work today, no heavenly harsh frugality. Grace is lavish, uncritical and personal, and generous to a fault. There is no counting out of coins or measured calculation of donations. All are given a windfall, a fantastic endowment, a greathearted present. Most of us, as our behaviors readily show, already are given far more than we know what to do with. And the gift is free of charge. To each is given according to his ability. "From each according to his ability, to each according to his need." Karl Marx took up the slogan about the time the church pawned it.

Sometimes children, like those receiving the strange world of the Bible today, live out ahead of us. You can see at Halloween. Here they come, up the path, ready to shine and receive. A nurse, a cowboy, a superhero, a monster. In our neighborhood this year we were cordially visited by Judas Maccabeus. (We live among Jews and Gentiles both). I also saw the best Halloween costume ever, a boy dressed as left over spaghetti: red suit, stringy attachments, meatball nose, and cullender for a hat. Into each bag free generosities are placed, and off they go into the future to invest the kindnesses received in youth in the use of talents in adulthood. The 2 year old nurse will manage Rochester General one day. The six year old cowboy will manage a Texas oil drill one day. The superhero will manage a communications company one day. The monster will manage to teach high school one day. Judas Maccabeus will manage to become a Rabbi. And Mr. Used Spaghetti? - definitely headed for the minstry. Gotta be. What do you say to the children who have a costume but cannot name it? And who are you? I cannot say. And what are you? I do not know. One day, we pray, they shall. They shall hear, on earth as it is in heaven, "Well done, though good and faithful servant. You have been faithful over a little. We will set you over much. Enter into the joy of the Master!"

And A Matthean Warning

What do you do with someone who will not receive what is given? Is that sin—the refusal to receive what is given? Is that sin - the mortal fear of using what is given? Is that sin the existential rejection of generosity?

It does not surprise us to find in Matthew a dark warning at the end of a great story. This is the Gospel of the wedding robe forgotten: "cast him into the outer darkness..." This is the Gospel of the sheep and goats: "you did it not to me - go away into eternal punishment". This is the Gospel of the Sermon on the Mount: "Not everyone who says to me Lord, Lord - but those who do the will of ..." This is the Gospel of houses built on sand and rock - 'and the rain fell, and the floods came..." This is the Gospel of maidens who trim not lamps - truly I do not know you; of a vineyard owner returning with vengeance - "put those wretches to a miserable death"; of a withering fig tree; of the miserly servant who is forgiven but does not forgive - delivered to jailers; and so on.

In these later parables, all of which end with a warning, as in the Gospel as a whole, Matthew has structured his teaching to carry this lifelong set of warnings. All 17 warnings (if I count them right) are the same. They are moral warnings: grace is free but not cheap. Straighten up and fly right. They are spiritual warnings: life is a tremendous gift! Dance don't droop, celebrate don't self-efface.

Perhaps, to finish today, we shall find faith and take courage from the divine silence, confidence and generosity proclaimed. If we do, we may be able to manage risk. The only way to manage risk, in this Gospel, is to risk management. The only way to manage our fearful risks is to risk management, in fear and trembling, of God's silent, confident, generous gifts to us. If you are going to manage risk this week, you will then risk a little management. You will manage to take responsibility.

> I'm a teacher. I couldn't possibly help manage the school.
> I'm a worker. I couldn't possibly run the place.
> I' m a preacher. I couldn't possibly manage a denomination.
> I'm an attorney. I couldn't possibly manage a corporation.
> I'm a mom. I couldn't possibly manage a nursery.
> I'm a doctor. I couldn't possibly manage a practice.
> I'm a busy taxpayer. I couldn't possibly manage a town.

But listen. The way the world gets better is when humble people manage the risk in life by risking their talents in management of a part of the world. Can't somebody else go to all those meetings? Sure. Who?

We can manage risk together if we all do our part. You can manage risk. Here is how: risk management.

"Mountainview"
Text: Luke 9: 28-36
Asbury First United Methodist Church
Transfiguration Sunday
Rev. Robert A. Hill
March 5, 2000

Whence Saving Insight?

When and how does a moment of insight come? What are the steps up along the mountain trail that give a moment of clarity that can save us?

Peter must have heard our Lord's ageless command: "If anyone would come after me, let him deny himself, and take up his cross, and follow." (Mark 8: 32). Then Peter is led, step by step, up a high mountain, where something…unearthly…occurs. He sees what cannot be seen. And, from this mountainview, for a moment, there is insight and there is clarity.

When and how does such a moment arrive, a moment of clarity that can save us from an anger that leads to murder, or a heartache that leads to suicide, or a despair over a gun-totting nation drenched in violence, or a chagrin about a country that ever more closely approximates Fosdick's verse, "rich in things and poor in soul"?

Today's Gospel promises you a mountain view, clarity and insight, found step by step along the rocky trail of life, that can lift us up above sin and death and the threat of meaninglessness.

Walk along with me, if you will, for just a few minutes…up the mountain path we go…and take, Come Sunday, a divergent road, like our Poet said,

Two roads diverged in a yellow wood
And sorry I could not travel both and be one traveler
Long I stood and looked down one as far as I could
To where it bent in the undergrowth

Then took the other as just as fair
Though having perhaps the better claim
For it was grassy and wanted wear
Though as for that the parting there
Had worn them both about the same...
I shall be telling this with a sigh
Somewhere ages and ages hence
Two roads diverged in a wood and I
Took the One less traveled by
And that has made all the difference.

1. Insight Through the Thicket of Personal Need

One step toward insight lies through the thicket of personal need. Careful, step carefully here. Here you recognize your mortality. "It is a great life, but few of us get out alive." Here you admit that the acts of desperation in news reports come from conditions you also know. Fear, anger, jealousy, hatred, dread. Here, step lightly, you see the shadow, and your shadow in the greater shadow. One called this "the feeling of absolute dependence". Here we are confessional. We say, "Hello. My name is John Smith and I am an alcoholic." We say, "We have erred and strayed from thy ways like lost sheep." We say, "There but for the grace of God, go I."

Today's Baptism reminds me of the first time I was left alone with our first child, to give her mother a night out. She had been the most pleasant of children, happy and bright, sleeping through the night. She hardly cried. But that hot August night, at the very moment the door closed and the car drove off, she began to wail. Not to whimper or weep, but to wail and shriek and scream. Five, twenty five, fifty minutes. I was really shaken, terrified, angry and frustrated, at my wit's end, and probably at the edge of some irrational behavior. Over the din of the howling daughter, I heard the doorbell. In came our church's lay leader, Bernice Danks, a veteran nurse and teacher of nurses who wordlessly took the child and somehow the howling ceased. "Oh, I like to make a few house visits a week. It's a little routine of mine...You know I tell my nursing students that we call the things that are most important, 'routine'...and I came by the parsonage and for some reason I decided to stop. I hope you don't mind the intrusion...What a pleasant baby she is!"

When we are helpless, insight can come.

Wesley is still with us to ask, "will you visit from house to house?" From Brentwood to Brighton and beyond? Insight sees inside the closed door of personal need, and measures the distance between public appearance and private reality.

2. *Insight Over the River of Others' Hurts*

A second step toward insight lies over the river of another's hurt. Here, we'll jump the river at the portage path, where we bear each other's burdens like canoes carried in tandem. A moment of clarity can come when you truly see another's plight, and feel it in your heart. Some insight comes from serving others, some from sensing others' hurt. It is really a matter of understanding power, this insight about others. Think of the Prince and the Pauper, or of Lazarus and Dives. Insight happens in the chorus of the common life, when we sing out, "so that's what is like to be you..."

The progressive tradition, theological and political, which is Rochester's hallmark (Rauschenbusch, Douglass, Anthony, and others) may be criticized as a "johnny one note" presentation. But if you have to choose just one note to play, this is the one to pick. Jesus means freedom. To learn about the nature of power, and the effects of power, we listen to the powerless.

Men, listen to the women about whom you care, as they describe being pulled over on the thruway in a winter night. With red lights flashing...sirens wailing...car door thudding...a tall male figure in uniform and wide brimmed hat...a revolver in the belt... "May I see your license please?"...Men, listen to women.

Majority, listen to the minority describe the feeling of being stopped on the front porch step, at night, after a long day of menial work, again with the lights flashing and the uniforms and hats and.."Gun!" 41 bullets later a tragedy—unintended to be sure—

has occurred. Not a gun but a wallet. Such a tragedy for all. But maybe it can help us to gain insight, to feel what others feel. Majority, listen to the minority.

Insight comes through the common song that recognizes another's hurt.

You know, we recognize this chance for insight every Sunday as we sing hymns together, to recognize that we are all in this together.

3. *Insight Scaling the Cliffs of Reason*

A third step toward insight lies over the cliff of reason. "Come let us reason together" says the Psalmist. God has entrusted us with freedom, and with minds to think through our use of freedom. While reason has its limits, it is reason, finally, that will help us learn the arts of disagreement—at home, at work, in church, in the community. We say, "try to be reasonable". And reason often prevails. If you ever doubt the power of reason to bring insight, remember the words of the Psalmist, and the voices of great minds through the ages. Josiah Royce's *Sources of Religious Insight*, which provides the outline for this sermon, comes to mind. Come let us reason together...

You know, we recognize this chance for insight, this moment of clarity, every Sunday through a sermon, a word fitly spoken (we hope).

4. *Insight Across the Gorge of the Will*

A fourth step toward insight lies across the great gorge of the will. Look before you leap. We are here ever closer to the mountaintop. Real insight comes in a moment of decision. Some say we learn to choose. But our experience is that we learn *by choosing*. Viktor Frankl spent his whole life developing the "logotherapy" around this one conviction: we grow by deciding. Choose. You cannot lose, in the fullest sense, and in the long run. Choose. Either way, you have learned, you will grow, you have changed, you will improve, you have developed. Choose.

Faith is not a matter of emotion or feeling or soul or heart or intellect only. First, faith is a decision. "If anyone would come after me, let him deny himself and take up his cross and follow."

As Kierkegaard put it, "either\or"... Either God exists or not. Decide. Either you see God in Christ or not. Decide. Either Jesus Christ has a claim on your life or not. Decide. Either every day is a chance for love or not. Decide. Either the way of love means particular consequent acts regarding your time, your money, your body, your community...or not. Decide.

Faith is not as much thrill as it is will.

You know, we recognize this chance for insight every Sunday, in a moment of invitation—to devotion, to discipline, to dedication.

5. *Insight Upon the Summit of Loyalty*

A fifth step toward insight brings us to the summit. There. Take a breath. Up here, the air is rarified. Up here, you may have a moment of clarity. For the fifth step toward insight brings us to the altar of loyalty.

Forgive the use of archaic words—loyalty, duty, chivalry. Beware though the sense that loyalty is a matter of sullen obedience. On the contrary! Loyalty is the red flame lit in the heart's chancel, lit with the mixture of personal need and social concern, illumined by the reason and ignited by the will. Loyalty combines the conservative concern for morality with the liberal hunger for justice. Loyalty is life, but life with a purpose.

Insight, real clarity, can come with a brush up with loyalty. Tell me what you give to, and I will tell you who you are. Tell me what you sacrifice for, and I will tell you who you are. Tell me what altar you face, and I will tell you who you are.

And real loyalty is magnanimous. Real loyalty is bighearted enough to honor an opponent's loyalty. At the summit, there can be a reverent respect for another's loyalty, truly lived, even when it clashes with our own. Maybe especially then. US Grant felt this at Appomatox as he took the sword from RE Lee. It is chivalry, this honoring of loyal opposition. We were once known for this kind of chivalry, a reverent respect for divergent loyalties, as long as they did not eclipse the one great loyalty.

Such a memory could help our political conversations, reminding us that at depth loyalties converge out of difference. Surface difference can occlude deeper agreements. Look at our supposedly varied political leaders, for example. George W. Bush is a Methodist. Hillary Clinton is a Methodist. Bob Dole is a Methodist. Tipper Gore is a Methodist! Loyalty has a magnanimous depth that honors other's divergent loyalties.

One of the strangest turns in the New Testament is found in 1 Corinthians 15. After Paul has reached the very summit of our faith, and sings of the resurrection in such heavenly tones, then, immediately, he turns to—do you remember?—the collection! A matter of loyalty.

Where your treasure is, there will your heart be also.

You know, we recognize this chance for insight every Sunday, through the presentation of gifts, an expression of loyalty, at the altar of grace and freedom and love.

Mountainview

Several years ago, we worshipped in the tiniest church in our area. A little Adirondack chapel, at the end of the trail, high up in the northern mountains. Beyond Owl's Head, and Chasm Falls and Wolf Pond, there is the summit of Mountainview, with its chapel and pump organ and wooden pews and simple pulpit, and humble service, still though a service like this one or any --- *a chance for saving insight as we recognize personal need, others' hurts, the power of reason, the importance of will, the force of loyalty—in the prayer of confession, the music of community, the preaching of the Word, the invitation to decision, and the loyal offering of gifts.*

Let insight abound on the curvaceous slopes of personal need! Let insight abound on the majestic mountains of social holiness! Let insight abound on the prodigious cliffs of reason and will! Let insight abound on the purple mountain summit of loyalty—from every mountainview, let insight abound! So that, to paraphrase the spiritual, we might sing, *insight at last, insight at last, thank God Almighty, we have saving insight at last.*

"Trust"
Text: Luke 13:1-9
Lent 2001
Asbury First United Methodist Church
March 18, 2001
Rev. Dr.Robert A. Hill

1. A Pasture View

A friend told me a story last winter.

He has friends who live on a farm in Michigan. The country landscape there is apparently similar to that in our region. This is a multi-generational family farm. If you were to visit this week, you would find three generations working together. The grandfather died a few years ago, but his sons, grandsons and great-grandsons still plow and harvest, milk and feed.

The matriarch of the family is now older and weaker. She was a typical farm wife of her generation, working alongside her children and husband. When plowing time came in the spring she would fix lunches for all hands, and deliver them into the fields. She delivered the meal, and while they ate, she would take over and plow. The same kinds of routines held for other seasons. The rhythms of seed and harvest, birth and decay set the beat for her life.

Now she is alone much of the time, in the old farm house. Her kids feed her breakfast in the morning and dinner at night. But every day, after breakfast, they settle her into a comfortable easy chair that rocks in front of an open bay window, from which she can look out onto the fields and forests and pastures of her home. Every day she watches, breakfast to dinner.

Now this is not an active scene. The barn and equipment are not in view. Most winter days there are no people to observe. A car on the road every half-hour is a lot of traffic. And snow lying on corn stubble looks about as exciting as it did one hundred years ago. Yet, she watches and looks. She seems to be deeply contented, as the late winter snow falls. She is eased and settled and comforted, looking out on a frosty field. There is something in that utterly ordinary scene that seizes her.

She has a sense, I think, of presence. Maybe she is weak and maybe she even has some mild dementia and maybe she doses every now and then, rocking in front of the window. But this ordinary winter story captivates me, because I think she is enthralled by something not quite visible to the naked eye, yet present. *There is something there, something alive, something at work, just beyond our comprehension.* She rocks and stays alert to presence. She has a hard won trust in Presence, a kind of trust for which life is meant and for which with all our hearts we do passionately long and hunger.

2. A Vineyard View

The lesson for today tells of another view, not a pasture view but a vineyard view, not from Michigan but from Palestine, not of wheat but of grapes, not in winter but in harvest. This is one of the parables of the fig tree.

Ah the fig tree. From the fig tree learn its lesson. You know what it means to be a fig tree in the New Testament. It is like being a turkey in late November, like the captured journalist chained to the Khmer Rouge in "The Killing Fields", or like being a helicopter pilot in a shooting war, or like being a green beer on St. Patrick's day. You know you are going down. It's like the American Airlines baggage attendant with whom we spoke after four days with no luggage and a wedding coming in the afternoon. "You will have to talk to my wife", I cautioned. "I understand", he empathized. *"You do not understand"*, she retorted, *"you do not. How would you like to go to a wedding dressed in your aunt's underwear?"* (I actually was interested in how he might respond to this, but I couldn't hear). No, like the fig tree, you know you are going down.

People step aside when they hear that the story is about a fig tree. They step back ten feet, because they know what is coming.

Sure enough, at least at the outset, doom descends. In stomps the owner. Stomp, stomp, stomp. Fee fie foe fum. Yes, we know what is coming. I have seen this lousy, lazy, no good, flee bitten moth eaten, barren, fruitless, faithless, heartless, ruthless fig tree for three years, and nothing. Where is the fruit? Where is the beef? Show me the money! Yes, we have a sinking feeling about the old fig tree, having heard a sermon or three. Is there not fruit? And here it comes... Cut it down, throw it in the fire, off with their heads.

And in the other Gospels, that is that. One dead fig tree, and let it be a warning to us. I came not to bring peace but a sword. Not a jot or a tittle will pass away. Woe to you...

Which is, of course, what makes today's lesson so interesting. Guess what? It's not over, at least according to Jesus in Luke 13. No, it's not over, yet. This is the Gospel according to Yogi Berra. "It ain't over 'til it's over". With a little bit of Irish blarney, a little Woody Allen, a little cunning and creativity, a little psalmist and saint in him, this lowly vinedresser says, "Well, hang on a minute..." *There is something there. He sees something. Something alive, something at work, just beyond our comprehension.*

3. A Pasture View

Meanwhile, down on the Michigan farm...

It is this same trust that keeps the woman at the farm house window, keeps her there and alive and attentive.

Picture her, this week, if you need and want reassurance. She has seen life from both sides. Hail and blizzard. Silo accident and depression. Birth and death. Happiness in youth and tragedy in age. She has seen her husband grow up and grow old and die, as most wives do. She has cleaned out the barn, stretched a budget to fit over many children, and kept the sabbath in the process. And now she just watches. Today there is a light snow falling to dust the corn stubble, and the wind is strong.

I mean this. Whether or not she knows about heaven, she certainly knows about hell. She knows about regret and anxiety. John Paul Sartre said that hell is other people, a continental dyspepsia that I have never understood (except during the sessions of Jurisdictional Conference). Two shorter, better definitions of hell are regret and anxiety. Our rocking farm wife has known them, too. How could she not? Regret when the son leaves the farm for dental school. Anxiety over the crop planted but not harvested. Regret at trips to Florida never taken when grandpa was well. Anxiety over aging and care and dependence. Regret over misdeeds in youth and mistakes in speech. Anxiety about all that is yet to be, on earth as it is in heaven. Regret is hell in the past tense. Anxiety is hell in the future tense.

Nevertheless (a sermon in a single word), Nevertheless, she rocks and watches and is comforted by what she sees. To you and me, what she sees is Andrew Wyeth on a bad day. But she sees something else. *There is something there. There is something alive, at work, just below the edge of our comprehension.* Maybe it helps the vision to have a mild dementia. What heals regret and what tempers anxiety is what we are given--in trust.

4. A Vineyard View

Meanwhile, back in Palestine...

Trust is what the vinedresser in our parable displays. He has a certain confidence, perhaps a confidence born of obedience to a great and loving Lord, yet still a confidence that where there is a will there is a way, no matter what the immediate cornstubble evidence suggests.

I struggle to intuit why this altered fig tree parable was so important for Luke and Luke's struggling church. As we saw last week, all these chapters 10 to 20 Luke has added to Mark's asperity. They must have had singular meaning for Luke's church fifty years after Jesus' death and resurrection. Perhaps, perhaps, the parable is meant to give trusting patience to those who are waiting out what scholars call the "delay of the parousia", or the expected but not actualized return of Christ on the clouds of heaven (1 Thess. 4-5). "Give me just a little more time…" sings the gardener.

Let it be, he says. Let it be.

His is not a naïve view. No, he recognizes that there comes a time when it is too late in every venture. He recognizes that the power to kill and give life is not his own. He recognizes that human labor and human investment is required for any progress. He recognizes the messiness of manure and dailyness of water. He recognizes that trust for the future is trust, not in human wisdom, but in divine grace. He recognizes the rigid limits of nature and history. He is a realist.

But he trusts that there is *something there, something alive, something not quite phenomenal, something just beyond our comprehension.*

I could compare his sense, his trust to a March day when it is still winter. Yet, there is a sense, a feeling. There are geese flying past, v by v. There is a blueish tint in the evergreens. There is more light and better light. There is wind, but not with quite the bite. One can fairly taste the maple syrup brewing miles away. Spring is coming.

Give me just a little more time, he asks. Do you have the feeling that he will ask the same a year from now, if things are no different? I do. He harbors an inexplicable but crucial sense of trust that things will work out.

As a Methodist Christian, I want that trust in my heart as I see the left and right fight. Some of us talk from the left, and yet live from the right. Others talk from the right and live from the left. We talk a good social liberal game, but support all manner of segregation and injustice in where we live, how we live, as we live. Pounding nails for Habitat we will do, but don't ask us to live in that neighborhood or have our children in those schools. We talk a good moral conservative game, but support all manner of waywardness when our own rights are at stake. Great leaders, too many to count, preach about righteousness and justice and civil rights, and go right ahead fathering children out of wedlock. If I read Amos right, social justice and personal morality go together, and where you lack one over time you lack the other. It looks like snow on cornstalks, an ugly sameness. I want to shout: "Give me just a little more time! Another generation, some manure and water, that is a few good preachers and a basket of money, and you just watch the figs fall, too many to count!" *I want that trust that there is something there, alive, incomprehensible, that may change the equation.*

As an eagle scout, I want that trust in my heart as I see a tragedy looming for boy scouting. Just at the time when our culture most needs the kind of mentoring between fathers and sons at which scouting excels--I am its witness-- the scouts are racing headlong toward a tragic collision, a collision of social justice and personal morality. Where have we heard this before? Before the shooting begins, perhaps today's vinedresser can help us to find a way through, with a sense of trust. Give it a little time, manure and water. (Personally, I think the scouts need to look at some optional local decisions and empowerments, and to listen to their leaders under age 40). Yes, today it looks like another case of snow on cornstubble, ugly and unchangeable. *I want that trust that there is something alive, incomprehensible, that may open up a different conversation, a new way that honestly respects both the plumb line of justice and the plumb line of righteousness, as well as the historical, organizational, relational and other peculiarities of the scouting program.*

As an American, I want that trust in my heart as I see the tragedy of family life across this great land. A baby conceived today runs the gauntlets of abortion, addiction, poverty, single parenting, neglect and abuse. The statistics are grim. Our bishops were so right to focus in our time on children and poverty. Snow on stubble. *I want that trust that there is something alive, incomprehensible, that may strangely bring fruit from a barren cultural fig tree.*

As a pastor, I want to be able to offer a sense of trust to you. Right now. Realistically, yes, but personally and truly. In place of your heartfelt regret, carried like a millstone for months or years. In place of your frightful and human anxiety, carried like a millstone for months and years. The anxieties of youth and the regrets of age. May they be gone, or at least placed in a "lock box" (!), tempered and tamed and tethered by trust. *I want that trust that there is something close to your heart, alive, maybe not quite comprehensible, that whispers...let it be...give it another year...maybe a little manure and water...let it be.*

And as a middle aged white guy, stuck somewhere between regret and anxiety *I want that trust, that simple trust like those who heard beside the Syrian sea, the gracious calling of the Lord, let us like them without a word rise up and follow thee.*

5. A Pasture View

Meanwhile, down on the farm...

Think about her this week, alone and content, looking out onto a gray pasture.

What keeps her going? What helps her see? What makes her happy? What brings her comfort and peace?

Is it that trust, that human response to the faith of Jesus Christ, that loving trust that "bears all things, believes all things, hopes all things and endures all things"? (1 Corinthians 13)

One early follower of Jesus said, "One thing I do, forgetting what lies behind and straining forward to what lies ahead, I press on toward the goal for the prize of the upward call of God in Christ Jesus?" (Paul of Tarsus).

An Irish man, Patrick, a killer of snakes and a lover of souls pronounced the same blessing, of "Christ before me Christ beneath?" (St. Patrick's breastplate).

Listen to that medieval convent maiden's prayer, "and all will be well and all will be well?" (Julian of Norwich).

As they sing at Taize, "ubi caritas, deus ibi est"?

There is something there. Alive and untamed. Creating trust, trust, trust, deep in the heart.

Paul Lehmann taught us, "God is at work in the world to make and keep human life human."

Ralph Harper learned, "Presence suggests an alternate way of thinking about time and space".

In an early pastoral visit, I heard a homebound octogenarian, eyes gleaming, affirm: "I know whom I can trust."

David sang in the Psalms, "The Lord is my light and my salvation, whom shall I fear?"

The soul that on Jesus still leans for repose
I will not, I will not desert to its foes
That soul though all hell should endeavor to shake
I will never, no never, no never forsake.

"There's No Place Like Home"
Text: Luke 19: 28-40
Asbury First United Methodist Church
April 8, 2001
Rev. Dr. Robert A Hill

Not So Long Ago

It is not so long ago that we greeted Jesus at his nativity, singing carols and lighting candles of hope. It is not so long ago that we witnessed his growth in wisdom and stature, in the knowledge and love of God, while as a teenager he taught in the temple. It is not so long ago that this mighty young man Jesus stooped, fully human, for baptism in the surging river Jordan, the river of death and life. It is not so long ago that we saw him take up his ministry among us, preaching and teaching and healing. It is not so long ago that with Peter and James and John we saw him ascend the Mountain of the Transfiguration. With him, up through the mountains we have climbed this Lent, step by step.

First, forgiveness. Second, salvation. Third, trust. Fourth, fasting. And now the passion. And now it is time to come down from the mountain, to take the full measure of this Man, and to have the courage to let Him take our full measure, too. The crisp air and vistas of the mountain pass have fed our souls. But now it is time to head home, and turn our face to Jerusalem.

Coming Home

The road down the Mount of Olives, or down any mountain, can tax the traveler. It reminds us all of earlier homecomings.

Odysseus walking the last few miles to Thebes. Socrates walking to the center of Athens and the cup of hemlock. Richard the Lionhearted sailing the English Channel, heading home. A prodigal son, scuffling up the last mile of country road toward a dreaded homecoming. You, returning at last to whatever you have long avoided, wandering as you have in Galilee for the rest of life. At last, there is the Emerald City, and the road home.

Today, I raise just one question. What was Jesus' state of mind? What was on his mind and heart, as he entered the Holy City?

There's No Place Like Home (Loneliness)

It is perilous, even arrogant, at this late date and from this great distance, to try to imagine Jesus' state of mind as he descends the Mountain and enters the City.

Albert Schweitzer, before he went off to heal the jungle sick, showed convincingly how inevitably errant are all such attempts. More recent attempts, even the best like that of Marcus Borg, only confirm Schweitzer's thesis. We paint our own inner lives into the life of Jesus, when we try to see what cannot be seen in Scripture. That is, against some more popular work of recent years, I still fully agree with Schweitzer. And yet, particularly at this point in his journey, at the entrance into the Holy City, and on the threshold of his own death, we are haunted - are we not? - by the desire to see what Jesus saw, feel what he felt and sense what he did sense, coming home.

Now Jesus is walking down into the city, down off the mountain, and down into the heart of his destiny. He is going to his grave.

Some of the Gospel today, as Jesus heads home, is too true to be good. He is not at home, not at home, in a world of injustice, abuse, violence, and death. For him, in such a benighted world, there is no place like home.

As are we all, though it seems sometimes to be a conspiratorially well kept secret. We all are walking down the Lenten mountain and into our lasting, our last future. Every one of us is going to die. We are going home.

Here are two possible sentiments in Jesus' heart and mind as he descends the Mount of Olives.

One, he looks back upon his ministry and feels that *there is no place like home.* He has found no lasting nest on earth, no lasting crib, no lasting domicile. He has found opposition and rejection. He has encountered misunderstanding and criticism. To a harsh world he has brought a gentle manner. To a wolfish world he has brought the labor of love. To a selfish community he has brought the summons to service. To an inconsistent dozen disciples, he has brought the steady presence of peace. He has not found a home, not here. *There is no place like home*, for Jesus, descending the Mount of Olives. He has even said of himself, "foxes have their holes, and birds of the air their nests, but the Son of Man has no place to lay his head."

Some of greatest sentences ever written in English are devoted to a similar ennui, a similar existential vagrancy.

And those of us who have been shot out of the saddle, riding for a righteous cause, as we dust ourselves off and bind our wounds, we do so in the best of company, in the company of the crucified, for whom, on this green earth, as yet, there is no place like home. Yes, we have lost a hospital in Rochester. In 1992 Rochester was praised in the national debates as the model city for health care - cooperative, high quality, moderate cost, comprehensively universal. Something happened, over eight years. And some - doctors, nurses, workers, volunteers, donors - who worked hard to save the Genesee, feel shot out of the saddle. But let me ask you something. What other saddle would they have rather ridden? Some losing causes are worth support even in defeat. I would rather be shot out of the right saddle than to canter comfortably all the live, long day in the wrong saddle. So dust off, bind the wound, and get ready to ride again.

For this city, the question is now sharply put. Are we going to hang together, over time, as a community, or are we going to hang separately? The definition of community in Rochester is hanging in the balance. Are we going to shuffle off to 15 little suburban pods, and live apart, or are we going to enjoy the full village green which life can offer us, if we will live together. The death of the Genesee is a stern warning to all urban regional nonprofit historic hundred year old Rochester institutions. Like AFUMC. Just because we were alive last year is no guarantee that we will be next year. We have not a person, dollar, idea or dream to spare. Not one. And it is, let us confess it, an uphill pull. But there is no other saddle I would ride in, for all the risk. This is the place to be!

Only, for this church to have a future we will have to tithe, worship, and invite with disciplined regularity. We are not doing so, yet. The condition of AFUMC in 2020, even its existence, is being worked out hourly this year and next year and the next. Give! Pray! Welcome! Or die.

There's No Place Like Home (Longing)

But there is something else alive in this homeless homecoming. Frederik Beuchner compares the feeling of faith to the feeling homesickness, that longing for the feeling of home. Faith is a heartfelt longing for the comforts of home.

Two, Jesus looks forward to his passion and feels that *there is no place like home*. He has come and now he must go. He tarries for a while, but he is going home. Only the greatest of the Gospels, that of John, fully and resoundingly displays this sentiment. But it is present, muted, in Luke as well. Jesus must endure the cross, just as we inevitably must endure tragedy, accident, betrayal, injustice, failure and death. We have the finest of company, the Lord Jesus Christ himself, when we endure life's damaging darkness. Some have lost loved ones to death this week. Some have lost beloved institutions to death this week. Some have lost beloved dreams to death this week. And Jesus walks beside you. In fact, this is his peculiarly chosen path, his way, his way of the cross. All of the passion, all of the passion music from a week ago, all of it, the cross itself, acclaim, in passion, the compassion of God in Christ our Lord. God has passion for compassion. So Jesus looks forward - does he not? - to the completion of his mission, to the last word in the soliloquy, to the transition to glory. Again, only John has fully held this diamond. Only he sees the cross as glory, without remainder. Only he has Jesus say, on the cross, "it is completed". But Luke too senses Jesus homesickness at his homeless homecoming. His longing for God. And we sense it too, because we feel it too: *there is no place like home.*

Some of the Gospel today, as Jesus heads home, is too good to be true. This greatest of passionate tragedies, the cross of Christ our Lord, is the passageway, strangely, wonderfully, to our heavenly home. He dies as we die. And we die with Him. We all die. We are not even temporarily immortal. Yet, attendant upon this road down the mountain and into the city, there resounds, softly at first, a carol of grace, a carol of love, a carol for all, like we, who are going home.

John sees it best. Only John places Jesus in Jerusalem thrice. Only in John does Jesus raise the dead at mid Gospel - "Lazarus, come out!" Only in John does Jesus preach for five chapters on the last evening, washing feet rather than celebrating mass. Only in John does Jesus make the Jerusalem road fully and only a road of glory, from Palm Sunday to Easter. Only in John does Jesus say, "In my Father's House there are many rooms…" He is going home, home. And somehow, again strangely, we know the way where he is going. For it is our way, too. Only in John does Jesus walk serenely to Golgotha. Only in John does Jesus walk to death like God striding upon the earth. Only in John does Jesus pronounce GLORY from the jaws of death. Remember his dying word. Not "eli, eli" as in Mark. Not "Father forgive them" as in Luke. Simply, serenely, powerful, triumphantly, yes, gloriously, he says, in John, "It is finished." It is done, completed, perfected - finished. He dies to rise, and go home, feeling and singing, "there's no place like home."

This homesickness, this spirited sense that home is over the next street, up the winding trail to the cross, this hunger for home, this is what Paul meant: *this slight momentary affliction is preparing for us an eternal weight of glory beyond all comparison* A Summons (5-6).

Conclusion

In Whittier's poem:

*I know not what the future hath of marvel or surprise
Assured alone that life and death God's mercy underlies.*

*And so beside the silent sea
I wait the muffled oar
No harm from Him can come to me
On ocean or on shore.*

*I know not where His islands lift
Their fronded palms in air
I only know I cannot drift
Beyond His love and care.*

"Surviving Survival"
Text: Luke 24:1-12
Easter Sunday 2001
Asbury First United Methodist Church
Rev. Dr. Robert A. Hill
April 15, 2001

Opening

Since it is Easter, we may as well go for broke.

Looking back at all of your life to this day, what is the single most traumatic experience that you have survived? You survivor, you.

Here you are, part of the Easter parade. You made it, you got through, you survived, you survivor you. Just what did you survive, though? Look back and be honest. You may never have spoken of this to anyone, and you may not need to. But for the next 17 minutes of a Gospel both too true to be good and too good to be true, pause before that one great frightening tomb of your life to date. What is the single most traumatic experience that you have survived to date? You survivor you.

Easter promises you resurrection power to survive your own survival, liberation from survivor's guilt - personal, generational and congenital. From the cross we learn to die. From the resurrection we learn to live! Why do you seek the living among the dead?

1. Peter and You: Personal Salvation

Our Scripture today, in the 12th verse, brings Peter to the tomb. Not a part of the original text, this later and highly appropriate addition reconnects the Easter Gospel with Peter. Peter comes and sees and wonders. He is waking up on Easter morning, a survivor.

Have you named your greatest trauma? Death of a brother. Loss of a son in law. Expiration of a mother. Pink slip. Bone cancer. Hospital closing. A phone call from the Bishop announcing your displacement. Moving after 25 years. Abuse at an earlier age. A child's suicide. An unexpected pregnancy. A plane crash. Divorce. A car accident. A run across an open field, with live ammunition coming at you.

Preaching without any sleep the one day the Bishop shows up.

In the first three Gospels, it is centrally Peter who faces trauma like this. He has left all. He has followed. He has stayed. He has loved. He has waited in the dark courtyard. But then - his singular existential trauma - he has denied his Lord thrice. And Jesus has died and Peter has survived, watching the death of his Beloved.

The Gospel accounts of Peter's denial, or betrayal, form the rich heart of the passion narrative. How powerfully Carol Trout read the passage on Thursday night. The pathos, the hurt with which the accounts are given reach to the depths of our hearts, even 2000 years later. Yet, through it all, Peter has survived. What remains for Peter, and for us, is to learn how to live as survivors, to survive our own survival.

I am not a psychologist, nor the son of a psychologist. But I know that "survivor's guilt" is real. Do you remember the film "Ordinary People" (based on Judith Guest's novel), about two brothers who capsize in a boat? One dies and one survives. Mary Tyler Moore oversees a spotless home where "everything is in its proper place - except the past." Berger, the counselor says at one point: "a little advice about feelings kiddo, don't expect it always to tickle." Conrad, the survivor, very nearly takes his own life, saved at the last by wise, loving, intervening words of his counselor, and friend, who asks repeatedly, "What is it that makes you feel so bad?" The answer, at last: "I survived."

Never doubt the saving power of personal presence and a word fitly spoken.

You too have survived. Something. Two years ago we were grieving the Columbine tragedy. The kids there testified, truly, that a strange guilt followed their grief. This is the tragic guilt of the innocent, survivor guilt. "Megan hid her tears behind sunglasses: 'I just feel so lucky to still be here." Greg Martinez said, "You almost feel guilty, about, you know, having your kid get out." Their counselor said those who feel guilty for making it out alive "need to be reassured that they can celebrate their survival." (AP, A Levinson, 4/99).

Here is a description of the effects of survivor's guilt: "general anxiety, depression, inability to sleep, poor memory, difficulty concentrating, difficulty completing tasks, an inexplicable sense of guilt." (Borgess).

That sounds a lot like human life in general!

In the light of Resurrection, Peter finds the power not only to survive but to prevail. He finds the power to enter a new life, to change, to risk. He finds courage that will take him beyond mere survival and will help him travel throughout the known world, and, if legend serves us, to die a martyr in the far off city of Rome. He survives his own survival.

Here is a promise for all of us. Whatever lingering survivor's guilt attends our survival through trauma, here is a power that frees us for a new life, beyond that great past tomb.

God had a purpose for Peter that went well beyond his late night denial. On this Rock, God built a church. God has a purpose for us that should lift us beyond whatever lingering connection still chains us to the past. Yes, you survived. Maybe another did not. But you did. This is the day of Resurrection. Are you ready to survive your own survival?

Even more. Something from that trauma you may fashion into a great gift for others, this side of Resurrection. Your loss will sensitize you to others. Your illness, to that of others. Your demotion, your failure, your dislocation - these now are gifts in your love for others.

For something happened, on Easter, that took a suffering survivor, bitterly weeping at the foot of the cross, and made him a fisherman for God, on whom the whole church has been built. What happened? Something happened. Something that saved Peter from his own survival.

Just as something has happened, that has taken a 175 year old church like ours, moved us through survival of location change, pastoral change, pastoral death, and given us the grace to survive our own survival.

2. Luke and Vietnam: Generational Salvation

What is true of individuals like you and Peter, is also promised today to generations, like yours and Luke's. What is the single greatest trauma your generation has survived?

For the people to whom Luke speaks, now toward the end of the first century, one great generational trauma overshadows their life. Thirty years earlier, in the year 66 AD, the Jews began a tragic, and losing, conflict with Rome. The war ended with the burning of Jerusalem and the destruction of the temple.

Did you ever wonder why Rome, not Jerusalem, is so central to Christianity? Jesus, Peter, John, James, Paul - all Jews, all focused on Jerusalem. The earliest church - that in Jerusalem. But by Luke's time, all that has been destroyed. And Luke's church is adrift. They have survived the destruction of Jerusalem. Others have died, including perhaps the brother of Jesus, James. But they have survived this central generational trauma. Now the question is whether they can survive their own survival.

Have you named your generation's greatest trauma?

For one generation today, located halfway between my father and me, that trauma is Vietnam. This conflict, in the rice paddies of the Mekong Delta, on the grassy lawns of Kent State, in the classrooms of Columbia University and the boardrooms of America, traumatized a whole generation. The trauma is not limited to one political perspective. All, all have been traumatized, to retranslate Romans 5: 12. All, the whole generation, all have been traumatized and stopped short of the glory of God. Tour the Eastman exhibit, and weep before the photographs of the fallen. Ask yourself, then, whether you doubt the venerable teaching about the "fall" of creation. Our Good Friday service spoke in eloquent image, music and silence of this generational trauma.

Still, as a generation, you have survived. You survivor, you. The Chevy 409 is gone. But here is the Chrysler Sebring. Arnold Palmer is retired. But here is Tiger Woods. You got through. Not all did. But you did. Do you come through with some generational survivor's guilt? Does it continue to carry the potential to hobble, maim and kill. For another generation, the trauma was that of *The Man in the Gray Flannel Suit*. (Still a great film). For you, it is *Coming Home, The Killing Fields, Apocalypse Now, Platoon*. Public trust, the place of authority, community commitments, and your relationships to other generations are overshadowed by trauma past. Yes, you survive. But the Easter gospel brings power to survive your own survival.

You remember *Apocalypse Now*. It is truly fascinating that Luke 21, three chapters before our reading, converts all of Mark's little apocalypse (we might call it *Apocalypse Then*), into an interpretation of his generation's greatest trauma, the fall of Jerusalem. For Luke, Jerusalem. For you, Saigon. Here is power to survive survival.

Here is historical fact. Something happened on Easter that 60 years later still had the power to take a generation like Luke's, a church that had lost its Jewish moorings and was adrift in a punishing and forbidding culture, and make a movement that became an Empire wide community, full of men and women ready to die in public rather than call Caesar God.

What happened? Something happened. Something that saved Luke's generation from its own survival.

Even more. Something from that generational trauma you will be able to carry forward, from many perspectives, to make a new way, for a new day. God had a purpose for Luke and his generation. And God has a purpose for you and your generation.

Resurrection is cutting you free from generational survivor's guilt. This is unspeakably good news, like fine wine, 30 years in the making. And one day, a generation we have hardly seen in church since teenager years will come home, surviving their own survival. Coming home, this generation situated half-way between my father and me. Coming home out of survivor's guilt, to explore the use of a great wave of treasure, a huge transfer of wealth (and I would like to speak to some of you personally!). Coming home to a new rebirth of wonder, and a new global community, with one shepherding Lord.

> Der Herr ist mein Hirte!
> El Senor es mi pastor!
> The Lord is my Shepherd!
> Kyrios Christos!

How will this occur? In church. But, you say, the church is so.... Yes, the church is always both a representation and a distortion of the divine. But how can you love God and hate the things of God? How can you come near to God at a distance from the grace of God? How can you experience God without praying, singing, communing, hearing, giving, serving? No, you will have to find a church. Maybe not this church, but a church.

3. *Christ and Humanity: Congenital Salvation*

Could it be that the salvation promised to you and Peter, the power given to your generation and Luke's, is also conferred upon the human race?

For a third time I ask a question. What is the single greatest trauma shared by the human race? All of us together?

Peter runs to the tomb, sees the linen clothes, marvels and wonders. It is Paul who puts the unspeakable into words. It takes him all of the Epistle to the Romans. He reminds us that all have been traumatized and fallen short of God's glory. Individuals, generations, races - all for some unknowable reason - are tinged with survivor's guilt. It is an irrational, inaccurate, unfair, untrue sense of ennui, gonewrongness, fallenness, exile. It is what the Bible means by sin - not something we do, but the air we breathe. Paul understands that God has subjected the whole creation to futility, for the final purpose of saving the whole creation.

Just here, St. Luke has much to give us. Luke emphasizes the will and plan of God. Luke explores the nature of the Kingdom of God, on earth as it is in heaven. Luke proclaims as far back as Christmas Eve: "all flesh shall see it together." Luke repeatedly uses a little Greek verb, found also in verse 7 of today's reading, *dei* - it is necessary, it is purposefully required, it is providentially needed, it is necessary. Luke holds all life in three parts: the time of Israel, the time of Jesus, and the time of the Church. For Luke, this time - our time - is the greatest of times, the time of the Kingdom of God, on earth as it is in heaven. For Luke, there abides a twin craving, held at the heart of the universe: a craving for a faith that appeals to culture and a culture that is attractive to faith. When church and city, faith and culture dance together on the bandstand of brotherhood - that is the Kingdom of God! And Luke, with scholarly Paul (Gal 3) and wondering Peter (Acts 10), means this for all people. All.

What great trauma do all people share? What great trauma has every one in this room experienced?

Birth.

You by virtue of your lonesome journey through birth are an heroic survivor. You by virtue of your gestation for nine long months, are an heroic survivor. You by virtue of your sudden, violent and cataclysmic deliverance, through natal Red Sea waters, are an heroic survivor. You made it. You got through. Others may not have. But you did. You survivor, you. And there you are, crying and all messy, pink and little fisted and wrinkled and wailing to beat the band. You survived.

Not unscathed, but undefeated. Bloodied but unbowed. I have not read it anywhere, and have not time to write my own book, but I think that with birth survival must come a kind of congenital survivor's guilt, way down deeper than words, that we all, every human one of us, we all share. Not something we have done, but the air we breath. All, all have been traumatized and stopped short of the Glory of God.

This is our condition. "Like the beating of the heart, it is always present." (Tillich). It? Tragedy, estrangement, sin, unbelief, hubris, concupiscence, separation, guilt, meaninglessness, despair, anxiety. Existential survivor's guilt. "It is experienced as something for which one is responsible, in spite of its universal, tragic actuality." (Tillich).

As Jim Croce might have written, had he survived: *I've got those steadily depressing, low down, mind messing, existential post-partem blues.*

Easter is a promise of salvation from survivor's guilt. You just may survive your own survival. The resurrection saves us from the lingering effects of birth by giving us - second birth. *"Born to raise the sons of earth, born to give them second birth."* Friends, on Easter we are set free to live in the Kingdom of God, a kingdom of love and light!

Look around the lake, and you will see what I mean. In Toronto there lives the great Jewish teacher, and Holocaust survivor, Emil Fackenheim. Once he was asked, "How can you practice faith in God after the horror of the Holocaust?" (That may be the single most important theological question of our time.) His reply: "I practice faith, in the face of Holocaust, *"in order not to permit Hitler any posthumous victories."* He survived, and survived his survival.

Look around the lake. In Montreal there lives a great French Canadian teacher, Jean Vanier. He left the pastoral life to create a movement of caring ministries with developmentally challenged people. Working with survivors to help them survive survival. His organization, *L'Arche*, has attracted great acclaim, including the service at the end of life of Henri Nouwen.

Look around the lake. When our first two little survivors arrived, we lived in a little cottage in Ithaca, around 1980. In the 1930's, Pearl Buck and her husband had lived there as he served that church and studied at Cornell. I think of her celebration of Chinese survival, and her effort to save the survivors there, here evocation of birth in the rice paddies of Canton.

With her contemporary William Faulkner, she trusted that the human race would not merely survive, but would *prevail*.

God is cutting us free from congenital survivor's guilt. We are set loose to risk, to try, to change, to laugh, to weep, to become who we were meant to be. Irenaeus: *"The glory of God is a human being fully alive."*

For something happened in the raising of Christ Jesus from the dead. What happened? The resurrection is more real than our experience, and that finally it is not we who question the resurrection but the resurrection that questions us. You ask what happened: *Something happened!* Something happened that even 2000 years later has men and women saying prayers, giving money, offering time, swinging hammers, sorting clothes, attending meetings, singing hymns, loving neighbors and on every day in every way building the kingdom of God. Luke would love it. What happened? Something happened, something that opens life up wide and frees us from our original survival and saves us for a new life, a new way, a new creation, a new heaven and a new earth!

Closing

In the cross, we learn to die. In the resurrection, we learn to live.

Our spirit is that of Harriet Beecher Stowe:

> *In the beauty of the lilies Christ was born across the sea*
> *With a glory in his bosom that transfigures you and me*
> *As he died to make men holy let us live to make men free*
> *Our God is marching on.*
>
> *He has sounded forth the trumpet that shall never call retreat*
> *He is sifting out the heart of men before his judgment seat*
> *O be swift my soul to answer him, be jubilant my feet*
> *Our God is marching on.*
>
> *He is coming like the glory of the morning on the wave*
> *He is wisdom to the mighty, He is honor to the brave*
> *So the world shall be his footstool and the soul of wrong his slave*
> *Our God is marching on.*

"The Great Embankment"
Text: Luke 24: 44-55
Sermon by Rev. Dr. Robert A. Hill
May 20, 2001
Asbury First United Methodist Church

Beloved: we are on a path together. Together we are taking a journey! Confirmation is not a location but a direction. Confirmation is not a spot but a trajectory. We're walking the path prepared for us by God's Grace.

Preface

At age twenty, some of us had the golden opportunity to study together in old Castile in the center of Spain. You know some of their traditions, eating dinner, *la cena*, from 11:00 PM to 1:00 AM, and later the needed tradition of *la siesta* the next day from two to four in the afternoon. But when the shops closed at 7:00 PM in this and in most communities, the town would gather for what was called *el paseo*, the walk. Together they would walk and shop and talk and stop for a coffee or other refreshments or a pastry. It was a time of conviviality.

One evening my friend Ed, from an Irish family in Ashtabula, and I stopped with some in the town and they began to sing songs of Segovia. After they finished, they asked if we would each sing a song that told them something about our identity, about our background. Well, I didn't think Ed was a very good singer, and I *knew* I wasn't so we were a little scared. But do you know, Ed, after the quiet, began to sing surprisingly, beautifully, a song about Molly Malone in Dublin's fair city, where the girls are so pretty. And again the quiet came and I realized it was my turn. So I began to sing what came to mind, "Had a mule, her name was Sal, fifteen miles on the Erie Canal." We translated roughly and our hosts said, "Is this the difference between Ohio and New York? He sings about a woman and you sing about a mule?!!"

Our imagery today is canal imagery--our home turf. Walk with me three steps, if you will, along the towpath. We could imagine ourselves somewhere between Pittsford and Bushnel's Basin, with the canal on the right and the moorings on the left. We're following the towpath. Step one as you are confirmed:

I. Believe

Confirmation gives us the grace to believe. To become a Christian this and each day means to believe in a certain way, to believe in almighty God. Whose power is known in the created order. Whose personality is seen in the face and mostly in the voice of Jesus Christ. Whose presence is trusted as our helping, saving spirit, day by day. We believe in a certain, specific way in almighty God. The Bible says: "if you confess with your lips that Jesus is Lord, and believe in your heart that God raised him from the dead, then you will be saved"(Rom 10:9). We believe---as the creeds express in a variety of ways. You know there have been creeds from the beginning of the Church. We are not a creedal denomination, but we use them, the Apostles' Creed and the Nicene Creed. The one regularly we use here is taken from the United Church of Canada: "We believe in God, who has created and is creating, who has come in the true person Jesus to reconcile and to make new". Our Confirmands for this day, have written their own several creeds. You know baseball players, now and then, give off a little bit of wisdom. We remember Yogi Beara saying, it's a good word for confirmation, "If you come to a fork in the road, take it." Sachel Page saying, "How old would you be if you didn't know how old you are?" But today, perhaps we could remember from thirty-two years ago, Tug McGraw, the great Mets pitcher saying, "You gotta believe, you gotta believe." To become a Christian in confirmation means to believe.

II.   Belong

Take another step with me will you along the canal path. On our left hand there are moorings where the canal boats once were tethered. In our life together, these can be images of sacramental rights, baptism and confirmation, communion, ordination, marriage, forgiveness, memorial--all very important means of grace. Not the center, the path, the journey is the center. But the moorings are still very important helps and provide security. To become a Christian means not only to believe but also to belong, to belong to the body of Christ, the church, The Bible says that "through the church the manifold wisdom of God might now be made known to the principalities and powers". There are no freelance Christians. We need one another! One person sharpens another like iron sharpens iron. And so in this great church we try week by week to summon the finest features of Christianity from every part of the globe and blend them together: Catholic tradition, Anglican sacraments, reformation faith, puritan discipline, pietist feelings. Yes, to be a Methodist (a Methodist is just like everybody else only more so) it's a blend.

III. Behave

To become a Christian means to belong to the community of faith and live among God's people, to be refreshed and restored. But take a third step along the path with me if you will, for to become a Christian also means to behave in a particular way. You know, along the canal path there are the moorings to the left and there is the canal itself to the right. And times of sheer delight come upon us in our life together, so savor them. That moment at summer camp in the evening, that quiet prayer hour when you heard a voice, that crusade in which you were converted for the first or second time, that moment at the communion rail when God's grace touched your heart deeply.

We are calling our young people, this and every generation, to behave in a certain way. Paul taught the Romans that they should love one another with "mutual affection" and so we say simply to our Confirmands, go to church, love your neighbor, tell the truth, keep your word, save your money, hug your father, kiss your mother, feed the poor, hear the hurt, learn to tithe, respect your body, and so live to the glory of Almighty God. To become a Christian means to behave in a certain set of ways.

The Great Embankment

Now if we go far enough out on the canal we'll come just toward Bushnel's Basin and there as we're arriving we'll find ourselves on "the great embankment." You know, in 1822 our forbears, these courageous pioneers, found a way to carry water, canal water, over water, the Irondequoit creek. Fearless they were, and so they put over a mile long and 70 feet in the air this great embankment upon whose path we are walking today (in the mind's eye).

Christ Jesus is our great embankment, carrying us in the water of faith across the river of life. Christ Jesus is our great embankment carrying us in the water of baptism, through the river of struggle, not only to the left and to the right but especially along that central path which we journey. Maybe this afternoon our young adults and their parents will go out to the Burgandy Basin and walk the canal and sense again the great embankment, but if we do today and every day let us do so especially listening for that one voice, that saving voice so equable, so pure and so serene: You know it well.

Blessed are the poor in spirit, blessed are the meek, blessed are the merciful, blessed are those who mourn, blessed are those who hunger and thirst for righteousness. You are the salt of the earth, you are the light of the world, let your light so shine before others that they may give glory to God in heaven. If someone asks you to go one mile, go two of them as well. If you're asked for a coat give a cloak as well. You have heard it said love your neighbor, hate your enemy, but I say to you love your enemy. So you will be children of the most high who is kind to the ungrateful and to the selfish.

Store ye not up treasure on earth, where moth and rust doth consume and thieves break in and steal; but store up treasure in heaven where neither moth or rust consume, nor do thieves break in and steal. Judge not, that ye be not judged, for the measure you give will be the measure you get. Ask and it shall be given, seek and ye shall find, knock and the door will be open. For enter in at the narrow gate, for broad is the gate and wide is the way that leads to perdition and many there be who go thereby; but narrow is the gate and straight is the way that leads to life and few there be who find it. To what shall we compare those who hear this word and heed it? They are like a wise man who built his house upon the rock and the rain fell and the flood came and the winds blew and beat upon that house but it did not fall because it was founded on the rock. To what shall we compare those who hear the word and do not heed it? They are like a man who built his house on the sand and the rain fell and the flood came and the wind blew and beat upon that house and it fell in and great was the fall of it.

Beloved, we are on a path, a journey together. Let us take three steps this and each day to believe, to belong and to behave as we become together in the body of Christ. Happy Confirmation Sunday! Amen.

"A Summer Thanksgiving"
Text: Luke 10: 38-42
Sermon preached by Rev. Dr. Robert A. Hill
July 22, 2001
Asbury First United Methodist Church

You all share with me in something inexpressible called grace, which is the spiritual equivalent of Wayne Gretsky on skates, graceful. God has loved us! And though there is still so much darkness, some of it doubly dark, I see flickering light in Christ's church.

We thank you lord for skillful, hard working, strong men and women who plow and seed, who fight with nature and who win from it our food. Grateful for farmers. Men who can raise and care for a herd of cattle. Who can help a cow through a difficult calving. Who can work with giant sums of money and not get too frightened, because they know, deep down, that money is something to use not be used by. Men who can be hurt-but never thank God defeated-by a turn in the weather. Men who like medieval knights on horseback can tractor the earth. People who can work by, for, and with themselves. I thank you Lord for what Thomas Jefferson called the backbone of the United States, the American farmer. (You have called them to force mother earth to give up her food wealth. She can be a stingy old goat. May rural America put her mind and heart in thee, and so make food...ungreedily. Mother nature is greedy. Must we be?).

We thank you Lord for gentle women and men. In this violent age and time...praise to the Lord there are still some gentle people. Gentle in speech. Awaiting the wish of another. Guessing what another wants or needs before the other has to cry out for it. Gently going about the work of parenting. Taking up collections for those hurt. Gently listening as someone else talks, trying with only a little success to find words that actually say something. Doing a little and doing that well. It is my wish that gentle people might abound, more and more, even as they keep a good head on their shoulders. Where are the gentle people? Quiet by the bedside...silent in the back pew...unnoticed doing the cleaning...teaching a child to read...listening in the back yard to hear the owl hoot...thinking a problem through...doing something for nothing...giving with no thought of getting.

We thank you Lord for people who have made tough choices and who live with their decision. People whom life has presented with difficult decisions. And they haven't turned tail and run. They've chosen. Now they live with their choice, knowing they might have done otherwise, but firm in the conviction that they've done the best they can. Not everyone agrees with their choice. It's threatening to have people disagree with you on something that really matters. Like salvation. Like love. Like family. Like politics. Like money. Like religion. Sometimes we have to make tough choices. Lord how happy we are to see people who make those decisions and live gracefully with them, without fretting, without dreaming that most perilous of dreams, presented in living technicolor under the title, "What might have been." These folks know that life is short and that we need not make excuses for spending our time on the wheat and kicking aside the chaff. They don't walk into life back end first. They don't get turned into a pillar of salt. We are grateful for people who live gracefully with past decisions.

Lord we thank you for tolerant people. People who aren't afraid even to be called wishy-washy if it means taking a chance on loving what is different. One Greek legend tells of a man who had only one guest bed. All his guests had to fit into that bed. If you were tall then late at night he'd come in hand saw off your legs just to make you fit his bed. If you were too short then late at night he'd come in and stretch you so that you made the right length for the guest bed. Intolerant of difference. Lord we thank you for people who are tolerant of difference. Who know that there is a wideness in God's mercy. Who can see life from more than one point of view. Who do not insist on the absolute right of their opinion. Who pray to have their eyes opened first and focused second. They can say, "He's different. I don't like him. But, then I don't have to like him. Christ has died for him. Only love will do." What variety there is in people, in places, in things, in insides, in thoughts, in sizes, in health, in taste, in color, in shade. Lord we can see that you love variety. I'm glad when others too are tolerant of difference.

I make this prayer with joy as I remember joyful people. People who could laugh from the belly up, twice a day. Did you laugh this morning? Laughing away crying is what makes us human. Who haven't lost the spirit of the Methodist camp tune, "I've got that joy down in my heart"...People for whom humor is natural, easy, smooth. People who can play a tambourine.

My God I thank Thee!
For industrious people.
For gentle people.
For decisive people.
For joyful people.
I see them in this church.

The Gifts of Summer
Text: Luke 11:1-13
July 29, 2001
Asbury First United Methodist Church
Rev. Dr. Robert A. Hill

Ant

The meaning of summer, *sub specie aeternitas,* and particularly in a climate, like yours, long in darkness and deep in cold, the meaning that is of the four score summers God gives you, at the largest extent of God's favor, is itself a matter for prayer, even if our Lord's Gospel today were not so fiercely invested in prayer. Let us pray together today for a few minutes by taking a homiletical walk, down a dusty summer road. In the mind's eye, and with the sun upon our backs, let us meander a moment, and see what we can see.

Start small. There in front of your left moccasin moves a lonely red ant, the lowliest of creatures, yet, like a Connecticut Yankee, bursting with the two revolutionary virtues, industry and frugality. Benjamin Franklin wrote, admiring such frugality and industry, and dubious of much dogmatic preaching, "none preaches better than the ant, and he says nothing." A good reminder.

While we step around the ant, the little insect recalls others: grasshoppers, flies, locusts. Simple creatures. Our current President, George W. Bush, prefers the locusts of Crawford, Texas to the blackflies of Kennebunkport, Maine. I remember driving past the Bush compound on the downeast coastline, and admiring its beauty. Why would our President prefer Central Texas? Its locusts, burning dry heat, flat arid landscape, and lack of water would seem to offer no competition. Yet, he flies to Crawford, and according to one recent NPR commentator, has a singularly good reason to do so. He loves the virtue of the simple people he has known there for most of his life. He likes the simple rhythm of town life. He enjoys the simple summer gatherings - reunions, little league, band concerts, parades. He must tire of the necessary urban emphasis on urbanity, the inevitable public relations concern for appearance and apparel. Or, as he said recently, "the people there - they are folks with good hearts." And as Jesus taught his students, "if people have some measure of goodness themselves, think how good their maker must be.

Maybe that is the meaning of summer, to pause and appreciate simple, good people, folks with good hearts.

Berry

We can stop up the path just a bit. Raspberries, blackberries, all kinds of wild fruit are plentiful now. Jesus taught us to ask, simply, for bread and a name. We daily need food and forgiveness. Give us each day our daily bread, and forgive us our sins, for we forgive all who are indebted to us. What bread does for the body, pardon does for the soul. One of the gifts of summer is the time and leisure to remember this. Church should be fullest in the summer, for this reason, this recognition of our ultimate needs.

Our neighbor has baked some of these wild berries into morning muffins. We stop to savor them, with butter and coffee. We listen to one another along the path. So we are nourished, by one another, and made ready for the next steps in the journey.

Maybe this is the meaning of summer, to pause and make space for real worship, for that which can feed our hungers, and set us free for the next adventure.

Fence

Up ahead there is an old fence. For a river to be a river, it needs riverbanks high enough to contain the flowing water. For a lake to hold its integrity it needs a shoreline that stands and lasts. For a field to retain any semblance of usefulness, it needs fences to mark its beginnings and endings. For an individual to have any identity one needs the limits of positive improvement, as Jesus taught about perseverance, and of protective caution, as Jesus taught about times of trial. For a life to have meaning and coherence, it needs those riverbanks, shorelines, fences, and limits that give life shape and substance.

We can spend some summer time mending fences. It is hard work, but utterly crucial. Keep your friendships in good repair, and mend the fences where they need it.   Think, heal, write, love.

The other day I came by this same old fence. I was walking with my dad, as it happened. We had some coffee and a muffin. Then we started off together, down the old road, he to walk with a gnarled walking stick, and I to jog after my own eccentric fashion. But for a mile up to the same fence, to the place where the road parts, we walked together. We shuffled and talked a little, remembering the name of a former neighbor, spotting a new garden planted, making a plan or two for later on. We remembered an old friend, a old style doctor, long dead. He remembered that Dr. Thro came to visit him the day his mother died. "It's hard when your mother dies," he said, "it gets you right in the chest!" I remembered Dr. Thro swimming the length of the lake and, while he did so, barking various orders at the universe and some of his patients along the shoreline, riverbank, fence - along the virtuous limits that make a life. We came to fork, one taking the high road and one the low, and with that an embrace and a word and a glance and we were alone again.

Maybe this is the meaning of summer, to set limits and keep them, to mend our fences and protect them, to honor one another in faith and love.

Cloud

This is a clear day, in our reverie, but even so there are a few dancing clouds, white and bright. We try to make sense of the summer, and to make space for the summer, and to honor this season, so different in New York than in Texas, one that brings together meteorological splendor and theological insight. In our church, we put together a dozen summer experiences, like next week's Summerfest, to allow meteorology and theology to dance well together.

There is a dimension of possibility alive in the summer that is hard to approximate in the rest of the year. We alter our summer hours of worship, not at all to suggest that worship is less central now, for in some ways summer ought to be the most worshipful of the seasons, but rather to accommodate our life to the necessary rhythms of life around us.

It is astounding to hear again in the Gospel that seeking, knocking and asking themselves bring discovery, opening and reception. But they do. Summer is the season and worship is the focus of all such wonder and possibility.

Maybe this is the meaning of summer, to pause and allow a fuller consideration of all the possibilities around us.

Breeze

A summer wind accompanies us as we walk farther down the dirt road. A fawn - or was it a fox? - darts into the brush. The smell of apples, already ripening, greets us at the turn. More sun, bigger and higher and hotter, makes us sweat.

I guess every family has a family secret or two, that one subject that dominates every present moment by the sheer weight of its hidden silence, that one taboo topic that somehow screams through its apparent muteness. Daddy's drinking. Junior's juvenile record. Grampa's prison term. The so-called elephant in the room. True of nations, too, and businesses, and projects and even churches. You find it, finally, by asking gently about what is feared.

The human family has this same kind of family secret. Something we avoid discussing, if at all possible, something that makes us fearful, something that dominates us through our code of silence. It is our mortality. Our coming death is the one thing that most makes us who we are, mortal, mortals, creatures, sheep in another's pasture, not perfect because not perfectible, the image of God but not God, "fear in a handful of dust". Yet we are so busy with so many other things that this elemental feature of existence we avoid.

Maybe this is the meaning of summer, to number our days that we get hearts of wisdom, to measure the mystery about us and give over our imaginations to a consideration of our limits, to <u>learn to pray.</u>

You

May the Good and Gracious God make of all of us prayerful people, simple and true our virtues of the heart, nourishing and nourished in pardon, disciplined by hard even bitter fences of peace, inspired by gracious clouds billowing and high, and supported all the day long by a summer wind, a spirited faith in the face of death.

"Have a Good Summer"
Summerfest 2001
Asbury First UMC
Hos. 11, Psalm 107, Col. 3, Luke 18
August 5, 2001
Dr. Robert A. Hill

Introduction

"Have a good summer!" Has someone said this to you recently? Or, something similar? "Are you having a good summer?" "How's the summer?" "What a great summer!"

For soon to become obvious, selfish, homiletical reasons, I listened, yesterday, all day, through a beautiful Trustees' picnic meeting and luncheon on Keuka Lake, and through a wonderful Stewardship Committee dinner and pool party, for this question, or its variants. Nine hits. Listen and count, tomorrow: "Have a good summer."

It is such a simple phrase, but to the needy, reflective ear, it raises a mortal question, a singular and, perhaps shattering, perhaps justifying question: What is a good summer?

Before addressing this question, I digress to offer a story. You perhaps know it. Or perhaps you have told it. A farmer had an odd habit of feeding his only pig in a distinctive way. He would hold the pig in his arms, and carry him under an apple tree. There the pig would happily eat his fill as the farmer, arms aching, waited. At last a neighbor asked: "John, that is one way to feed a pig, but, in addition to straining your back and arms, it must take a whole lot of time. Aren't you worried about that lost time?" "Oh", said the farmer, "Of course you are right, it is a lot of time, but, then...*what's time to a pig?"*

It is a warning to those of us, like me, who raise such questions, and those of us, like you, who chew on them. A mortal question, to be understood, and a saving truth, to be told, depend on hearing. Faith, that is, comes by right hearing, and such hearing by the word of God.

Thus the simple sentence, "Have a good summer," is, like much in life, a very thin ordinary veneer covering a deep, existential interrogative: just what is a good summer?

What constitutes a good, a godly summer? Perhaps with your help, and under the shadow of the Holy Scripture, which towers over our experience like a steeple towers over our communion today, we can respond by raising other questions. One good question deserves another.

1. Interruption

Has your summer allowed an interruption? Of what? Of routine, of the usual of set patterns, of your own plotting and planning, of comfort, of discomfort, of what has been. Has summer provided a pause?

The parable of the Rich Fool, read today, is a warning word from Jesus for the followers of Jesus. "A man's life does not consist in the abundance of his possessions."

Wait, stop, think, heal write.

A Hindu proverb says: During its lifetime, the lordly goose looks down upon the humble mushroom. But in the end, they are both served up on the same platter.

Life is meant to become a rich offering toward God, not a laying up of treasure on earth where moth and rust consume, and thieves break in and steal. And speaking of thieves breaking in, please allow this brief digressive interruption. After all, it is summer...

It reminds us of the ostensibly humorous story of the burglar, speaking of greed and covetousness, who slipped with his flashlight into a dark suburban home. He took jewelry and cash. Then in the dark he heard a voice: "Jesus is watching. I'm warning you." The burglar trembled, wondering who had spoken. Turning on the light, he saw a parrot in a cage, who said, "My name is Moses, and I warn you, Jesus is watching." Relieved, for the moment, the burglar smiled and said, "What kind of silly suburban people name their parrot Moses?" The parrot replied, "The same kind of silly people who name their longtoothed, ferocious dog, Jesus. I warned you, Jesus is watching."

Life is more than security. The best things about life are free. Travel light.

2. *Inflammation*

Has your summer involved some inflammation? Has the season brought spirit to a fever pitch? Is there around now any love on fire? The mid-west is scorching hot. Mt. Aetna in Sicily is flowing with lava. And in your heart? Where is the fire? What is it that you love so much that it makes you…now nostalgic, now tender, now torrid, now angry, now remorseful, now hot, now vengeful, now envious, now determined, now happy?

The Bible readers among us are right to suspect that Hosea 11, another of today's readings, smolders here. Listen to this loveliest of passages again: "When Israel was a child I loved him…"

I am not talking about passion only, eros only, the body only, feeling only. Though I mean all that. I mean, rather, something beyond mere 'sloppy agape'. I mean the heart. Where your treasure is, there will your heart be also.

Julia Kristeva, French philosopher, who recently, and categorically and stridently rejected the 'political correctness' once labeled as her offspring, said this summer that there are "three great things in life: to think, to heal, and to write." A Schweitzer would have agreed, and said, "There are three great instruments—the Bible, the pipe organ, and the stethescope." I say: find a way, your way, every day, to preach and to sing and to love.

Somewhere in every life there is a hot, scorched, midwestern summer. Remember it. Somewhere in every life there is a potent lava flow, about to burst, bursting, having burst. Seek it. Somewhere in every life there is the love of Hosea 11, God like a mother holding an infant to the cheek. Recover it.

Has your summer involved some inflamation?

3. *Institution*

Has your summer included the care and feeding of an institution? Yes, I could have used another word like 'incarnation', more theological and perhaps more accurate. But then we all would have gone home unclear, unconflicted, unconfronted, and unhelped. Operational incarnation means insitution.

Life does not give ground before individuals apart from institutions. Transformation, lasting good change, in history, happens not through individuals only, nor through movements only. Real traction in history involves institutions. Like corporations, governments, businesses, schools, parties, associations, cities, and, yes, churches. In this, as in most things, the radicals have it wrong. A movement is not superior to an institution. A movement is an institution that has not grown up.

Today's Psalm the 107th, recites the tradition of deliverance, liberation, rescue, redemption, that is your birthright…"Until they reached a city in which to dwell." The Lord has redeemed us from trouble.

Marguerite Brown, whom we buried this week, knew this. Hers is a story of a woman who made space for a very worthy institution, Asbury First UMC.

Has your summer involved an institution? .

4. *Inspiration*

Has this summer brought inspiration? Something? Something fine and true? Something sensual? Something grand and loving? I truly hope so. "A man's life does not consist in the abundance of his possessions." This very night one's soul may be required.

The last lesson, today's epistle, Colossians 3 (I commend to you this wonderful chapter) tells us to "set your affections on things above, not on things on the earth."" Rid your life of immorality and lying, so that Christ, your lips, Christ, your reward, Christ, your glory, Christ, your new person, Christ, your Lord may truly be revealed in and through you.

I saw an eagle soaring over our lake last Tuesday. Barth, I recalled, said that "the gospel is the freedom of a bird in flight". And I remembered the proverb: "Three things are too wonderful for me, and four I cannot understand. The way of an eagle in the sky, the way of a ship upon the high sea, the way of a serpent on a rock, and the way of a man with a woman."

Has the summer brought inspiration?

Coda

Have a good summer
A summer that allows interruption
A summer that involves inflammation
A summer that includes an institution
A summer that brings some inspiration

(And, as you probably suspect that the sermon more deeply intends, in the same ways, have a good life).

"Get Well Soon"
Text: Luke 13: 10-17
Asbury First United Methodist Church
August 26, 2001
Rev. Dr. Robert A. Hill

Preface

You are courageous people, you who have come today to hear the Word of God. You have braved the summer heat, and you have risen above the warm summer temptation to sit a little longer by the pool, or to browse a little longer through the paper. You have chosen again to place yourself within earshot, at least, of the Lord Jesus Christ, and so to give praise to Almighty God. To do so, you have sailed out between the Scyla of the sacrament alone and the Charybdis of the spirit alone. This is no small achievement. Most Christians in our region are Roman Catholic, and most new Christian churches are Anabaptist. Still, you have come here to worship in the broad tradition of the great church, fully catholic and fully reformed and fully ecumenical, and, perhaps, to wait for the Word of God, even from a mere Methodist pulpit.

Perhaps the breath of the Spirit will whisper to you this morning: "You count. You matter. You are real and really beloved. I love you. Get well soon."

Perhaps the Risen Christ this morning will whisper to you, if you are sick, and especially if you have suffered in ailment for 18 years: "Get well soon." Or maybe the voice will rise to much more of a whisper, and you will walk home, sensing, after two decades, "I am well. It is well." Get well soon.

Your courage is further to be acknowledged, because you come to listen with curiosity to the Scripture, and you reflect with respect upon the Church, and you judge honestly about life as you have experienced all of life. Curiosity about Scripture, respect for the Church, honesty about life - these are your own gifts of interpretation for the morning. You know that one requires the scholar's imagination, and the other requires the pastor's heart, and the third requires the preacher's guts. You have been given reason to trust, over generations, that somewhere the three will meet again before the noon hour strikes. So, as a loving and addressable assembly, you do not fear. You do not fear...not the strange world of the Scripture, with its spirits, angels, demons, and divinity.... Not the community of strangers that is the church, with its wheat, tares, heroes, villains, friends, opponents and its troubling capacity both to represent and to distort the divine, the church where we pretend, intend and contend to know one another, with a baseball slugger's level of success (30%)... Nor even the estrangement of your own daily life, with its betrayals, ambiguities, losses of meaning, inexplicable horrors, random hurts and just plain boredom. You fear neither God nor man. Upon the strange world of the Bible you radiate curiosity. Toward the community of strangers in church you radiate respect. Into the estrangement of experience you send a glimmer, a gleam, a glistening honesty that is to be prized far above much pious hooting. To church you dare to come. In this, I salute you. For your courageous curiosity, respect, and honesty are themselves, curiously enough, and quite honestly, to be fully respected. There is Good News awaiting behind all that is so very strange today.

For today we celebrate the mysterious presence of Christ, the Healer. He stands among us, this perennially young man, knowing our own ailments and like a feudal baron placing and unfurling his flag for battle, and announces: "Get well soon!"

Scripture

In the reading of his Word and the preaching of his Gospel, Jesus discloses himself to us today, though his person, it seems, is never quite devoid of that shrouding, that misty, mystical aplomb that is never fully to be had, to be captured, to be held. He stands above us, high as a lifted pulpit. He waits above us, high upon a raised altar. He moves before us, and whether or not we are worthy to touch the hem of his garment or to gather the crumbs from his table, neither motion holds him. He comes, he speaks, he heals, he judges, and he leaves, pushing us against the wall with a question - "ought not one so ill be set free?"

Strange is the world he inhabits. I picture Luke retelling this story in a house, perhaps in Antioch. There are thirty or forty in the room, gathering to pray, to commune, and to listen. "Now he was teaching..." Did Luke find it stunning, as we do, that the worship service into which Jesus had been invited, is toppled by the appearance (the apocalypse) of a sick woman? Years ago, Lily Tomlin, opening a one woman Broadway show, had her act disrupted by an unruly street woman, who had a spirit that had crippled her for at least 18 years. The ticket buying customers in the front row had had enough and were about to throw her out, bodily. Tomlin came on stage, halted the proceedings, ushered the vagabond to center stage, and addressed the house: "Let me introduce you to...a fellow human being." We learn so much from the dreams of drama, as my own daughter has taught me and as our new Christian Educator, Jennifer Martin, with a degree in ministry and theater, will further show us.

Jesus speaks among us from atop his Lukan stage, in a voice of command. I suppose you could call it a voice of compassionate command. He notices hurt. He cares about individual ailment. He cares enough about sickness to make its healing more important than organized religion. And most dramatically of all, in a word of exorcism, he eternally launches into our life the potential for healing. As striking, for century one, as is Luke's recollection of Jesus' notice of women - of this woman and countless others in the Lukan record - more striking still is the fundamental Good News of the reading, that Jesus Christ cares to heal. We celebrate the elusive presence, the mystery of a strange healer. Nature brings healing. Time brings healing. Medicine brings healing. Prayer brings healing. There is a conspiracy of healing at work in the universe.

I cannot answer at all to my own satisfaction why some and not others. In the air my breath touches I see a friend's brother, a colleague's sibling, a sister-in-law, a youth, a close friend, none of whom apparently are going to be healed. I am angry as well as frightened as well as sad. Yet Luke the Physician must have known as many or more. But he reminds us of the main thing:

there is healing, there is healing. And Jesus has shouted healing into the very core of being: "you are set free." The very tragedy of sickness, which we rightly hate and fight, takes its full outline and design as shadow from another truth: the Mysterious Lord desires healing. Its lack, its absence is the moon, but its presence the sun. How healthy it is to pause, once this week, to be greeted by the healing voice of Jesus Christ.

Sometimes, not often, in the languid long history of theology, one meets a paragraph full of courage. I remember reading St. Augustine on sickness and health. He was whistling past the graveyard, a little, it is true, but his defiance, his courage stay with me. "Why sickness wouldn't exist, if it weren't for health. In fact, sickness does not exist. It has no being. It is only a corruption of being."

He said what we feel. Sickness sickens us because we know that healing is primary, and we chafe at those unhealed hurts. No, we more than chafe. We howl, we moan, we lament, we shake our fists and curse.

More, let us say, we cannot say.

Church

Speaking of endless contention and intractable difference, we reflect now with respect on the community of faith. Do you find it humorous (and did Luke?), to notice that the immediate response to a miraculous, physical act of healing, performed by the way, in public, upon the aisle of the synagogue no less, is - doctrinal bickering? There is a conspiracy of healing moving through the universe, and the immediate response erupts as cultural disputation. It makes us wonder how best to proceed with our common life, including our life in the church. It is the kind of thing that gives religious wrangling a bad name.

As strange us the setting in Scripture seems for the Person of Christ, the collection of strangers in the church of every age seems stranger still. What good news, for us, for you who have given your time and money and prayer and good will and forgiveness to the church, to hear again the reminder that the church is the Body of Christ, the physical expression of his life in our world. Jesus reproves his opponents. Notice. Jesus has opponents. There is conflict. There is difference of view, culminating in a short term victory for one side but a resurrectional victory for the other. Jesus connects even this woman, even this cripple, even this ritual outsider, to the main project of the community. Healing. His fight this morning is to make space in the church for those who appear and hunt for healing. I still find it funny, though, that for the community the main gift of healing is immediately forgotten in the ensuing debate about Sabbath. There is a little humor here, like that which gently mocks the despondent prophet Jonah, gloomy under the fig tree.

The Gospel which is given into the hands of the stewards of the mysteries of Christ - the Church - celebrates healing on the grand scale. There is ever a corporate consequence to the intrusion of Jesus' voice. Eighteen years is a long time. So long that sometimes we forget to celebrate when the time has changed.

Think of AIDS. Twenty years ago, AIDS was an immediate death sentence. Today much healing is possible, and much prolonged life. Because the change has come incrementally, we have not paused to praise God. Of course the scourge and the plague continue, and of course our battle against it continues. But look. Bound for 18 years, this set of children of Abraham have partial freedom. This is good news.

Think of stem cell research. Twenty years ago, most of the debate now occurring did not exist. Yet today, potential further healing, with all the potential risks to the fundamental sanctity of life, is on the move. I for one think the President handled this issue quite well. But even if he did not, the rising sun of new potential healing is waxing, not waning, in this new area. Silent for 18 years, other daughters of Abraham may find health.

Luke the Physician has had spiritual siblings throughout the ages. Elizabeth Blackwell, Florence Nightengale, the Mayo Brothers, and many others. Our church today is supported by the kind and intelligent ministry and presence of many fine physicians, nurses, and other health care providers. What gifts they offer, on a daily basis, to many who have had crippled spirits for 18 years! In this community of strangers, as well as friends, the Lord Jesus Christ is present in the healing voices of the real community and order of St. Luke - the healing professions.

Life

You though may wonder whether any of this finally touches your eighteen years of pain. The Christ of Scripture, whose Body is the Church, meets us for healing in the prisons of estrangement we know in life, when we are honest. The Gospel, if nothing else, gives us the freedom to be honest about what we experience. For once, today, let the word go forth. Your life is now within earshot of the Master Healer.

It may not seem so after 18 years of addiction. Alcohol addiction can come on slowly, insidiously over a decade or two. One night a week becomes five and two beers become ten. Spirits cripple. I mean literally. We have four AA groups in this church which begin with a recognition that one is powerless, alone, to healed. One turns to a Higher Authority. You need not suffer, endlessly bound to drink. 18 years is plenty. There are ways and there are programs and there is every possibility for healing. Get well soon.

Nor may it seem that Jesus is close when one is fighting a culture of obesity. In fact, our culture is under daily attack from diets that come at us as if we had spent every day milking at 4 am, in the hay mow for 10 hours, and milking at 4 pm. Do so, and you do need 5000 calories a day. But how many of us do so? Our kitchens, our cooking, our cuisine come from 2 generations ago. We need a new way of eating, and the church is the place to start. Nobody likes food more than I do. I like only two kinds of pie (hot and cold) and only two kinds of ice cream (vanilla and non-vanilla). But as a people we are drowning in a sea of fat. High blood pressure, diabetes, hardened arteries, heart disease - all traceable back to the kitchens, cooking, cuisine of our culture. We eat like farmers. Once we were farmers. No longer. 18 years is a long time, but things can change even after decades. There are ways and there are programs and there is every possibility for healing. Get well soon.

Nor may it seem like Jesus knows the spirit that cripples you in the soul, the dark depression that takes life. We lost a boy in Brighton this week. How I wish we as a people were more versed and more sensitive regarding depression. Like the spirit that crippled for 18 years, it is a powerful enemy. It would not be Sunday, at least on this green earth, if someone were not wrestling again and mightily with depression. It is healthy just to name our ailment, our malady. Even if healing does not come immediately, naming and recognition and honesty help. It may seem that the church with all its celebration and hymnody and affirmation of faith does not get it. Today's Gospel does. 18 years is a long time, but things can change even after decades. Jesus sees you, crippled underneath an ailing spirit. He speaks. He speaks in order to free you, at the very least by announcing the irremediable presence of the potential for healing. There are ways and there are programs. Get well soon.

Endnote

Here is Good News, a reason for affirmation and celebration! The Lord Jesus Christ meets us mysteriously out the strange world of the Bible, in the midst of the community of strangers in the church, and right in the heart of our existential estrangement. Our Lord is a Healer, *the* Healer in whom we trust. And his healing has a further purpose, as Luke, the Physician, would want remembered. You are set free to set others free. You are healed to become a healer. You are blessed to a blessing. So get well soon. I mean: get well… Soon! We've got work to do.

"The Lamp of the Poor"
Text: Luke 14: 25-33
Together in Ministry Sunday
Asbury First United Methodist Church
September 9, 2001
Rev. Dr. Robert A. Hill

Opening

"The lamp of the poor", Canadian Hemingwayesque novelist Alistair Macleod has recently recalled, is the translation for the Gaelic term meaning "moon", *'lochran aigh namb boch'*. Christ Jesus is the lamp of the poor for this world. You, budding disciple, are becoming a lamp of the poor, in his name. This great congregation, Asbury First, dreams of itself as a 21st century lamp of the poor. And we are children of the dream, so let us dream away.

A dream lives at night, in moonlight, and walks in the dark (Luther's phrase for faith). Now a vision - a vision is a child of the day. Picture an aerial photograph. Imagine a carpet ride. A vision needs sight and daylight. But a dream, a dream is a nocturnal beast. (Who hopes for what he sees? We hope for what we do not see.) You enter a dream, not from the bird's eye, but from the mind's eye. You take up a lamp, let us say, and you begin to browse here a little, there a little. You enter a dream on foot. A dream is a human, a man-sized mystery. Now you pick up your torch, in the darkly dusk, and you meet the future. It's scary to walk in the dark. Poe caught it best.

And the silken, sad, uncertain rustling of each purple curtain
Filled me, thrilled me with fantastic terrors never felt before
So again to still the beating of my heart I stood repeating
'Tis some visitor entreating entrance at my chamber door
Only this - nothing more.

There is a visitor, the mysterious Lord Christ Jesus, who enters upon us, stealthily, in our dreams this day.

Perhaps the greatest, most internationally influential architect of the modern period, a Swiss known as 'le corbusier' (the raven, speaking of ravens), once remarked, "what makes our dreams so daring is that they can be realized." We have some dreams, you and I. What makes them so daring is that they can be realized.

Your courage is further to be acknowledged, because you come to listen with curiosity to the Scripture, and you reflect with respect upon the Church, and you judge honestly about life as you have experienced all of life. Curiosity about Scripture, respect for the Church, honesty about life, these are your own gifts of interpretation for the morning. You know that one requires the scholar's imagination, and the other requires the pastor's heart, and the third requires the preacher's guts. You have been given reason to trust, over generations, that somewhere the three will meet again before the noon hour strikes. So, as a loving and addressable assembly, you do not fear. You do not fear…lot the strange world of the Scripture, with its spirits, angels, demons, and divinity…. Not the community of strangers that is the church, with its wheat, tares, heroes, villains, friends, opponents and its troubling capacity both to represent and to distort the divine, the church where we pretend, intend and contend to know one another, with a baseball slugger's level of success (30%)…Nor even the estrangement of your own daily life, with its betrayals, ambiguities, losses of meaning, inexplicable horrors, random hurts and just plain boredom. You fear neither God nor man. Upon the strange world of the Bible you radiate curiousity. Toward the community of strangers in church you radiate respect. Into the estrangement of experience you send a glimmer, a gleam, a glistening honesty that is to be prized far above much pious hooting. To church you dare to come. In this, I salute you. For your courageous curiosity, respect, and honesty are themselves, curiously enough, and quite honestly, to be fully respected. There is Good News awaiting behind all that is so very strange today.

1. Christ Jesus: God's Lamp for the Poor

It will not surprise you that the first of three encounters for us, today, looms in the Scripture herself. Jesus has with him, for once, a great crowd. As he is heading toward Jerusalem, and as every step, word, and deed in this soft underbelly of St. Luke (chapters 9-19) falls underneath the shadow of Jesus' looming cross, and as the stark reality of that 'magnificent defeat' (Buechner), seems not to occur to the 'oi polloi' (vs. 25), Jesus speaks harshly.

This is not quite the passage one wants for a festive 'Together in Ministry' Sunday. We are following the lectionary (a series of ecumenically selected passages) this fall, however, so we must face it. I would not otherwise have chosen to do so. It is too tough a passage for the first fall Sunday. Having plighted my troth to the lectionary, however, I am bound. I am like the man who complained loudly in the lunchroom, year after year, about how much he disliked what he had in his brown bag. "Look what is packed here-just tunafish! Just peanut butter! Just cottage cheese!" Finally his lunchmates asked him who on earth was responsible for preparing those loathsome victuals. "Oh", he said, "I make my own lunch". To the lectionary, then, and without complaint.

Jesus wants to make sure that the crowd understands the cost, the literal cost, of a great dream. The dream is daringly great largely because-it can be achieved. They may become his disciples. But discipleship comes at a price. Salvation may be God's gift, free of charge, but discipleship, the way of salvation, costs. Grace, free to receive, is not cheap to live. In our time, as you well know, it was Dietrich Bonhoeffer who wrote so eloquently about costly grace.

Here Luke, in arranging a series of Jesus' sayings, advances the hyperbole of a dominical warning. The dream who is Christ is greater than family. Even life itself is a part, one part only, of this dream, which surpasses the limits of life. Luke, looking back 60 years to Calvary, places on Jesus' lips, "carry the cross". In sum: all our holdings, all our possessions are at risk, in the encounter with this dream.

Your many, quick questions about all this, scholars have also readily hurled into the path of this pronouncement ("you must give up all your possessions"). Did Jesus really say it? Did he really mean it? Does it hold true for us?...Yes, Yes, and Yes. Those who approach Dream Incarnate cannot proceed unless lightened they are and freed they are from being possessed by possessions. Unless they can let go, and *give up what does not last in order to lay hold of what does.*

Behold, lamp in hand, He stands in the doorway, well on into the night of longing. He knocks. To open, one must let go of all hand filling, soul trapping possessions which possess, things that master their masters. Behold Jesus Christ, the Lamp of the Poor!

2. You are His Disciple: One Lamp of the Poor

The Gospel of Luke is fascinating in its treatment of possessions, wealth, economics, because a great transition propels it. 1. The church is growing up in Luke's day. 2. The church is finding its place in the Roman world. 3. The church is finding its voice among educated gentiles. 4. The church is finding its way as it becomes an institution. 5. The church is finding its earthly footing, even as it anticipates a heavenly home. 6. Luke's Christ, as he remembers Christ, has things to say about money. We may hazard a summary: *DO NOT BE POSSESSED BY YOUR POSSESSIONS!*

Several odd features complete this Lukan portrait of the mysterious Christ. 1. The Greek for 'hate' bears a technical meaning, less emotional and more relational (Ringe). 2. It is clear that the Lukan Christ is speaking to men, "father and mother, wife and children" (Ringe), which tarnishes somewhat Luke's reputed affirmation of women. 3. The daily bearing, and bearing up under, a heavy cross (the regular, recurrent earthly defeat of things eternal) is assumed for the disciple, requiring only the briefest comment (vs. 23). 4. Prudence, economic realism, fiscal restraint, careful planning constitute the body of this teaching, found in the images of tower and battle. 5. They lead, logically, to a very practical teaching: at one point or another, all of your possessions will be 'given up', in the course of your discipleship. In the end, you lose them all.

For our time, a few pastoral suggestions about possessions may be in order. *One:* Get out of debt. Debt shackles, limits, hobbles. It is the very measure of how much your possessions possess you. Give up...your debt. All debt is bad, much is truly evil. *Two:* Participate in life by giving of your possessions. Give up...by giving away. *Three:* Grow in generosity, by percentage, in kind, through creativity. Give up...in increasing measure. *Four:* Maximize varieties and options in giving. *Five:* Tithe. Like marital fidelity is to relationship, it is the map, the compass of fiscal love. Give up...with discipline. So, therefore, give up your possessions: debt, self, sloth, doubt, ego. In this way, your life will radiate. You will become, yourself, a lamp of the poor.

3. *Asbury First: A Lamp of the Poor*

And what if all 2139 of us did so? What if we met Jesus, God's Lamp of the Poor, by living individual lives that did shine like lamps for the poor? Then we could live the dream. We would walk in peace and joy along the *Village Green* of life. Here, take a lantern. It is night time. We leave the sanctuary. We walk through the spacious, open welcome area. Then (for this is only a start), we tour the expanded grounds of our ministry. At every turn, in this dream, there is a lamp lit. Look: just here is a new United Methodist conference office, for a combined upstate conference. Look: just here is a pastoral counseling center which specializes in the needs of women, created and guided by a retired pastor. Look: just here you find a lamp lit on the porch of an Urban Retreat Center, spiritually led by a spirited minister committed to this cause. *(And each of these projects tithes from their own budget back to the mother church that created them, thus providing the possibility of further growth. They learned to do so, over time, from the Storehouse, Dining Center, Nursery School, Daycare and others, who were inspired to do so by this sermon! Hey, why not really dream?)* Look: just here there is the lamp of the porch of the county wide Wesley Foundation, a center for student ministry. Look: just here a lamp is lit over the door of a Hemispheric Hispanic ministry Center, from Emmanuel to Amor Fe y Vida. Our lamp leads us further: just here you find a religious drama center, K-12, and an elder care program, and.....Behold Asbury First United Methodist Church, The Lamp of the Poor!

Endnote

And what Emma Lazarus write? Perhaps she had Christ, she had you, she had this church in view:

Give me your tired, your poor
Your huddled masses yearning to breathe free
The wretched refuse of your teeming shore
Send these, the tempest tossed, to me
*I lift my **lamp** beside the golden door.*

On Meeting Sin Again for the First Time
Text: Luke 15:1-10
Asbury First United Methodist Church
September 16, 2001
The Rev. Dr. Robert A. Hill

Opening

Today our hearts are heavy. With our children, and with the world's human family, we have had to watch the sinful, terrorist destruction of a part of our one city, New York.

It recalls the night, July 1977, our first year of marriage, in which we stood atop the Union Seminary roof and looked out at a completely darkened New York, shut down by the blackout of that hot summer weekend. Not a light burning, save the cabs rocketing down Broadway. Like the darkness of sin, which is our natural condition, East of Eden.

It further recalls an evening in the Union Seminary quadrangle, June 1979. The President made an effort to mention something personal about each graduate. Of me, he said, I thought it odd at the time, "we shall miss Bob's love of New York". He was remembering, I guess, a poem I had written about walking from Battery Park, underneath where the World Trade Center once was, north, and gradually, to Spanish Harlem. Wall Street. The West Village. Soho. Times Square. Columbus Circle. Central Park West. Morningside Heights. A city of such lust, avarice, pride, like the sin which the Scripture describes, yet one that in the autumn is as dazzling in color and sound and life as any place on earth. (The stickers for our children last week, the Van Gogh prints, came from 54th street, the Museum of Modern Art.) In heaven it is always autumn, said John Donne. And in New York the autumn is just heavenly. Which has made this week's attack all the more hellish.

Perhaps it is fitting that this week's lesson presents Jesus, in his primary colors, not as teacher of righteousness, but as savior of sinners. Perhaps this is one week, maybe the best week in my 24 pension years of ministry, to think about sin. Maybe we are ready to meet sin again for the first time. For when, only when we have brought ample appreciation to the nature and power of sin, will we ever be able amply to appreciate the grace of God in Christ, who has come into the world to save us from our sin, both collective and personal. Once we have met sin again for the first time, we may be ready to meet Jesus again for the first time. For "where sin abounds, grace over abounds".

Truth to tell, we do not use well or regularly the verb "to sin", the noun "sin", or the related personification "sinner". Our use of these words, in general, lacks any significant confidence or regularity. As Gardner Taylor so memorably said 25 years ago, "sin may be out of our personal lexicons, but it is not out of our lives". In 24 years of ministry, I cannot recall a single week in which such a consideration of sin would have been more timely than this week terror and loss.

For the most part, the word resides outside of our regular vocabularies, at least our workday verbal wardrobe. The word does not seem to fit well, any longer. It droops in the midriff, and the collar, ever stiff, runs high and starchy. Thoreau said, "nature is right, but man is straight." Sin is neither, neither right nor straight, and so the word is ill-fitting. This puts us worlds apart from the author of the Third Gospel, for whom the word (verb, noun, all) carries a meaning so readily clear that it needs (much to our later misunderstanding and consternation) no definition or clarification. Luke says "sinner" with the same unselfconsciousness that we would use with words like felon, patient, criminal, or victim. What does it mean? What does this ancient word, propped for a moment on the lips of the Lord, tell us about the hidden, mysterious, strange Jesus of this far too familiar set of stories?

1. Scripture

a. It is curious that church-wide (for the most part), the other numinous oddities of language in Luke 15 we do understand and use. We hear you use these great words, and use them well. One says to his son, in the pew, as the Scripture is read, "I remember—a parable is a story with a message, and I remember that Jesus always taught using parables. He taught by telling stories. These parables were set in the countryside, and were about people and about justice. Jesus taught adults with simple stories." You understand 'parable'. Someone else, driving home today, interprets the word 'joy' for her rider: "Joy is God's delight, given us by God's spirit. You are one of the footprints, hallmarks, earmarks, landmarks, benchmarks of the Holy Spirit. What pleasure is to the body, joy is to the soul." I might have thought that 'repentance' would throw you, but no. In the choir, disrobing, an alto tells a bass, "Repentance means to turn around, to head home, to dust off and try again, like that story about the son and the pigs." And angel means messenger, and presence means joy, and heaven means the message of the presence of joy. You have passed, and more the Scriptural SAT, to this point.

b. But what is a sinner, and what does this tell us about the grand mystery of Christ? Our passage holds itself several clues, but finally the two fundamental meanings for 'sin' we shall have to intuit, congruent with Luke's usage, from the rest of the Bible. For Luke uses the word as if we all did know what he meant. And maybe after this week, we clearly do.

Here are some random clues, found in Luke 15:1-10. A sinner is somehow a cousin to a tax collector, one who represents, that is, an alien unjust power, who inflicts that power for ill upon the children of God, and who yet has a conscience with which to listen and draw near to God (vs. 1).

A sinner, next, is one whom Christ Jesus welcomes and with whom Jesus shares the intimacy of the common table (vs. 2).

Jesus comes for others, as Paul said, "the saying is sure and worthy of full acceptance, that Christ Jesus came into the world to save sinners—of whom I am the foremost". A sinner, primarily here and also in the later account of the Welcoming Father, is lost, dislocated, and alone. For this reason, then, a sinner found is the cause of inexpressible delight, joy. Including the lonely, discovering the dislocated, reconnecting with the disappeared—these moments provide a heavenly joy, a consequence of the discovery of the sinner (vs.7)

c. Luke trusts, as he recalls or recasts or casts these parables out of his own past, that there is a divine purpose coursing through history, building the church, propounding the Gospel, and saving the lost, and gradually and expensively and individually finding people who have been lost in the rubble of life, darkened and dislocated by sin. But what is sin?

2. *Personal Sin*

In the first place, sin is utterly personal. This we understand. The covenantal commands of the decalogue have a personal consequence (Exodus 20). For we confess, too a personal dimension to the apocalyptic sway of sin. The angels in heaven—and perhaps a few others—may "need no repentance". As grace touches ground in Jesus Christ, sin touches sand in personal confessions. We get lost. It is our nature, east of Eden. We get lost in sex without love: lust. We get lost in consumption without nourishment: gluttony. We get lost in accumulation without investment: avarice. We get lost in rest without weariness, in happiness without struggle: sloth. We get lost in righteousness without restraint: anger. We get lost in desire without ration or respect: envy. And most regularly, we get lost in integrity without humility: pride. If you have never known lust, gluttony, avarice, sloth, anger, envy or pride you are not a sinner, you are outside the cloud of sin, and you need no repentance. (You also may not be quite human).

3. *Pervasive Sin*

a. In the second place, sin is pervasive. (On this point, today's sermon bears down, because its sibling is so much better understood.) Sin has a corporate, expansive, even institutional reality. We mistake its power, if we see only, say, several dozen individuals acting to destroy property and life in lower Manhattan. That of course is real, and true. But sin is the power of death, throughout life. Sin is the condition of life under which such treachery takes place. Sin is the absence of God. Sin is an orb of confusion in the world. Sin is the advance or retreat of a great thunderstorm, a frontal advance, though theological not meteorological. Sin is like a city blacked out, a power far beyond any individual lamp turned down, any individual light switch-hit. Sin is a shadow, the one great shadow. Whatever is not of faith, is sin. And that is quite a lot in this world. All have sinned and all have fallen short of the glory of God. All. Sin is the air we breathe. Sin is the architectural design for our natural state, east of Eden. Sin is the controlling legal authority of our being. Sin is the occupying army that has our beloved homeland, love, under siege. Hence, sin is the knock at the garret door, late at night, and the thud of the storm troopers' boots, and suicide bombing of the terrorist. Sin is a force, a wind, a phalanx, a competing entity. Sin is all that mutes the voice. Do we blame sheep for being lost—hardly by the way a comprehensively intelligent beast—for getting lost? It is his nature. Do we blame the coin—inanimate, hardly noticeable—for getting lost? It is Isaac Newton's gravity at work. But we only sin clearly when we are ready to see it, by revelation, and often only once we have left its borders behind. Like all lasting reality, we know it in retrospect. Read again the works of William Stringfellow.

b. That is, the power of sin vastly surpasses any individual, human attempt at cure. You might as well try to stop a reeling boat hoist wheel, holding 2000 lbs., with your bare arm. It is just that impossible, that foolish. Individuals may behave morally or immorally, usually some of both. But corporate sin marches on, R Neibuhr showed in 1932: "Man's capacity for justice makes democracy possible, but man's inclination to injustice makes democracy necessary". Sin is that 'inclination'. "If social cohesion is impossible without coercion, and coercion is impossible without the creation of social injustice, and the destruction of injustice is impossible without the use of further coercion, are we not in an endless cycle of social conflict?" Sin is that 'impossible'. As a rule, in American Protestant Christianity, we vastly underestimate this primary, pervasive form of sin. This is both our achievement and our defeat.

Perhaps the stock market symbolism may work again for us, 70 years later. The power of sin is as free before any single individual, as is the stock market before any lone investor. The market moves due largely to corporate, institutional, fiduciary choices, which themselves are not influence by individual courage, but first by the fiduciary responsibility of corporate officers, thinking of and for the collective. The same is tragically true of nation states, and alliances. They march to the beat of a different drum. The chief weakness of my beloved Methodism, so American and so optimistic, is its congenital naivete about pervasive sin. While it took individuals to knock down the twin towers and kill thousands, it took more than individuals, too. That 'more' is sin.

Getting rid of males or females will not destroy sin, or the exodus of Caucasians, or the ostracism of the wealthy, nor the browbeating of heterosexuals. Sin is a pervasive, brute, existential reality, which does not give ground before any merely ideological assault. As Wesley, "sin remains even when it does not reign."

Sin traps us in an endless cycle of social conflict. For this theological reason, some US response to Tuesday's heinous crime is probably inevitable. We may hope that as a nation we shall have the courage not to overreact, and, indeed not to react at all, but to respond. It is devilishly difficult not to overreact when you have been humiliated, even as an individual, and perhaps impossible for a collective. But let us hope not to react, but to respond, and to respond justly, mercifully, humbly, prudently, rightly, and effectively.

That is, if we are to use force to bring order and protect peace, then may it be force that does not create more disorder and less peace.

If we are tragically to find military action necessary to address a clear and present danger, then may it be action wisely chosen that makes danger less present rather than more.

Let us summon the faithful courage of collective patience, and take our time. We have all the time we need.

We recognize that there are times when force, alone, is the required and necessary response (December 1941), but that there are also times when force is wrongly used and unnecessary (August 1998), bringing only further retribution. Not to have responded to Hitler militarily in 1941 would have been as lasting a collective sin upon the conscience of this country as we could imagine. We may be entering such a time, both similar in tragedy and different in scope.

May we respond with courage, not react with vengeance, as, in Christ, we grapple with pervasive sin.

4. *Christus Victor*

Luke's little stories assume a recognition of sin, pervasive and personal. You know, it takes a while in life to know what you are up against. Once you begin to see, you begin to appreciate. Once you see the reality of sin, you can appreciate the awesome gospel, "Christ died for our sin." You come to yourself. But that is another, nearby, parable. Once we have fully met sin again for the first time, we may also meet Jesus again for the first time. Not the Jesus of Marcus Borg's self-portrait (wisdom teacher, religious mystic, social prophet), but the Jesus of Luke's Gospel. Jesus Christ is not a teacher, only, but a Savior, a Lord. And his grace, alone, carries enough power to grapple with sin, pervasive and personal. That is why, on this Lord's day, with heavy hearts, and nostrils still full of the stench of body parts in lower Manhattan, we may yet lift our heaviness to God. Sursum corda! Lift up your hearts.

We have much to do. Jane Addams said it of our nation, but her insight now fits our world: "The blessings which we associate with a life of refinement and cultivation must be made universal if they are to be permanent. The good we secure for ourselves is precarious and uncertain, is floating in midair, until it is secured for all of us and incorporated into our common life". How prophetic her words do sound this week.

Have faith, people of faith.

Terror may topple the World Trade Center, but no terror can topple the World Truth Center, Jesus the Christ.

The World Trade Center, hub of global economies may fall, the economy of grace still stands in the World Truth Center, Jesus the Christ.

The World Trade Center, communications nexus for many may fall, but the communication of the gospel stands, the World Truth Center, Jesus Christ.

The World Trade Center, legal library for the country may fall, but grace and truth, which stand, through the World Truth Center, Jesus the Christ.

The World Trade Center, symbol of national pride may fall, but divine humility stands, through the World Truth Center, Jesus the Christ.

The World Trade Center, material bulwark against loss may fall, but the possibility in your life of developing a spiritual discipline against resentment (Niehbuhr) still stands, through the World Truth Center, Jesus the Christ.

> *The soul that on Jesus still leans for repose,*
> *I will not, I will not desert to his foes*
> *That soul though all Hell should endeavor to shake*
> *I will never, no never, no never forsake.*

"Faith Handles Change"
Text: Luke 16: 1-13
Asbury First United Methodist Church
September 23, 2001
Rev. Dr. Robert A. Hill

Opening

Before us today stands Jesus Christ, robed in mystery and announced in a strange parable. There is no easy interpretation for this parable. Why is its hero, my favorite accountant, commended for dishonesty, which is a breach of the ninth commandment? We do not know. Why is his master happy to be cheated? We cannot say. Why is an accountant's swindle upheld, in this parable here attributed to Jesus, as a preparation, somehow, for heaven? No one can tell. What, please, does verse 9, as tangled in the Greek as it is in your bulletin, intend? We do not see. What possible connection is there between the story, and the four trailing proverbs? Little at all, except that they all deal with money. How did this mess make it into Luke's travel narrative? It is not clear. Is this dishonest manager our role model, in the church, as we try to "manage wealth in the direction of justice?" (Ringe) Perhaps! And, most of all, where is Jesus, The Divine Mystery Incarnate, to be found in our reading today?

For some weeks we have ridden hard for three points a sermon. We will rest the horse a minute, a little feed and little water. Easy big fella. Get well soon, we said: Healing in Christ, and healing in society, and healing in people. The lamp of the poor we cried: Christ, church, disciple. Meet sin again, we implored: Sin is personal, sin is pervasive, Christ saves us from sin. Three points, and a poem. But the horse is tired. And our fellow bandits, interpreters Craddock and Ringe and Tittle, are tired too, at least in reference to this passage. I continue to curse the lectionary. The parable of the dishonest steward has really just one meaning, and it is very good news.

1. L'Etranger

Let us recall the mystery of Christ, the Stranger in our midst. We can announce his presence today, again today. He is among us: dealing with issues we dismiss...speaking with people whom we dislike...considering options we disdain...selecting vocations that do not yet fully exist...expanding spaces that we constrict...accepting lifestyles that we reject...attending to possibilities that we ignore...approaching horizons that we avoid...healing wounds that we disguise...questioning assumptions that we enjoy...protecting persons whom we mistreat...making allowances that we distrust. So, strangely, is He among us.

For the mystery of Jesus Christ falls upon us, approaches us, and enchants us, when and where we least expect Him. In the strange world of the Bible. In the midst of the community of strangers that is the Church. Hidden in the brutal estrangement of our personal life. Here, behold, the Lord Christ Jesus, "L'Etranger".

Contrary to much preaching, televised and popular today, his presence is neither simple, nor surface, nor easy, nor fundamental, nor shallow, nor ideological, nor one dimensional, nor ahistorical, nor primarily political. He draws us, lures us, and enchants us. So he sets us free.

For St. Luke has captured a collage of portraits of Jesus, "On the Road". We are on a journey, as Luke reminds the church. We are making a trip to the promised land. We are headed in a certain direction. With our spiritual forebears, we are traveling, on a journey. Israel left Canaan to go to Egypt to find bread. There they became the slaves of Pharaoh. But Moses led them out, parted the Red Sea, and guided them through the wilderness. He brought them the ten commandments. At last, he sent them forth, with Joshua, to inhabit the land flowing with milk and honey. In such a glorious land, they hunted and farmed. They even built a temple, and chose a King. Samuel, Saul, David, and Solomon reigned, but were followed by others less wise and less strong. Although the prophets did warn them, the children of Israel left their covenant and their covenant God, and at last suffered the greatest of defeats, the destruction of Jerusalem and the return to slavery in Babylon, 587bc. Cried Jeremiah, "O that my head were a spring of water, and my eyes a fountain of tears, so that I might weep, night and day, for the slain of my poor people." (9:1) Like Israel marching in chains to Babylon, and then trudging home again two generations later, we people of faith are on a journey, from slavery to freedom.

Luke's mysterious Christ meets us today, hidden in the calamity of unexpected change and economic crisis. On the road, the journey of faith, Luke has most to say, and Jesus most regularly addresses the issue of money. Remember how Luke traces the Gospel. Mary in the Magnificat honors the poor. John the Baptist preaches justice, in the great, unique tradition of the Hebrew prophets, from Amos forward. Isaiah's words and hopes are affirmed. Jesus blesses the poor, not just the poor in spirit, in his 'sermon on the plain'. Remember the parable of the 'rich fool', "tonight is your soul required of you, and these riches, whose shall they be?" Luke sets Christian discipleship at odds with, in contest with, anxiety about possessions. And in conclusion, meet Lazarus and Dives. Jesus Christ calls us to manage our possessions toward justice, both as a church and as individuals.

2. An Initial Personal Application

But you may wonder whether this parable speaks to you, especially if you are in financial calamity. Along Luke's Jerusalem road, Jesus has a healing word to say about possessions, money, wealth.

To me it is clear that the chief communal issue before Luke's (Antioch?) congregation was the management of wealth. This means that they had money. This also means that they did not immediately throw it away. This further means that they reasoned that the apocalypse of the end was not so very near that no financial planning was necessary. This additionally means, as Luke's writing shows, that they were trying to learn to become prudent, astute, imaginative, shrewd, clever, insightful, accountable, interpreneurial managers. So they are reminded, in argument from less to more: "Keep faith in the little things, to be ready for the big ones." An ounce of prevention is worth a pound of cure. "Be faithful with money, which belongs to God, so that you will become faithful in soul, which belongs to you." A stitch in time saves nine. "Do your pre-season training with possessions, so that you will be ready for the regular gridiron season of the spirit." Look before you leap. Be penny wise, not pound foolish.

In other words, "use possessions so as to gain, not to lose, your future" (Craddock). Be creative. "For all the dangers of possessions, it is possible to manage goods in ways appropriate to life in the Kingdom of God" (Ringe). Remember that you are a manager of someone else's accounts, an absentee landlord who has a claim. And go ahead, be clever. Be creative and loyal, but if you have to choose - be creative.

3. *The Gospel of the Dishonest Manager*

The deeper truth in this passage, though, is simply that faith handles change. Faith carries the power to master the vicissitudes of change. Ultimately, this parable cannot be interpreted along moral, or economic, or even political lines. So read, it makes no real sense. Luke has gone ahead to read the parable so, in part, by appending the four parables about fiduciary fidelity. We have honored his teaching. But the parable itself says something else. Like the mystery of Christ itself, the story is not moral but mystical, not theoretical but theological, not law but grace. It is *good news*.

The good news is that faith handles change. A man gets the pink slip, and leaves under suspicion, with the sheriff on the way. He is looking at doing time. He is on the lamb. He is headed for jail, prison, the lockup, the pokey, hoosegow, calaboose, the slammer, the joint, the tank, in stir, goin' up the river, doin' time, in the brig, the gray bar hotel, the big house, the can. (Isn't language wonderful? As the steel magnolias said, "accessorize - it's the only thing that separates us from the animal kingdom". I would add speech.) He is not a moral exemplar. But just as his ingenuity handles the sudden change in his circumstance, so the powerful grace of faith, the faith of Jesus Christ, handles the constant change of life. Faith manages change, masters change. So Paul can shout, "I have been crucified with Christ. It is no longer I who live, but Christ who lives in me and the life I live in the flesh I live by the faith of the Son of God who loved me and gave himself up for me." (Gal. 2:20). The faith of Jesus Christ, working heteronomously through life, handles change. Faith is nimble, not flatfooted; agile not stolid; creative not loyal; shrewd not complacent; quick not quiescent; fast not slow.

Notice what my favorite accountant does not do. He does not pray, go to temple, seek ministerial counsel, bellyache, celebrate his victimhood, join the choir, or leave it all up to Jesus. He does not say, 'let Go let God'. Unlike Jerry Falwell this week, he does not claim that God has done this to him. In fact, the faith here acclaimed has no religious clothing at all. No, he does none of that. Rather, he responds, shrewdly. He finds the faith to handle change, and lives the faith that handles change. Change is real hard, and real good. Like life, like love, like faith, like...any of the things of God.

Of course, this week, I cannot help think of the young father, RIT graduate, and others on the plane that crashed in Pennsylvania. Somehow, amid sudden and calamitous change, they found the courage to act in a way that, at least in part, handled change. They even had the presence of mind to call home first. Faith handles change. I cannot help think of the men who carried a person in a wheelchair down dozens of flights of stairs. Faith handles change. I cannot help think of the several firemen's boots you have put dollars into. Faith handles change (literally). I cannot help think of Mayor Giuliani, in his finest hour. Faith handles change. I cannot help mention our President, who found a grand phrase when he needed it, this young leader of such few words: "We shall meet violence with patient justice." Beautiful. Subject, verb, predicate. May our actions be as eloquent as that old Yankee sentence. Faith handles change. The faith of Jesus Christ, our salvation, does not fear to change, nor does faith fear change. Faith manages change. This is the grace and beauty of church meetings. You can see this ordinary grace at work in most church meetings, where faith is called upon to handle change.

It makes you wonder whether there is collectively an unforeseen, creative, shrewd response to our changed circumstance as a people. How to meet violence with patient justice…hmmm…in the trust that faith handles change. This is the faith of Jesus Christ, apart from which all else is sin.

Keep this portrait of the shrewd manager in your wallet, especially for the days your wallet is empty. He meets the report of his mismanagement, itself possibly false, with calm. He does not try to change the world, or this news. He raises the basic question with courage: "What shall I do?" He thinks creatively, acts enterpreneurially, communicates astutely, relates cleverly, strategizes shrewdly…and lands on his feet. When the cheese moves, he does too. And Jesus commends him, I guess. And Luke commends him, I guess. And even his old boss commends him, I guess. You can't help but love the guy.

And I have no idea what verse 9 means.

"For the Freedom We Have Received, Lord Make Us Truly Thankful"
Text: 1 Corinthians 11: 23-26 and Luke 17: 1-11
World Communion Sunday
October 7, 2001
The Rev. Dr. Robert A. Hill
Asbury First United Methodist Church

"Affliction is a good man's shining hour".

"Suffering produces character, character endurance, endurance hope, and hope does not disappoint because of the Love God shed abroad in Jesus Christ our Lord."

"Count it all joy, siblings, when various trials beset you."

"As often as you eat this bread, and drink this cup, you do preach the Lord's death until he comes."

In this autumn, suddenly, we realize again how much we owe to those who won our freedom, both temporal and spiritual.

A. *Temporal Freedom*

Freedom from the Tyranny of Kings

We think of Washington's army, shivering along the Hudson River, in the first cold winter of Independence, 1776. Thomas Paine:

"These are the times that try men's souls. The summer soldier and the sunshine patriot will, in this crisis, shrink from the service of their country; but he that stands it now deserves the love and thanks of man and woman. Tyranny, like hell, is not easily conquered; yet we have this consolation with us, that the harder the conflict, the more glorious the triumph. What we obtain too cheap, we esteem too lightly; 'tis dearness only that gives everything its value. Heaven knows how to put a proper price

upon its goods; and it would be strange indeed, if so celestial an article as Freedom should not be highly rated."

Freedom from the Bondage of Slavery

We think of Lincoln, exhausted and soon to die, riddled with worry, conflict, risk, chance, decision and death for four years. Yet he lived out of this affliction to announce a great hope. Abraham Lincoln:

"With malice toward none, with charity for all, with firmness in the right as God gives us to see the right, let us strive on to finish the work that we are in...to do all that may achieve a just and a lasting peace for us and for all the nations."

Freedom from the Threat of Dictatorship

We think of Franklin Roosevelt, bound to his wheelchair, yet out of that bondage finding the rhetoric and courage to lead his people from fear to faith. Nothing to fear but fear itself. A day that will live in infamy. A world founded on four freedoms. Arsenal of democracy...FDR:

"We, too, born to freedom, and believing in freedom, are willing to fight to maintain freedom. We, and all others who believe as deeply as we do, would rather die on our feet than live on our knees (1941)...We have learned that we cannot live alone, at peace; that our own well-being is dependent on the well-being of other nations, far away. We have learned that we must live as men, and not as ostriches, nor as dogs in the manger. We have learned to be citizens of the world, members of the human community (1945).

Freedom from the Despotism of Ideology

We think of John Kennedy, wearing the anxiety of the cold war, and meeting that cold with warm words, warmly worded. A profile in courage. JFK:

"Let the word go forth from this time and place, to friend and foe alike, that the torch has been passed to a new generation of Americans, born in this century, tempered by war, disciplined by a hard and bitter peace, proud of our ancient heritage, and unwilling to witness or permit the slow undoing of those human rights to which this nation has always been committed, and to which we are committed today at home and around the world...Let every nation know, whether it wishes us well or ill, that we shall pay any price, bear any burden, meet any hardship, support any friend, oppose any foe to assure the survival and success of liberty."

<u>Freedom from the Fear of Terrorism</u>

There have been few if any such Presidential or national rhetorical flourishes, like those of Paine, Lincoln, Roosevelt, and Kennedy, since 1963. In fact, to this ear, there have been none. That alone should help us assess our recent past. There have truths told, words fitly spoken, rhetorical flashes, to be sure, but they have been from lesser voices, and from pulpits, and they have been largely ignored. I name only one national sentence, of high rhetorical value, since Kennedy. It was spoken this fall. G. W. Bush: *"We shall meet violence with patient justice."*

Yes, this fall, in our loss, we can more clearly see the high worth of the human freedom we have received. We can be thankful, at eucharist, for human freedom, humanly wrought.

B. Spiritual Freedom

But I must ask you: if the value of our temporal freedom is now so clearly and even starkly visible, *how much more*, then, is the higher value of our spiritual freedom even more clearly and more starkly visible, in this Sacrament of Holy Communion, through which we do preach the Lord's death until He come? If the ringing rhetoric of our national heritage can so move us, today, *how much more* are we transformed by the freedom we have received in Jesus Christ? For it is this freedom, wrought by Almighty God, upon which we depend for our salvation, for eternal life, for forgiveness, for heaven, and for heavenly peace on earth. This is God's own work, enacted in the death of Christ, whom we preach until He come. As God's act for us, for us men and women, and for our salvation, it is not susceptible, finally, to terrorist assault of any kind.

Freedom from the Tyranny of Religion

We think of Paul of Tarsus, who was seized by this same freedom, and who could fly free from the fetters of his inherited religion. Religion, untamed, can do so much harm. The death of Jesus set Paul free, to love and to serve. *"I have been crucified with Christ. It is no longer I who live, but Christ who lives in me. The life I now live in the flesh, I live by the faithfulness of the Son of God, who loved me, and gave himself up for me."* Take this sacrament to your comfort, as an altar call to freedom from the tyranny of religion.

Freedom from the Bondage of the Flesh

We think of Augustine of Hippo, who wrestled, grappled with the desires of the flesh for much of his life. A man of great learning, he nonetheless found himself unable to put away temptations that he was powerless to resist. Then, once in a garden, he heard a voice, like of a child, saying, "take and read". He picked up a copy of the letters of Paul that he had been reading, and he saw these words: *"Not in rioting and drunkenness, not in chambering and wantonness, not in strife and envying, but put ye on the Lord Jesus Christ, and make not provision for the flesh, to fulfil the lusts thereof."* From that moment he found peace of mind. Take this sacrament to your comfort, as an altar call to freedom from temptation.

Freedom from the Threat of Judgment

We think of John Wesley, who though he had as much or more formal religion than any of his contemporaries, was made to wait until middle age before he exchanged the form of religion for its power. Wesley on Aldersgate Street: *"About a quarter to nine, while he was describing the change which God works in the heart through faith in Christ, I felt my heart strangely warmed. I felt I did trust in Christ, Christ alone, for salvation; and an assurance was given me, that He had taken away my sins, even mine, and saved me from the law of sin and death."(5/24/1738)* Take this sacrament to your comfort, as an altar call to freedom from the threat of judgment.

Freedom from the Despotism of Defeat

We think of Weldon Crossland, one of the former pastors of this church, bringing a proposal for a new church to his doubtful Board of Trustees, and doing so amid depression and war. The year is 1939. He dedicated his idea to the glory of God and the service of Rochester. On the front page, as I have learned thanks to a friend's research, he placed this quotation, an inscription he had found on a country church in England: *"In the year 1643, when all things sacred were either demolished or profaned, this Church was built by one whose singular praise is to have done the best things in the worst times and to have hoped them in the most calamitous."* Take this sacrament to your comfort, as an altar call to freedom from the despotism of defeatism.

Freedom from the Fear of the Future

We think of Ernest Freemont Tittle, who more than most in his generation fifty years ago, saw the contours of the future. Tittle: *We of this generation are confronted with the revelation of divine purpose given in a human interrelatedness and interdependence that justifies the term "one world". We find ourselves in a situation where no one nation can prosper unless all prosper, no one people can dwell secure unless security is assured to all. This situation was brought about through human agents, through the activities of scientists, inventors, traders, imperialists; but it is not a result of human planning. Not even the most ardent imperialist will claim that empire was devised as a means of drawing the world together, nor will anyone claim that science or invention or international trade was carried on with a view to bringing about the interdependence of nations and peoples. The situation in which we now find ourselves, so far from being a result that we human creatures purposed and planned, has to a large extent been brought about despite our purposes, which for the most part were selfish and shortsighted enough. It has come to pass through the providence of God, who, through science and technology, through improved means of transportation and communication, through the extension of trade and credit, has brought it to pass that we have got to act with due consideration for the rest of mankind if we ourselves are to prosper and dwell secure. Something beyond us, a superhuman purpose and power, is working in history, bringing about the increasing interdependence of men and nations, so that our sheer survival becomes ever more contingent upon the establishment of justice and fair play in all our relations to one another."*

Takes this sacrament to your comfort, as an altar call to freedom from fear of the future.

"A Tale of Two Persistent Women"
Text: Luke 18:1-8
October 21, 2001
Asbury First United Methodist Church
Rev. Dr. Robert A. Hill

1. Persistence in Luke

We begin today in the town court of Nazareth, the honorable UnJ Judge presiding. Hear ye, hear ye. Hizzoner awaits. And Behold the Lord Jesus Christ dressed today in the apparel of a poor woman: He told them a parable about their need to pray always and not to lose heart.

In our autumn of anxiety, as we read the obituaries of the dead in the New York Times, we can readily appreciate the Scripture's utter realism. Luke too needed to remember that Jesus told them about "losing heart". This phrase communicates, in a season of anthrax, terrorism, uncertainty, economic pain. Greater souls in easier times have felt such ennui. So we are not surprised today to hear reports of increased therapy, medication and consumption of comfort food. We can feel the depression. Robert Pinsky, past poet laureate, at the U of R last week commented on the search dogs in lower Manhattan, unable to find any living beings, and increasingly depressed by their lack of success and their lack of reward. There is so much that we cannot influence or control. When we feel terrorized or hijacked, our animal reaction is to terrorize or hijack. Someone. Something. We are in danger of losing heart. The greatest threat is not that we will *succumb* to the terrorists, but that we will *become* terrorists, verbal and civic, ourselves.

We fear, and try to find our security in larger automobiles or drug supplies or stock collections or homes or layers of disconnection, gated communities of the mind and heart. But security comes not through possession, but through relationship. Do you want to be safe and secure? Invest your self in a lifetime of building and keeping healthy relationships. There is your security, where neither moth nor rust consumes.

Jesus pointed to the Town Court of Nazareth and therein to the simple figure of a persistent woman. See her at the bench. Watch her in the aisle. Listen to her steady voice. Feel her stolid forbearance. Says she: "Grant me justice." We leave her there for a moment.

2. *A Summer Run*

Instead, jog for a moment along a familiar village green. For there is a second persistent woman today, not of Scripture but of experience. It is largely in the interplay between these two women, Scripture and Experience, that we discover truth. You can see her in your own past, your own gallery of saints. Name the most persistent woman you ever met. Bella Abzug. Betty Bone Scheiss. Florence Nightengale. Elizabeth Cady Stanton. Eleanor Roosevelt. Esther. Barbara Streisand. That uppity Syropheonician woman. Harriet Tubman. Sojourner Truth. Susanna Wesley. Your grandmother. Whomever. I was thinking of one such persistent woman on a 90 degree day in the summer. For that summer day, hot and humid and happy, I took the car into Hamilton for repair. They needed much skill and two hours and some money to do the job. So in the great heat I was free to run through a familiar village, and across a village green, where long ago I was raised in a patchwork complex of relationships, durable and healthy.

Running along, with no deeds to do no promises to keep, I recalled an earlier age...There is a lanky Baptist preacher, heralding the promise of truth; and a musician on the bandstand, singing for justice; and a postmaster protecting communications; and a library, awaiting the emergence of justice; and a church and a store, and a graveyard with night falling. All in the mind's eye.

Through the familiar streets I ran thinking, steadily and especially, of my teacher, Marjorie Shafer. In the sixth grade she opened the world to us - by teaching us to read. As a teacher, she used the resources she had available, namely, her time and her voice. She persisted, through those years, prayerfully using the common resources of time and voice. You have time and you have a voice, too. You have need of persistent prayer, too. You have a desire not to lose heart, too. I was impressed, with the dogs barking in the summer heat, by the persistent memory of her persistence. It was good to remember the time given and the voice lifted, in 1966 in the 6th grade—SRA reading, sock hop, changes in classmates, baseball—Sandy Kofax and Orlando Cepeda, the Beatles, James Bond, memorizing the map of Africa, a mock debate about Vietnam, and the long great story of Bilbo Baggins. And, suddenly, girls.

> *Three things I do not understand*
> *Four are too wonderful for me*
> *The way of a ship on the high sea*
> *The way of an eagle in the sky*
> *The way of the serpent on the rock*
> *And the way of a man with a woman*

So continued this reverie, in a summer run, on a hot day, along a village green.

3. An Unexpected Christ

Meanwhile, back in Bethlehem town court, all rise, hear ye, hear ye, the honorable U J Judge presiding, another persistent woman employs time and voice. You have time and you have voice. Like Christ himself, she implores the implacable world to grant justice. Like Christ himself, she comes on a donkey of tongue and patience. Like Christ himself, she continues to plead, to intercede. Like Christ himself, she importunes the enduring injustice of this world. Like Christ himself she prays without ceasing. Like Christ himself she persists. She is an example to us of how we should use whatever time we have and whatever breath remains - to pray. It is prayer that is the most realistic and wisest repose of the anxious of this autumn of attack, and anthrax and exasperation. By prayer I mean formal prayer, yes. But by prayer I mean the persistent daily leaning toward justice, the continuous pressure in history from the voice of the voiceless and the time of the time bound.

What drove Luke, alone, to remember or construct this parable? The lengthening years, without ultimate victory, since the cross? The long decades of living without Jesus? The uncertainties of institution and culture and citizenship and multiple responsibilities? The daily stresses of managing a budget? It is the primitive church that can give an example to an America waiting to meet violence with patient justice. They waited for Jesus to return. And he delayed. And he delays, still. And there is rampant, hateful hurt, across God's village green earth. It is enough to make you lose heart.

Though with a scornful wonder we see her sore oppressed
By schism rent asunder by heresy distressed
Yet saints their watch are keeping their cry goes up 'howlong'?
And soon the night of weeping will be the morn of song.

It is a long wait. And that is just the point. Like the bridesmaids who waited with lamps trimmed, we feel the length of the wait.

Notice, waiting with us, is a poor widow. She lacks power, authority, status, position, wealth. She has her voice and all the time in the world. Like Jesus Christ, whose faith comes by hearing and hearing by the preaching of the word. We shut the courtroom door for a moment.

4. *Persistence in Life*

Meanwhile, back along the village green of experience, not the town court of Scripture, the heat hangs heavy on happy halcyon Hamilton. I run over to the Golf course, up the willow walk, past the artesian well, around the library, by the road to Chapel House, down Fraternity row, along the swan pond. I am carried by the wings of love and faith, and Al Childs now dead runs with me and Dale Winter now dead runs with me. Goodness and mercy - got my back.

This summer my friend said: "In my life I want to focus on relationships and flexibility". I said: "yes, on love and faith, relationships and flexibility."

I decided, with still more than an hour left of repairs, to run over to the school, down Kendrick Ave.

This one persistent woman, Marjorie Shafer, gave us a love of books - Tom Sawyer, Huckleberry Finn, the Hobbit, Harriet the Spy, the biographies of the Presidents, the Gospel of Luke. I suppose she looked out for the day when every voice would be lifted in praise. I perceive in hindsight that she, and your own favorite feckless female, persisted by faith. She was already old when she taught us. She was at least 40. I suppose she was one of those saints waiting with persistence. I guess maybe she rode down to Washington on a bus a few years earlier and heard a good sermon:

One day every valley shall be exalted...
With this faith we will be able to hew out of the mountain of
despair a stone of hope...
With this faith we will be able to work together...
This will be the day when all God's children will be able to sing
with new meaning...

And she taught for several more decades, persistent, tough, helpful, kind.

She found a corner of the world in which she could have some influence for good, and invested her time and her voice in another generation. She persisted.

5. Persistent Prayer and Justice

We enter again the Nazareth Town Court. The Honorable U J Judge presiding, and falling asleep. The Bishop fell asleep at Conference a few years ago. It was a memorable moment.

If we are not to lose heart, in the seemingly unending search for justice, we shall need to pray always, to "relax into the truth", and to give ourselves over to the divine presence in our midst.

Ernest Fremont Tittle was the greatest Methodist preacher of his mid twentieth century generation. Tougher than Sockman, truer than Peale, Tittle preached in Chicago until he died at his desk, writing about Luke. This is his book, only at best half written, and published after his death. It reads like someone cleaned off his desk into a printer. Yet I prize this volume.

There is special need for persistence in prayer when the object sought is the redressing of social wrongs. God will see justice done if the human instruments of his justice do not give way to weariness, impatience, or discouragement, but persevere in prayer and labor for the improvement of world conditions. Here we can learn from the scientist. Medical research is a prayer for the relief of suffering, the abolition of disease, the conservation of life - a prayer in which the scientist perseveres in the face of whatever odds, whatever darkness and delay. More especially we can learn from great religious leader like Luther, Wesley, Wilberforce, Shaftsbury, who year upon year prayed and fought for the causes to which they dedicated their lives. The need for persistence in prayer arises not only from the intransigence of the oppressor, but also from the immaturity and imperfection of the would-be reformer. We have a lot to learn and much in ourselves to overcome before we can be used of God as instruments of his justice. Recognizing this, Gandhi spent hours each day in prayer and meditation, and maintained a weekly day of silence.

The importunate widow continues, simply continues, and by her continuation comes to personify the divine. All this, behind the humble door of the Nazareth Town Court.

6. Surprise!

And meanwhile, jogging on the village green, the sun is getting higher as noon approaches. It is time to head back out toward the garage, and pay the piper. I have been running in such a sweet reverie, a happy retrospective, that the hour has come too fast. I have been thinking all morning of my old teacher. Now the school is a block away. I wonder if she is still active. I remember how it felt to walk to school at age 12, excited for the start of every day, arriving 20 minutes early, entering the school that marked the portal to the future. What a persistent presence in so many lives she was! Behind the school there is a large parking lot, and a long park. The park sometimes is used for family reunions. Almost choosing otherwise, I decide to run out to the back, to see the park. This has been a long run, and I am tired. It has been a long run in the ministry. It has been a long run in the church. It has been a long run in the conference. I am feeling the burning in the calves, some ache in breathing. It is hot.

Where do we find the persistence that keeps us going through adversity so that we do not lose heart? Do we not find it, given to us in prayer? Is this not our source of sustaining grace? How shall we have any lasting life without prayer, worship, study, tithing, service, song, fellowship, loving conversation?

Do you ever have a feeling that something is going to happen and then it does? A kind of premonition? I turned down into the back lot, empty for summer vacation, and saw just one lone car. It was hot and I was sweating, so I could not see too clearly for a time. And there was a kind of haze in the hot air. I saw the car move and stop, two women in the front seat. I slowed, the car paused. I paused, the car waited. I looked, and then I looked again. There in the rider's seat, to my utter astonished amazement, sat Mrs. Shafer, as old as ever, teaching, still teaching, using her voice and her time, teaching her granddaughter to drive. "Hello Mrs Shafer", I said. "Hello Bobby", she bemusedly replied, "it's nice to see you."

Sometimes, with a little persistence, just a little more running, just one more street, *keep going just one more block, don't stop for quitting, for suicide, for divorce, for giving up, for leaving*, you run headlong into Presence. "In thy presence there is fullness of joy."

And ran on to get my car, confident I had at least one sermon illustration for the fall.

7. Coda

Pray always
Labor Omnia Vincit
Do not lose heart
Work conquers all
Pray always
All of us are better when we are loved
Do not lose heart
Early to bed and early to bed and early to rise
Pray always
A stitch in time
Do not lose heart
Waste not want not
Pray always
Rome was not built in a day
Do not lose heart
Only the devil has no time
Pray always
God is time and voice
Do not lose heart

"Family Ties"
Text: Luke 17: 5-10
October 28, 2001
Rev. Dr. Robert A. Hill
Asbury First United Methodist Church

Chancing an encounter with the Divine, as you have by coming to worship, you also step toward the threshold of help for family trouble. Solutions start with reverence, prayer. It is my experience, observation, and personal confession that our troubles continue often out of our own desire to see them continue. Said one distraught husband, "I enjoy fighting with her". Said another angry daughter, "I'll teach him a lesson". Said a grandparent, reacting out of the deep pain of loneliness, "This needs to go on a little longer, if only to who is right". In other words, we aren't always genuinely seeking peace. Warfare breaks the monotony. Squabbling has its entertainment value. And, fortunately, we are always right. I know I am. You see, its one thing to seek peace if you recognize you might be wrong. But we're right, you and I. We would rather be right than happy. We would rather be right than happy.

Christian homes are not immune to this general disease of relational strife. Baptism and belief do not magically eliminate trouble on the home front. Nor does piety abroad discount our calling for love at home. In Luke 17 Jesus tells about a worker who has been 12 hours in the wheat fields, pouring out his life and sweat. The worker comes home. What word is given when he come home? Rest, thou weary and languid disciple? No. Come and eat, thou hungry and needy pilgrim? No. Take thine ease, thou faithful servant? No. Says the Lord, "Up, serve, work again, love, strive, your field work does not exempt you from your domestic duties." Our religious faith does not exempt us from domestic duty. Rather we are more intensely involved and concerned.

The Bible and our experience teach together three sturdy and reliable lessons about family ties.

1. The child has the opportunity to initiate peace and love.

2. The parent has the opportunity to humble himself.
3. The church has the opportunity to practice forgiveness.

One word for the child, and one for the parent, and one for the church.

1. First. The child has the opportunity to initiate peace and love. This is, you probably recognize, a modern paraphrase of the fifth commandment. "Honor your father and mother that your days may be long upon the earth" (Ex. 20:12). Notice as ever that humans do not break the commandments. We may be broken by them, over a lifetime. They are themselves, unbreakable. We may abide in them, be broken by them and so be open to real forgiveness, or try to live apart from them. They are, like the rest of the Bible, more real than anything else in life. More real than The Today Show, or chinese food, or Doug Flutie, or music. Here, the Bible indicates for us a path toward peace. The child, son or daughter, has the initiative. What an opportunity! The parent does not have the same freedom to initiate. Here is the wisdom of the Scripture, life down deep. The child has the chance to set things right! With the child, you as a child, lies the initiative. You can do it without losing face, without false pretense, without seeming disingenuous. The parent is caught in the parental role, bound by history and tradition and the approach of death. The child is free to dance and recover what is lost. The ball is in your court. You have power, opportunity that your seemingly omnipotent parent lacks. Make that phone call.

For three years one daughter, call her Prudence, fought the necessary and good fight for family peace. This involved setting limits, telling the truth, rejecting past manipulation, becoming a child not of man but of God. This is unbearably hard work. Avoiding it though is even harder work. When the dust had settled, and they saw what had occurred, it became clear that any further relationship would need the child's initiative. This is the daughter's opportunity, to be at hand as God breathes new life into old relations. She hated to make that extra, gratuitous, phone call, because, she was in the right. And she was. But any peace would only come because right and wrong were displaced by love and forgiveness. This is not to deny the place of honesty. There is absolutely no reconciliation without confrontation. The child has the freedom to set a new course. Prudence made her call on a Sunday afternoon. A lunch date was set, the air was cleared, the future again lies open. Make that phone call. Honor your father and mother. You have the upper hand, the initiative, the opportunity.

A warning: It happens that some relationships die. The Bible recognizes this and enshrines this eternal truth in the wisdom saying in Matthew 10:14, "If any one will not receive you or listen to your words, shake the dust from your feet as you leave that house or town."

2. Second. The parent has the opportunity to humble himself. The radical freedom of the Christian faith falls here at the doorstep of father and mother. You may not have the initiative with the children, you may have to wait for them to come around, but throughout life you do have the initiative with the heavenly Father. You have the opportunity to live humbly with God. Authority in the father/son and mother/daughter relationships is not at the center. Not authority but authenticity is the key. A parent who reveres the Divine love is an authentically loving parent. You are free, dear parent, to humble yourself before God.

This opportunity is taught in Ephesians 6. "Parents, do not provoke your children to anger, but bring them up in the discipline and instruction of the Lord." How does one teach discipline and instruction, especially to grown children who are now themselves parents? By humble example.

Parents do a lot of waiting. Waiting for the school bus to arrive. Waiting for Jill to finish her lesson. Waiting for Jack to come home. Waiting for the car to come home with Jack in it. Waiting and hoping that Jack and said car are in one piece.

I didn't notice right off just how hard that waiting can be. I worked late nights in High School, flipping burgers at an old Red Barn in Syracuse. "You want fries with that?" is the vocabulary of that work, and I know it well. We would close by 1 A. M. and then clean up. I would head home, walking up hill toward Allen Street, and rest. One winter night, it must have been a Friday because it was payday, I took a shortcut over a wire fence. It was a beautiful cold night, about 3 A. M. I was in a dream world, walking along, flakes of snow dropping quiet like love. It's fun to be young, off of work, with a paycheck in your pocket. Paycheck. Crossing E. Genesee I checked my pocket. It was gone! $89.00! Gone! In the dark I retraced my steps back down hill and over that same fence and there, just against the wire fence was the check. I headed up home happy. The clock was striking 3:30 as I came in and padded down the hall. "Glad you're home" came a voice, not clearly male or female, but distinctly parental. "I'm never asleep until I hear you come in." Parents wait and watch.

In the waiting is the chance to display a humble walk with God. This is the power of example, the parent's opportunity.

3. Third. The church has the opportunity to practice forgiveness. The word of scripture which confirms this for us is found in Luke 6: 32ff. Just as parents and children have words of command for family troubles, so the church has a distinct role to play, an avuncular, serendipitous, creative role to play in bringing peace to families. It takes women and men of heart and courage to bring it off.

Don is such a man. Deep in the heart of Texas, this Yankee turned Texan runs a school district in a medium size prairie town. He is a Christian hero in my book because he went out of his way to practice forgiveness. Two years ago Marie came to work for him. She is a graduate of a teacher's college in Upstate New York. She left the Empire State hoping to leave parts of her background behind. Marie is a stellar elementary school teacher. She loves kids. She hugs and laughs with and cries with her kids. She is a born teacher. Thank the Lord there are some left. Quickly she became a favorite in her little Texas town, where "damnyankee" is one word. She is a plump and happy young woman. In February she came to Don in tears, bearing with her her resignation effective immediately. Marie was with child. In this Texas town, she knew from her opening interview, this is grounds for immediate dismissal. She had no other intention and no other desire than to bear her child and place it for adoption. To do that she had to sacrifice her job and her dream of escaping her Empire State past. She quietly explained her situation and left.

Don saw a chance to save a vocation and a person by enacting a route to forgiveness. He intervened. He prayerfully telephoned and cajoled and politicked a solution to her problem. Don found a way to place Marie in another town and another job for four months until her delivery. He found a way to preserve her original position, even her original classroom. He found a way to keep her from panicking at the first sign of family trouble. He found a way to love, do good, and lend to someone who could give him nothing but some trouble in return. He restored her life and some of her soul. And all this from a back-sliding Episcopalian. Luke 6:32 says it all.

1. The child has the opportunity to initiate peace and love.
2. The parent has the opportunity to humble himself.
3. The church has the opportunity to practice forgiveness.

Let us live our faith this week.

"We cannot do more than we owe to God. Can we ever do as much? If we fail to see this, it is because of our inveterate habit of taking for granted things that might well serve to remind us what utterly dependent creatures we are.

We take for granted the cosmic setting of our lives, seldom or never stopping to reflect upon the fact that the sky does not cave in on us; or the fact that "seedtime and harvest, and cold and heat, and summer and winter, and day and night (do) not cease." (Gen. 8:22).

We take for granted our daily bread, especially those of us who live in cities, unmindful of the fact that we are dependent not only on the farmer, the miller, the baker, and the grocer but also on cosmic forces-soil and rain and sunshine, the whole order of nature.

We take for granted a beauty of earth and sea and sky whereby our spirits once and again are calmed and healed and uplifted. Natural beauty, so far as we can see, is not a necessary condition of bodily existence. Only our souls would be impoverished if it were denied to us, but how very great that impoverishment!

We take for granted the lighting and heating of our houses, the delivery of our mail, the working of our telephones, the policing of our cities, the teaching of our children-unmindful of our dependence on fidelities, devotions, and co-operative undertakings that are themselves dependent on a sense of duty whose source and secret is God

We take for granted a tradition of service that derives from the love of God made manifest in Christ, a tradition of mercy and compassion and unfailing ministry to others without which the world of today would seem hardly endurable and the future most dreadfully dark.

We may even take for granted a divine mercy that does not abandon us but gives us another chance when we have played the fool and brought disaster upon ourselves and others."

(E. F. Tittle)

"Come Down Zaccheus!"
Text: Luke 19: 1-10
Stewardship Sunday
Asbury First United Methodist Church
November 4, 2001
Rev. Dr. Robert A. Hill

It is hard for me to tell, from this angle, which tree you are in. Given the guns of this autumn, it is hard for me to tell which tree I am in myself, day to day. Has life chased you up the tree of doubt? Or are you treed in the branches of loyalty? Is that you in the religion tree? Or are we shaking or shaking in the money tree? Jesus Christ calls us today, to come down out of the tree forts of our own making, and accept a loving relationship with Him. May measure all with a measure of love.

Doubting Zaccheus

Perhaps the presence of unexplained wrong provokes you to doubt the benevolence or the power of God. No one can explain why terrible things happen, as they do. But if you will come down a limb or two from your philosophical tree of doubt, the tree of the knowledge of good and evil, you may hear faith. God can bring good out of evil, and make bad things work to good. This is not a theological declamation, but just something we can notice together.

We played golf the other day. On the last hole, I pulled out a three wood and hit a grounder, that nonetheless rolled right to the green. If I had connected, I would have smashed the clubhouse window, for it was way too much club. Sometimes a bad thing, a worm burner golf shot, interferes with a really bad thing, a $1000 broken window.

Two Sundays ago Chris and I drove late to church. I usually run early Sunday and finish memorizing the sermon along the way, as I did on October 21. I just forgot the time. We raced here, and in so doing I cut a corner, literally, and so popped a car tire. I was not happy to hear my son say, "haste makes waste". You know, though, both rear tires were thin. I had replaced the front in

August, and forgot about the rear ones. I have to admit, it was good that I had reason to replace them, before I had a blowout, in a convertible, on the highway. Sometimes it happens that a bad thing prevents a really terrible thing from happening.

Joseph was thrown into a pit, and sold into slavery. He had to find his way, as a Jew, in the service of the mighty Pharaoh. He did so with skill, and rose to a position of influence, even with Potiphar's wife chasing him around in his underwear. Then, a full generation later, a great famine came upon those brothers who had earlier sold Joseph down the river. They went to Pharaoh, looking for food. And who met them, as they came to plead? There was Joseph. He so memorably said, as written in Genesis 50: "You meant this for evil, but God meant it for good, that many might be saved." Sometimes it happens that a bad thing in one generation prevents starvation in the next.

In Jericho, as Jesus found the little man up in the tree, his fellows grumbled (vs. 8). Why would he take time with such a greedy, selfish person who makes his living off the sweat of others' brows? That hurts, to see divine attention given to those who have harmed you. Why would he have a meal with someone who takes no thought for the hurt of God's people? This is bad! And it is. We miss the power of the parable if we do not see this. This is Jesus taking up with those who have wished the church ill, who have used the church for their own very well intended but nonetheless self-centered reasons. This is Jesus consorting with sinners. But sometimes a bad thing in the little brings a good thing in the large. Zaccheus changes, and in so doing provides great wealth for others' benefit.

Come down from this one tree, doubting Zaccheus. I know that bad things happen to good people, and as a pastor hardly anything troubles me more. Sometimes, though, sometimes—not always, just sometimes, a bad thing early averts a really bad thing late. I have seen it, and you have too. It is enough to give someone up the doubting tree a reason to come down at least a branch. Think of it as existential vaccination.

It is the labor of faith to trust that where sin abounds, grace overabounds. Even in this autumn of terror. September 11 is the quintessence of all things bad. I want to be very nimble, careful in what I say here, so that I am not misheard. This is a bad thing. But one of the redeeming possibilities in this disaster is the chance that as a result, enough of us, now, will become enough committed to the realization of global peace and justice, that these dead shall not have died in vain, and that their demise will be a warning to us that we do not have forever in the quest for peace on earth. Sometimes a bad thing in one part of history protects us from a worse thing in another part.

Let us not lose sight of the horizons of biblical hope, as improbable as they can seem. The lion and the lamb. No crying or thirst. The crooked straight. All flesh.

The divine delight comes still from saving the lost, including the forgotten, seeking the outcast, retrieving the wayward sons and daughters of Abraham. God wants your salvation. Your salvation "has personal, domestic, social, and economic consequences" (Craddock). Jesus Christ saves us from doubt.

So come down Zaccheus, come down from your perch in that comfortable sycamore tree, that comfortable pew, that skeptical reserve, that doubt. Come down Zaccheus! The Lord Jesus Christ has need of your household and your money, and He responds to your doubt.

Zealous Zaccheus

Come down Zaccheus, down from your zealous leanings, hanging out on the branch of life. Idolatry comes when we make one or more of the lesser, though significant, loyalties in life to become a shadow of the one great loyalty, that which the heart owes alone to God. Zaccheus had governmental responsibility, community status, a welcoming home, a fine family, and we can suspect he was loyal in these regards. Curious as he was, up on his branch, he had no relationship with the divine. Into this relationship, Jesus invites him. More precisely, Jesus invites himself into relationship with a man up a tree. He is invited into a whole new life, a new world of loving and faithful relationships, that stem from the one great loyalty.

We need to be careful about lesser loyalties this fall. Again, I want to speak nimbly and not be misunderstood. To me, it is clear that there are times when police work, force and even the violence of some warfare tragically must be used to prevent, as we just said, even greater horrors in the future.

Our priorities, ("God, family, the Packers" as Lomardi said) become clear in a time of loss. Read with me one of the many obituaries posted in the New York Times:

This year, Sheila Scandole carved the pumpkin for Halloween, a job that had always fallen to her husband, Robert Scandole. But he is not here anymore, so with a little help, she carefully etched a spider on a pumpkin.

And when she took their two daughters out trick-or-treating in their Pelham Manor neighborhood in Westchester County, she could not help but think about him. "He would have been right there with us," she said. "I felt horrible, but I tried to carve the pumpkin the best that I could. I wanted to make it real special."

Mr. Scandole, 35, a trader with Cantor Fitzgerald, doted on the girls, Emma, 4, and Katie, 2. He worked on Wall Street, but he always clung to his old neighborhood, in Breezy Point, Queens, even taking part in a basketball league with some of the guys he grew up with. He and Sheila met at Breezy Point, where their parents still live. "I lost the greatest love of my life," she said.

Yet all of this involves a lesser loyalty than the one owed to God. We can forget whose water we were baptized into, if we are not careful.

Do you see the danger? Come down Zaccheus, come down, before it is too late. Make sure your lesser loyalties - to government, family, home, all - do not cover over, do not shadow the one great loyalty.

Religious Zaccheus

Let's talk for a moment about religion, shall we? Come down Zaccheus, come down! No amount of religious apparatus can ever substitute for what Jesus is offering today, and that is loving relationship. No amount of theological astuteness can ever substitute for loving relationship. No amount of sturdy churchmanship can ever substitute for loving relationship. No amount of righteous indignation can ever substitute for loving relationship. No amount of church music, instrumental or vocal, can ever substitute for loving relationship. No amount of formal religion can ever substitute for the power of loving relationship. Jesus invites us into loving relationship with him, and so with each other. That is salvation. Are we lovers anymore?

Sometimes it is easier to see things in others. Let's talk about Islam, shall we? I love Huston Smith's happy review of the religion of Mohammed. We can certainly learn much from our Islamic neighbors. I commend our President for his tolerant care of our Moslem citizens, and, with some few exceptions thus far, our nation's civility. We can do no less.

You remember your high school review of Islam. The word means 'submission', and Moslem is one who submits to God. The five pillars of Islam, like the 'tulip' summary of Calvinism, have shorthand value. You remember them: 1. One God. 2. 5 times daily prayer. 3. Tithing (2.5%). 4. Fasting at Ramadan. 5. Pilgrimage to Mecca. It is a worthy religion.

Without being critical, can we though be honest? Islam is a religion, like our own. But Zaccheus had religion, and that a good one. He even had God, the real God. But religion alone, even our own, is God without Jesus, order without freedom, authority without personality, transcendence without immanence, heaven without heaven on earth, and much masculinity without much femininity. O come down Zaccheus! Come down from certainty, whether of five pillars or five points, and walk the daily dusty path of the cross. No amount of religion can take the place of loving relationship.

Wealthy Zaccheus

Come down Zaccheus, come down, at last. Impediments to faith come through doubt and idolatry and religion, but none of these holds a candle to the harm that wealth can bring. In global terms and in historical terms, every one of us in this room is wealthy. Luke's entire gospel, especially its central chapters, is aimed at this point. For Luke's community, the remembered teachings of Jesus about wealth were most important. That tells me that the Lukan church had money, and so do we. This is what makes the account of Zaccheus, "one who lined his own pockets at other people's expense", so dramatic for Luke, and so Luke concludes his travel narrative with this clarion call: come down. Be careful as you do not to trip over wealth, power or health. We lose them all, give them all away, over time. They are impermanences. They go. Better that we see so early.

Wouldn't you love to know what Jesus said to Zaccheus that caused him to give away half of what he had? I would. Especially on pledge Sunday.

It is in this light, three years later, that I still see my unsuccessful wrestling match with a boat hoist that resulted in a broken arm. Whatever else may have happened, at least, for once, I had the insight that comes with that kind of pain and ill health. I would wish it on no one, but there is no better way to see that this is a two handed world, than to lose one for a while. It is not only a two handed world. It is a western, white, male, educated, wealthy, healthy, heterosexual, middle class, two handed world. I need to be reminded of that. Come down Zaccheus, and feel the pain of others.

In our church, over 25 years, we have seen power pushed around from some to others, and taken by some from others, and given by some for others. Racism is not limited to whites, nor gender bias to men. It has been an important, and tragic time, both. I have seen some bitter things done, through the misuse of power. I am sure other institutions have the same troubles. The church, though, has a higher calling, and so our failings in this regard are worse. We should know better. I should have known better than to have said and done some of the things I have said and done over the years. Through the misery of black against white, north against south, male against female, clergy against laity, though, if nothing else, one insight inevitably emerges. Soon we will all be dead. Maybe we could find ways to use whatever power we have now to honor God, love our neighbor, reflect our mortality, and affirm the powerless. Come down Zaccheus, come down!

Before we left seminary, on the day after Thanksgiving in 1978, an odd event befell us. I worked nights as a security guard in those years (along with former President James Evans of CRDS, by the way), and would come home to sleep at 7am. Jan had the day off, and left to shop, but left the door to our little apartment ajar, by accident. About noon a street woman found her way into the building and up into our floor, and then into our room. I woke up to see a very poor, deranged woman, fingering rosary beads, and mumbling just over my head. Boy did I shout. She ran into the next room and I stumbled downstairs to call the police. By the time three of New York's finest and I returned to the apartment, the poor lady was in the bathtub, singing and washing. They took her away. Jan came back at 3 and asked how I had slept. The moment has stayed in the memory, though, as an omen. Our wealth is meant for the cleansing of the poor of the earth. I think the Lord wanted me to remember that in ministry, so I have tried to. Come down Zaccheus, and use your wealth for the poor.

God at Night
Luke 24: 44-53
May 28, 2006
Asbury First United Methodist Church
Dr. Robert Allan Hill
Valedictory Series #1

Dark

Faith is a walk in the dark.

Darkness need not surprise you. There may be no darkness in God, as 1 John declares. But there is a lot of God in darkness. There may be no darkness in divinity, but there surely is divinity in darkness. The Bible tells us so.

In its very first sentence. In its very first sentence, the Bible tells us so. Darkness was upon the face of the deep, when the divine sermon spoke creation. Darkness. Darker than a hundred midnights down in a cypress swamp. In the beginning, there was darkness—infused with divinity.

Darkness lurks in every Scriptural nook and darkness lurks in every Biblical cranny. Jacob scurries to the river called Jabbok. At night. The children of Israel would neither have heeded nor have needed a great pillar of fire, across the wilderness, except that they traveled...at night. Yahweh gave them a cloud of smoke—his daily obscurity—and a pillar of fire—his nightly obscurity, with which to chart their course. Obscurity squared. You remember the university professor of theology and culture, Nicodemus. Nicodemus saw the light, at night. Every Holy Week encounter happens at night. Jesus prays at night. Peter betrays at night. Thomas doubts at night. Mary shouts at night. All the crucial passion scenes occur at night. And Paul? Paul and Silas, past midnight, have their chains ripped off in a Roman prison. Their guard is petrified. But they are not surprised. The night time—is the right time...

You would like faith to be simple and sunny and clear? You would prefer that faith be as plain as the nose on your face? Or, plainer still, as plain as the nose on MY face? Really. When has that ever been so? With Jeremiah, walking, by night, in chains, to Babylon? With Samson, blinded, seeing a lifelong night? With Paul shipwrecked? With George Washington, Christmas Eve of 1776, marching in the snow at midnight, crossing the river to Trenton, with all the chips on the table? With Harriet Tubman, listening at 2am for bloodhounds along the Susquehanna? Or maybe with Dwight Eisenhower, at 3am, on June 6, 1944? Or with Nelson Mandela in the 28 years of darkness behind bars? No. Darkness surprises no one who lives in friendship with God, least of all you who have been baptized to the cross.

Our account, in Luke 24, of Jesus' last leave taking, in Ascension, transpires at night, too. Here we find a lot of night travel. They know Him in the breaking of bread, and then immediately, "at the same hour", that is, late at night, they head in from Emmaus to Jerusalem, to wake the sleepers, to tell the story. Like most sermons, their news has to be delivered to the drowsy, the nearly napping. The word comes at night. First at night, in the Genesis pattern, "evening and morning..." The true light that enlightens everyone was coming into the world. The light shines—IN THE DARKNESS. Even Luke's victory banquet, the lasting triumph of a lasting future on earth, the feast of Ascension, happens…at night.

Now, if we are honest, darkness is frightening. But not unexpected. Frightening, but not surprising. It is sobering to see a loved one taken off in a stretcher, down the long night hallway of uncertainty. Human life in a nuclear age is anxious life, ever shadowed life, lived against the background of a potential nuclear winter. Who would not sleep with one eye open, come hurricane season, when the wind begins to blow, after Tsunami and Katrina? Beware, beware a cheery, cozy, quasi Christ, unfamiliar with the dark. Beware a Jesus who has not been given his night license. Beware a loud, light, boxy, bongo, easy Christ. There are plenty around today. Steven Prothero's *American Jesus* will show you the historical bestiary.

Today Jesus ascends. He leaves. His leaving is the nighttime hallmark of his loving. In fact, in sum, his leaving is his loving. His leaving is the heart of his loving. You know from your experience about loving and leaving. Like a mother leaving a daughter at school, or a father leaving a son at camp, or a teacher leaving a student at graduation, or a boss leaving an apprentice at retirement, or a parent, perhaps a mother or father memorialized here today, leaving this earth. As Bonhoeffer's sturdy words remind us, the leaving is the loving:

Nothing can make up for the absence of someone whom we love, and it would be wrong to try to find a substitute; we must simply hold out and see it through. That sounds very hard at first, but at the same time it is a great consolation, for the gap, as long as it remains unfilled, preserves the bond between us. It is nonsense to say that God fills the gap. He does not fill it, but on the contrary, He keeps it empty, and so helps us to keep alive our former communion with each other, even at the cost of pain.

The darkness is frightening, but you need not fear it. The edgy fragments of a post-modern sensibility—every generation and identity group for itself and the devil take the hindmost—is frightening, but you need not fear it. The cataclysmic demise of authentic Christianity in the Northeast— lovely, large, lasting and liberal, and increasingly gone apart from Asbury First—is frightening, but you need not fear it. The emptiness of the world when your spouse dies and the thought of emptying the closets is a prospect worse than death itself is indeed frightening, but you need not fear it. Here is why. You come from a long line of women and men who have practiced discipleship in the dark. Who have earned their night licenses, as you also have done. Your people knew God…at night. You will too. Miguel de Unamuno had it right: "Warmth, warmth, warmth! We are dying of cold not of darkness. It is not the night that kills. It is the frost."

Our memorialized saints share with the Lukan church an experience of God, at night. At their best, they knew how to take responsible risk. At their best, they knew both how to come and to go, to enter and to leave. At their highest, they trusted their instincts. At their finest, they had the guts to start out before dawn, before the fog lifted, before daybreak. They hoped, that is, for what they did not see. Who hopes for what he sees? We hope for what we do not see.

Do we minimize the obscurity of the future, the dark night of the unforeseen? Do we repress the forebodings of the subconscious? Do we deny the complexities of power? Do we call darkness light and night day? No. No. No. No. No.

Nothing of the night is foreign to us, nothing of darkness is foreign to us. We avoid nothing, nothing, though this world with devils filled should threaten to undo us. Darkness is no surprise.

Walk

We have learned to walk in the dark.

You will not want to race in the dark, like a cabbie hurtling down Broadway at midnight in the blackout. We do not hurl ourselves like fools into the black beyond. You know the value of virtue: prudence, temperance, courage, patience.

Walk.

Walk humbly. If we walk…we have fellowship. Walk by faith not sight. Walk with God. At night, especially, walk. Do not run. Walk.

Slow and steady wins the day. A stitch in time saves nine. An ounce of prevention is worth a pound of cure. Let your head save your heels. Look before you leap.

Thunders Isaiah, "They that wait upon the Lord shall renew their strength. They shall mount up with wings like eagles. They shall run and not be weary. They shall walk and not faint."

Ghandi weighed 100lbs, wore a sari, and looked sorrier. He walked four miles a day. And, oh, by the way, he changed the world for the better. Jesus never left Palestine. He walked, preaching and teaching and healing. John Wesley walked slowly to Aldersgate Street, and more slowly home, a changed man. His horse walked all over England. Morality, generosity, piety followed the man on horseback. Said Wesley, "I am always in haste, but never in a hurry."

Self-destruction awaits a hasty pace in the dark. Take your time at night. Feel your way. Step along. Be careful. Once the toothpaste is out of the tube, it is very hard to get it back in. Let your eyesight grow accustomed to the obscurity of experience and the hidden nature of God. Befriend shadows. Walk. Skulk. Lurk. Who hopes for what he sees? Said Alice Walker, "at middle age I slowed down so that whatever was trying to catch up to me would have an easier time of it."

Instinctively, as a congregation, you have known how to walk, in the dark. It has taken us seven years, here at Asbury First, to bring our new building to fruition. You knew how to walk. Not to run, to walk. Not to crawl, to walk.

Abraham Heschel would call this Sabbath living:

> *There is a realm of time where the goal is not to have, but to be, not to own, but to give, not to control, but to share, not to subdue but to be in accord...The higher goal of spiritual living is not to amass a wealth of information, but to face sacred moments. (Sabbath, 9-11)*

To face sacred moments.

Walk. Swing your arms. Smile. Greet your neighbors and their wayward kids. Take your time. Only the devil has no time to let things grow. It is a foolish farmer who pulls up his carrots every week to check their progress. Easy, easy.

Otherwise, you will miss the fullness of life and faith.

Dietrich Bonhoeffer, born 100 years ago this year, is best remembered for his teaching, by word and sacrifice, about grace:

> *Cheap grace is the preaching of forgiveness without requiring repentance, baptism without church discipline, communion without confession, absolution without contrition.*
>
> *Cheap grace is grace without discipleship, grace without the cross, grace without Jesus Christ, living and incarnate.*
>
> *Costly grace is the gospel which must be SOUGHT again and again, the gift which must be ASKED FOR, the door on which a person must KNOCK. Such grace is costly because it calls us to follow, and it is grace because it calls us to follow Jesus Christ. It is costly because it costs us our life, and it is grace because it gives us our only true life.*

Costly grace takes time. It requires us to walk, and not faint. Costly grace takes time. Time to invite, and to tithe. Time to fish and to plant.

The only way to make headway in the dark is to walk. The night time is the right time—if you will walk.

Victor Hugo wrote, *Have courage for the great sorrows of life and patience for the small ones; and when you have laboriously accomplished your daily task, go to sleep in peace. God is awake.*

Here is the good news of God at night: Faith...is a walk...in the dark.

God at Dawn
Acts 2:1-21
Asbury First United Methodist Church
Dr. Robert Allan Hill
June 4, 2006
Valedictory Series #2

Preface

I love the prairie! So often I have seen the dawn come and the light flood over the land and everything turn radiant at once, that word 'good' so profoundly affirmed in my soul that I am amazed I should be allowed to witness such a thing. There may have been a more wonderful first moment 'when the morning stars sang together and all the sons of God shouted for joy', but for all I know to the contrary, they still do sing and shout, and they certainly might well. Here on the prairie there is nothing to distract attention from the evening and the morning, nothing on the horizon to abbreviate or to delay. Mountains would seem an impertinence from that point of view.

So M Robinson finishes *Gilead*. At dawn, with an aching heart, a full chest weight of the sense of …the unnamable. Radiant. Good. Wonderful. Song. Joy.

Have you forgotten the love you had at first? When did breathing become such an ordinary thing to your mind? And prayer? Have you begun with the spirit to end with the flesh? Has the vocation, the sense of self and soul that is the real marrow of Pentecost given way to drift, ennui, languid doldrums?

Wake up! It is morning! Dawn is breaking! Come Pentecost…

In our Scripture lesson today, Luke is surely reminding his church, and reminding us, of the love we had at first. Every single one has a tongue of fire given, that makes effective connection with others. Every one is called, has a vocation, a measure of spirit.

Jacob finally won his name at dawn: Israel, he who wrestles with God.

David wrote of dawn as the feeling of a groom after the wedding night.

The disciples enter the tomb at dawn.

John ends with breakfast at dawn, and a catch of 153 numbered fish.

For some, this call has been a call to the ministry.

The sermon today is an unapologetic, unabashed, direct appeal to you to consider whether, come Pentecost, you are meant to preach. Has a flame got your tongue? Were you meant to be in ministry?

Two dozen women and men have been called and sent into the ministry through you in the last 10 years.

They heard the wind of Pentecost, and the call at dawn. Early some morning, and no they were not drunk, at least not most of them, they heard something, and heeded.

Would that all God's people were prophets

Prepare for a profession that does not yet fully exist...

Where your deep gladness meets the world's deep need...

Where your deep sadness meets the world's deep greed...

How shall they hear without a preacher?...

Let your life shine...

Be ashamed to die before you have won some victory for the human race...

Who told you who you was?

If you see a turtle on top of a fence post, you know he didn't get there by himself...

Prepare to depart this life 'in the friendship of Christ'...

Some read RM Miller on E Tittle, some R Lischer on small church ministry, some Bernanos and the life of a country priest, some Hempton on Methodism, some BB Taylor on the preaching life, some R Hill on ministry in the Northeast, some P Palmer on calling....

Pentecost is God at dawn. This morning is the morning of tongues of fire, of firey tongues, of speech that burns, heals, warms, enflames, inspires.

How shall we rightly admire the prairie dawn? How shall we sense whether, and how, we are called? How do you know what you are called to be and do?

Things that really matter are ultimately relational, whether that relationship is with others, with self, or with God. Our friends give us ourselves. Our instincts give us ourselves. Our sense of presence gives us ourselves.

1. Close Relationships

Here is one account, one testimony, no worse nor better than any other.

We learned to love Jesus in the simple rhythms of the ordinary. We learned to love Jesus in the pause before meals, with grace in his name. We learned to love Jesus singing hymns to Him, in church, at camp, in the car. We learned to love Jesus as we read about his life in the Bible. We learned to love Jesus by celebrating his birth in snowy December, and his destiny in snow melting April. We learned to love Jesus by seeing older people love him, really love him, with their hands, and their money and their time and most especially with their choices, and within that, with their choices about things not to say, not to be, not to do. We learned to love Jesus like we learned to speak English, one lisp at a time, one dangling preposition at a time, one new word at a time. The music of Jesus played the accompaniment to all of the growth and decay of life around us. There was no wall of separation, neither artificial, nor sacramental, nor communal, between our life and his. His was our life, and our life was his.

This sounds romantic, but it is not meant to be. Conflict, envy, hurt, gossip, anger, misjudgment, unfairness, tragedy, hatred, fear, abuse, neglect, betrayal, addiction, and loneliness sat around the table too—around the kitchen table, around the picnic table, around the coffee table, around the communion table.

Still there was a closeness in the Christ who raised us—a pine needle Adirondack Christ, with the dawn scent of the forest primeval, a sunlit Finger Lake Christ, a blue collar Erie Canal Christ, a blizzard Christ, an autumn peak Christ, a high summer Christ, a Christ with mud on Easter shoes. You could say that we were more Gospel people than Letter people, more Peter than Paul, more good Samaritan than justification by faith, more Methodist than Presbyterian. There was no forced or feigned distance between Jesus and us, between his life and our own.

He was with us in school. Our teachers attended church, and when they scolded us for talking or not wearing our eyeglasses, Jesus walked past us and smiled.

He was with us at home. Our parents entertained college students, all then of just one gender, with sandwiches and pickles. The men stood when their hostess entered the room. They wore ties. Jesus sampled the pickles, with us.

He was with us in the summer. He felt the glow of a warm campfire on a cool mountain night. When the ministers worried whether there was too much kissing, too much holding hands, Jesus worried too, and then you could see him, almost, holding a young couple as they held each other.

He was with us when we grew up and became teenagers ourselves.

He was with us when all hell broke loose. When older boys, or younger men, went off in pressed uniforms to someplace on a map we had seen in school. When some came home, and when some partly came home, and when some did not come home, He wept.

He was with us in college, at marriage, in studies, at work.

You go with your friends. So if your friends go off to college, you may too. If they enlist, you may too. If they take a job in the south, you may too. It is a natural thing.

If people you know and love go into the ministry, you may too. If you respect somebody who is in the ministry, you may be inclined to preach. If your parents, with pride, have the pastor to Sunday dinner, you might think about taking that seat, and holding that fork, and intoning that prayer. If you grow up with Rev. Jones, and sense he is a real human being, you might try to become one such yourself. If the kind of people who are your kind of people enter Christian service, you might, too. And if your mother, father, grandparents, spiritual aunts and uncles, and a boyfriend or two study for the ministry, you may too.

Trust your experience. Honor your instincts. Listen to your heart.

Your relationships are crucial, crucial in the dawning of a sense of vocation.

In eighth grade the choir director, Ruth Tubbs, commented on the resonance in my speaking voice, following the usual desultory youth service. In college, the chaplain, Jim Leslie, took seriously my interest and gave advice. At church camp, Lou Broadbent and Jim Legro showed me you could be a minister and still be a real young man with heart and life. At home both parents somehow said just enough without saying too much. After college, Bob Homer gave me two churches, and checked in on me and checked up on me. It takes a long time to grow a preacher. Relationships hold the key.

Hold that thought. You might want to continue to dance with the one who brung you. For as crucial as our relations and relationships are at vocational dawn, they are more significant, even as the sun begins to rise.

2. Work Relationships

So now you are beginning to work, to hold a job. What counts in your work relationships? Can you honestly list what is meaningful and what is not about what you do? There are clues here, terribly important ones. Do not, do not enslave yourself to something that diseases your soul.

It is Richard Florida in *The Rise of the Creative Class* that gives me hope about the future of the culture, the church, and the ministry. He surveyed people about what they want in work—a kind of white collar Studs Turkel. Regarding work, he found, the question 'what?' is often secondary to the question, 'with whom?' People prefer the hair salon to the machine shop, for relational reasons. Hear his report on surveys of what people most want in work:

> I. Responsibility
> Being able to contribute and have impact
> Knowing that ones work makes a difference
> Being seriously challenged
>
> II. Flexibility
> A flexible schedule and a flexible work environment
> The ability to shape one's own work to some degree

III. Stability
> A stable work environment and a relatively secure job
> Not lifetime security with mind numbing sameness but not a daily diet of chaos and uncertainty either

IV. Compensation
> Especially base pay and core benefits
> Money you can count on

V. Growth
> Personal and professional development
> The chance to learn and grow
> To expand one's horizons

...cut new ground...feel at home...be creative...design your own work space...define your own role...have peer recognition...enjoy a work\life balance...

Now hear the good news! The ministry gets A+ in four of these five. There is no greater challenge or responsibility than shepherding souls. No one has more daily flexibility in determining one's use of time. As an itinerant preacher you are guaranteed a pulpit—somewhere. Reading a book a day, or the equivalent, is a guarantee of personal growth. Responsibility! Flexibility! Stability! Growth!

The culture around us is starting itself to move away from the rank materialism of an earlier time. The deep sorrow we have at the suicide of the church meets the deep falsehood of our culture, here. It is false that an ever bigger mortgage will make you happier. It is false that several credit cards to the maximum will bring joy. It is false that accumulation of things will bring peace. It is false that $100,000 of college debt is a doorway to nirvana.

So, we get a D in compensation. This is a real issue, particularly for those acculturated to see the bottom line as the measure of worth. It is no accident that the church struggles to attract young, heterosexual, middle class, white males. We must do what other generations have done, and make this an opportunity for heroic living. You learn the value of a dollar. You learn to make every opportunity count. You learn the danger of debt. You learn the power of giving. You learn the shrewdness of frugality. You learn to hike, hard with a heavy backpack. See it as a physical challenge, like a 7 mile run in the winter, at 10 degrees. Add a little snow. And some wind. Yes...

Growing segments of the population work for challenge, enjoyment, to do good, to make a contribution, and to learn. Such motivations will eventually eclipse compensation as the most important motives for work ... People on their death beds never wish they had spent more time in the office (Robert Fogel)

3. A Relationship with God

A longing deeper than the relationships of belonging in family, and the relationships of meaning, in work, exploded from human hearts on Pentecost. This dawn day of spirit! This dawn day of fire! This dawn day of translation, interpretation, preaching, ecumenism! This dawn day of world Christianity! This dawn day of the church! This early morning dawn day! A deeper longing burst forth on Pentecost. Theirs, and ours, is a deeper longing, a longing for a relationship with God.

St. Augustine of Hippo at long last found himself, his soul, and his true vocation, by finding a personal relationship to God. Yes, Augustine entered the ministry. He became priest and bishop in North Africa about 400ad. He wrote 500 letters, 200 sermons, 2 great books. In an age, like yours, of intercultural conflict, Augustine made sense of faith's highest vision...the city of God. In a culture, like yours, that wore the nametag of Christianity without fully understanding its meaning, Augustine celebrated...the grace of God. In a political climate, like ours, that honored highly individualized freedom and the power to choose, Augustine praised God's freedom to choose, and acclaimed...the freedom of God. In a highly sexualized age, like ours, Augustine colorfully confessed his own wandering, his own mistakes, which, he attested, did test but did not exhaust the …patience of God. In a religious climate, like ours, which buffeted a truly biblical belief, Augustine praised his maker, and so reminded the church of the proper…praise of God. His *Confessions*—perhaps part of your summer reading—his great autobiography, is a prayer—for the city of God, by the grace of God, in the freedom of God, to the patience of God, as the praise of God. Augustine found a relationship with God and was ordained. And vice versa.

It may be that the only way God has to relate to some of us, to get our attention, to mute our pride, to kindle our affection, is to get us into the ministry. Baptism and confirmation suffice for most. But for the real hard cases—the guy who wrote the book on pride, the gal whose picture is alongside the dictionary definition of sloth, the one who embodies real falsehood—like us, like Augustine….like you?...God keeps ordination in reserve.

Long ye for God? Preach. Preach until you believe it, then preach because you believe it. Long ye for God? Preach.

At dawn, God called. Some answered…

Brad Benson
Jennie Barrett
Jennie Castle
Ginny Cross
Stephen Cady II
Rick Danielson
Linda Hickmon Evans
Heidi Geib
Keith Griswold
Kim Hines
Janet James
Tom Lebeaux
Barb Nelson
Bryant Oskvig
Daven Oskvig
David Payne

Todd Phillips
Caroline Simmons
Andre Spivey
Carol Wenske

Et toi?

Thirty years ago today I preached my first sermon, in New Hope New York. It does not take long to go from being a young turk to becoming an old turkey. Who will come along to take our places?

Think about it...

God at Noon
Romans 8: 22-27
June 11, 2006
Asbury First United Methodist Church
Dr. Robert Allan Hill
Valedictory Series #3

Along the Genesee River, our fellow Christians at the Abbey of the Genesee offer prayers at 2am, 6am, 11am and 6pm. They pray to God at night, at dawn, at noon, and at dusk. We do too, in our own ways, trying to receive the grace to leave aside the troubles of accumulation for the fairer fields of the sacred. We live to face sacred moments. To cling to faith and face the dark is to face a sacred moment, at night. To discern a calling and face the future is to face a sacred moment, at dawn. To work steadily and face the heat of the midday sun is to face a sacred moment, at noon. To sing a vesper song, at dusk, and to face partial parting is to face a sacred moment, at dusk.

Midday is one such moment. At the Abbey these prayers are known as sext prayers, that is, sixth hour prayers. Six hours after dawn. In the heat of the day. In the full sunlight of work.

With all creation they, and we, as the Apostle teaches, await redemption. Here Paul is offering his mature thought about life, work, groaning, struggle, hope, patience, weakness, sighs, and Spirit.

He wrote earlier, "When I was a child I thought like a child, I acted like a child, I reasoned like a child; when I became a man I gave up childish ways." What a remarkable verse! Mr. justication by faith himself, Mr. God is not mocked himself, Mr. by grace ye are saved himself, Mr. I have been crucified with Christ himself—Paul, right here in the Bible, plain as noonday sun indicates that he may just now and then, here and there, once in a while, he may have learned from his experience. He grew. He changed. He matured. He learned. What he thought at dawn, he rethought at noon. Go figure. Wouldn't you love to know what he thought as a child that he gave up as an adult?

At the midday we pause to pray and rest. Here are six midday thoughts and prayers for Asbury First into the future.

A. Asbury First United Methodist Church is a wonderful, gracious and loving church, truly a delightful community in which to serve.

Architecture, Music, Pulpit, Missions, Adult Classes, Local Outreach, Pastoral Care, Endowment, Worship, Organ, Teak Room, Office…and People! Asbury First includes features that compare favorably to the best anywhere in American Methodism…

Its pulpit and preaching…Its nave and organs…Its music…Its liturgy and pastoral care…Its local missions…Its teak room and pastor's office…Its endowment…Its Christmas and Easter services…Its campus…Its spiritual liberality…Its people!

B. Our theology of preaching and practice begins in grace and ends in freedom.

For over a decade you have listened for, and so given birth to, the announcement of good news of grace and freedom.

Said Gospel has been spoken in a traditional sermon of 22 minutes.

Its interpretation has scoured the several continents of the whole Bible: the gospels, Paul, John, the Apocalypse, the Prophets, some stories of the Law, some proverbs and ways of wisdom.

Your preached gospel, born in the longsuffering of presence and listening, has scoured the Scripture. We name its good: freedom and grace. A Methodist freedom to resist a purpose driven life. A Wesleyan grace to resist the certainties of an atheistic scientism. Saving grace, healthy freedom, both of which allow you to be confident even when you cannot be certain. Who needs faith if you already know all? Who needs faith if you are already that certain? If you are, already that certain that is, who needs the life of faith?

Or prayer? Or friends? Or community? Or others? Or memory? Or hope?

No, you affirm that older, thinner, more Biblical inkling of glory, that confidence that is faith. Not arrogance, confidence. Not blind faith, confidence. Not bullheadedness, confidence. Not certainty, confidence. The confidence born of obedience, "the obedience of faith" of which Paul writes in Romans (as tasty an oxymoron as one can chew).

> **C. The bright sunlight of opportunity for the next decade here shines out on an open meadow of robust stewardship, focused on tithing.**

How do people learn stewardship? I wish I could say that the 26 stewardship Sunday sermons I have preached since 1979 have changed the world of giving. They have not. These practical guides only work when your heart is in it. When your heart is in it. How does that happen? That only happens when your heart is changed, warmed, healed. How does that happen? Usually it happens in a very humble way. It happens when you are ready to let it happen, and it happens then when you hear something. A word. Oh I do not discount the example that others set that makes us think and act, but we only come in earshot of such examples when our heart is changed. And that change comes, whenever it does, when we wake up to how much we have been given. As in this story from my friend Doug Mullins:

> *Belinda was a single parent, trying to take care of herself and raise five-year old Ryan. She was single because her husband had left her. One evening Belinda tucked Ryan into bed and was reading a book to him. He interrupted her to ask if she had bought that book for him. "Yes" she said. He then inquired if she had also bought the bed in which he slept. Again the answer was "yes". Had she the bought the house they called home? Yes, she had. And what about the new sweater he liked so much? "Yes", she said, she had bought that too. He thought about how good she had been to him, supplying his needs, and he finally said, "Mommy, get my piggy bank. There are seven pennies in it. Take*

them and get something you really want for you." As is so often the case, we have much to learn from our children. Ryan realized that everything he had was a gift from his mother. His response was to offer her his seven cents, everything he had. Our relationship to God is just like Ryan's relationship to his mother. Everything we have is a gift from God. Ryan offered his mother seven cents. It was not much, but it was all he had.

D. Now we need to suspend our efforts at reconstructive engagement with our beloved denomination, and aim rather at peaceful coexistence.

The Troy Conference (Albany) lost 17% of its worshipping attendance in one year, last year. This was the largest loss in the denomination for that year.

The Wyoming Conference (Binghamton) lost 5% of its actual membership is one year, two years ago. This was the largest loss in the denomination for that year.

The North Central Conference (Syracuse) had a membership of 150,000 when I was ordained there in 1979. Today its membership is under 75,000.

The Western New York Conference (Buffalo) has a membership of 55,000, a membership smaller than many single districts in the rest of the United Methodist Church.

The New Jersey Conference had a membership of more than 200,000 in 1970. Today its membership is under 100,000.

What kind of organization accepts this sort of collapse with no accountability admitted by or demanded from its leadership?

E. In short, ministry is preaching the gospel and loving the people (especially the least—children, the last—the poor, the lost—the isolated).

1. The interruptions are the work.

2. The nominations report is the most important thing you do each year.

3. It is the one-on-one conversations that matter most.

4. No secrets, no surprises, no subversion.

5. When you put your gift on the altar, don't look back.

6. What you do speaks so loudly that I can't hear what you say.

7. You only have what you can give away.

8. The rubber band only stretches so far before it breaks.

9. Preach what you know.

10. *Don't inhale. (That is, remember that ministry is service).*

F. Asbury First, by the way, has grown 25% in the last decade, and is poised to do the same in the next.

Membership has moved from 2009 to 2315, endowment from $2M to $6M, worship services and attendance from 2/558 to 4/731, lay participation from 40% to 60%, assessed building values to (with new build) $25M+; program development (musical ensembles, adult classes, educational offerings, mission offerings, church program offerings, and other) has had similar increases as has total revenue: calendar 2005 (endowment income, capital campaign income, annual plan income, special giving income) is approximately 3x that of 1995 ($1M, $3M).

God at Dusk
June 18, 2006
Exodus 30
Asbury First United Methodist Church
Dr Robert Allan Hill
Valedictory Series #4

All of us are better when we are loved.

In closing, these four weeks, we have announced the gifts of God for the people of God. The gift of God at night is *faith*. A two point sermon: faith is a walk in the dark. The gift of God at dawn is *calling*. A three point sermon: your calling is where your deep gladness meets the world's deep need. The gift of God at noon is *work*. A six point sermon: the fun in life is in planting and fishing, stewardship and evangelism. The gift of God at dusk is *word*. We live by the word of God. (By extrapolation this should be a twelve point sermon, but it is only eight. Fear not.)! A word of valediction in transition. *A vesper hymn of love. A word of love.* All of us are better when we are loved (BWL). Which reminds me of a story…

1. Word

I remember the account, historical and hysterical, of the preacher who was about to move from one pulpit to another. His community arranged to recognize him at a chicken dinner.

(Chickens have paid dearly for our love of fellowship and our native in frugality in the Methodist church. They seem to be the right bird at the right price somehow.)

The local florist agreed, free of charge, to provide a table bouquet. The preacher wanted to thank every single member and friend. *Thank you.* And every single group—choir, class, study group, all. *Thank you.* And especially every group leader, the real shepherds in church. *Thank you.* After the remaining florid comments, the bouquet was presented to the preacher and his family. All were amazed to read its banner: "Rest in Peace". The preacher reddened, and then laughed, and then said something about the next appointment needing resurrection. The florist was mortified, but readily and joyfully forgiven. The festivities proceeded along their clumsy way, as such things have a wont to do.

Our local florist, however, was sullen and would not be comforted. The preacher asked him again to let it go, but like Rachel weeping for her children, the florist would not be consoled. At last he confessed the reason. "Rest in Peace" he could easily live with at the ministerial recognition. But he had to admit the other bouquet had been sent to the graveyard where a group was gathering for burial, a floral piece meant to honor the deceased. And he could only imagine their disappointment and shock when they opened that arrangement and read its banner: "we hope you will be happy in your new location".

The gift of God at dusk is a word, a valediction in transition, a valediction in transition. All of us are better when we are loved.

2. Biblical Valediction

The Bible is a long chain of valedictions in transition.

It is the gracious humanity of the Holy Scripture, its divine grace that is, which of course makes space for valedictory words. Listen again to Jacob, that dear old man, as he bids farewell to a host of progeny, ill fed, unlead, widely spread, nearly dead. Then listen to his favorite son—such a burden to be the favorite son—Joseph, as he bids farewell, as he says, "you meant it for evil, but God meant it for good". Is it an accident that M ML King, the last night of his life, quoted Moses, on the last night of Moses' life? The words, the valediction from Mt. Nebo? Look out on the land of milk and honey, says Moses, Moses, the man of stone and commandment and prophecy and courage, who too bids adieu. What about blind Samuel, dear old man, warning against kings and those who want kings, that dear old man as he says goodbye? Are not the books of the prophets, all, at the last, a last will and testament, and a collection of how they would have their words remembered?

Hosea—God loves. Amos—God makes just. Jeremiah—God reigns. Micah—God sees. It is as if, before these great people of faith must finally leave the world stage, they want with Hamlet to name their demons, their hurts, their truth, and their faith, especially their faith.

Father, if it be thy will, let this cup pass from me. Eli, Eli, lama sabach thani. Father forgive them, for they know not what they do. It is finished. We remember the last words best.

From an early age we learn the importance of valediction. At odds with mom and dad, the eight year old decides to run away. He speaks his last word. He packs his suit case, and dons his cap. Out the door he goes at dusk. The family cat watches and purrs. Parents watch through the blinds. He sits under the lamppost, and night falls. And after a respectable time, he comes back inside, closes the door. His parents know better than to say anything. They wait, reading the paper and smoking the pipe. The cat purrs, and rubs a long brown tail against the boy's legs. The boy has grown. Having said a real good bye *in* life, he is ready now to say a real hello *to* life! With the maturity of someone who has now said farewell, and survived it, he says, to show his adulthood, "Well, it's good to be back....I see you still have the same old cat."

All of us are better when we are...

3. The Voice from Mount Nebo

The valediction in transition—that Mosaic valedictory trajectory---from Moses on Mount Nebo reminds us of "a sense of dynamism of reality in the hands of a future creating God" (Brueggeman).

In our first sermon, July 9, 1995, we announced the same good news, "God keeps God's promises". Though their fulfillment is yet incomplete, though their fullness is yet more at hand than in hand, though we see now in a mirror dimly—the God of divine promises lives!

You may think it presumptuous to read about Mount Nebo in the closing service. "Who does he think he is, Moses?" Well, I refer to Woody Allen, who visited East Avenue earlier this spring. Allen who told us, "90% of life is showing up" (Good to remember on Sunday mornings…). Allen who wondered, "How do I find happiness and meaning in a finite world given my waste and shirt size?" Diane Keaton listens to him raving and citing Torah, and says, "Who do you think you are, God?" Allen responds, "Well, I have to model myself after somebody…"

Of course, there is only one Moses. There is one Moses and we are not him. Yet we know his experience, at dusk, of leaving at the river's edge, leaving at the edge of something new—unforeseen, exciting, happy.

Two of the finest church organists in America during the late twentieth century had the same last name, shared the same post office address, and both lived, together, in Rochester, New York. They lived on the same suburban street, nestled in the leaves and furrows of the upstate lake region. In fact, they lived in the same house. As husband and wife, it seemed the right thing to do.

David Craighead brought his wife Marian, in the last month of her life, to sit one last time on her organ bench. It was a mortal struggle for her to make it from home to church, this last time, a trip that she had made with relative ease, hundreds of times, since 1960. The Austin organ had been refurbished, at her direction and with her supervision and on her approval. Before she died she wanted to sit at the bench and assess the work. They came in the afternoon of Ash Wednesday, 1996. Few words were spoken in the hour visit. She sat and looked and touched. She did not play. At last, with a lifted eyebrow, she summoned her husband to take her home. Home. As we left, in the deepest of pain that one loving human can have at the imminent departure of another, and in some tears, David said, "Watching her there…So hard…It is like Moses on Nebo…She can see the land ahead, but it will not be hers to enjoy…Like Moses, on Mount Nebo…" One heard that afternoon a distinctively faithful, distinctively loving, Christian way of speaking, the Biblical narrative summoned without preparation or pretense, to give voice and response to the day's own trouble.

All of us are better when…

4. Moses' Word

In Deuteronomy, Moses offers three speeches, at the edge of the river Jordan. Here his voice is remembered to carefully reinterpret the past. The Moses of Mt Nebo is bringing a word of challenge and change.

A community needs one leader for the journey, another for the arrival; one for the wilderness, another for the promise. *One for the travel to the new space, another to inhabit and settle the new space.*

Are you picking up what I am putting down?

Deuteronomy replaces holiness with compassion. Truth without love is brutality. Love without truth is sentimentality. You need both, both holiness and compassion. But the Bible, and the communities of faith it undergirds, lean toward compassion. James Sanders (once of Rochester) defined the 'montheizing tendency' of the Old Testament. We might define an 'agapetizing tendency'—a listing toward compassion—in the whole of Scripture. And its place of demarcation is the end of Deuteronomy.

Genesis to Numbers wants purity. Deuteronomy affirms justice. The former wants tidiness, the later righteousness. The first wants holiness, the second compassion. The Bible lives this tension, as does our church. Both are important, both are Biblical, both are part of faith. Remember, though, that at Mt Nebo, the concern for levitical purity, pronounced from Genesis to Numbers, gives way to the Deuternomist's concern for justice.

Salvation is not only a state of mind—salvation is a *state of affairs*.

So for thirty chapters (see how easy you have it, thirty minutes not thirty chapters) Moses reminds the people about those shackled in debt, about those shackled by unfettered public authority, about those shackled by poverty.

5. A Village Green

It is Moses' later view, the second law view, that evokes a vision of a village green (our church's vision), a place where all things lastingly good, spiritually enriching, religiously excellent from across Monroe county, converge. We have the center of the green nearly done. A decade from now, or two, we may own the block from East to University, and 1010 to Granger.

Then we could live the dream. We would walk in peace and joy along the *Village Green* of life. Here, take a moment. It is dusk. We leave the sanctuary. We walk through the spacious, open welcome area. Then (for this is only a start), we tour the expanded grounds of our ministry. At every turn, in this dream, there is a lamp lit. Look: just here is a new United Methodist conference office, for a combined upstate conference. Look: just here is a pastoral counseling center which specializes in the needs of women, created and guided by a retired pastor. Look: just here you find a lamp lit on the porch of an Urban Retreat Center, spiritually led by a spirited minister committed to this cause. *(And each of these projects tithes from their own budget back to the mother church that created them, thus providing the possibility of further growth. They learned to do so, over time, from the Storehouse, Dining Center, Nursery School, Daycare and others, who were inspired to do so by this sermon! Hey, why not really dream?)* Look: just here there is the lamp of the porch of the county wide Wesley Foundation, a center for student ministry. Look: just here a lamp is lit over the door of a Hemispheric Hispanic ministry Center, from Emmanuel to Amor Fe y Vida. Our lamp leads us further: just here you find a religious drama center, k-12, and an elder care program, and.....

All of us come marked, BWL: "better when loved". Good when made. Better when loved. Best when shared.

All of us are better...

6. Gospel Valediction

But there is a gospel valediction that is rooted in the biblical word.

We remember the last words best. Every spring we hear our Senior youth intone their valedictions. We remember what they say.

Martin Luther King, we remember, last said, "I have been to the mountain top and seen the promised land".

Douglass Macarthur told the houses of congress, "Old soldiers never die, they just fade away".

Or Nathan Hale, "I regret that I have but one life to give for my country".

At church camp, and at great revivals both, in Methodism it is Wesley's dying sentence that is preached: "The best of all is God is with us."

Amadeus Mozart, at the end, with Solieri taking down his every whispered note—who could forget it?

Why, after thousands of pages, and a lifetime of writing, does Aquinas' last self-deprecation remain: "all my work, before Grace, is so much straw"?

Did I neglect the greatest of historical valedictions? What would Lincoln's Second Inaugural sound like today?

With malice toward none—including as he did those who have done us physical harm, and who pray in different ways to the One God.

With charity for all—male and female, poorer and richer, religious and unreligious, gay and straight, black and white.

With firmness in the right—that combination of charity and magnanimity that seeks first to understand, and then to be understood.

Let us to do all to achieve a just and lasting peace, for ourselves, and for all the nations.

7. Word at Dusk

We remember words at dusk.

We returned from four months in Switzerland in late summer of 1978. We arrived too late to attend the funeral of our sister in law, a twenty something red haired mother and husband, our MYF treasurer. At birth, you are old enough to die, we know, yet…

The family, widower, and toddler son went up into the Adirondacks to lick wounds following the funeral. We met them there. A hot summer night, corn and steak, a family in grief, at dusk. At dinner, something clicked and the little boy realized, maybe, what had happened. A little guy. He shrieked, he howled, he would not be consoled. No sermon can ever live beyond earshot of his crying at the summer table…Mom…At last Dad scooped him up and went down to the lake in the redolent sunset, a mountain cool dusk, with the woods and all creation groaning at the boy's howling. Dad put him between his legs and rowed the old boat. The son's heart howl and the dad's feathering of the oars made a strange evening duet. A cry, feather the oars. A shout, feather the oars. A shriek, feather the oars. Until at last, the little boy fell asleep, his first night as a motherless child. Sometimes I feel like a motherless child…

There is no explaining such tragedy. Our faith gives us not the capacity to understand, but *the power to withstand* such hurt. Love is stronger than death. Last summer we say that boy, now, himself, a thirty something husband and father. Laughing, smiling, carrying his mother's voice and charm into the unforeseen tomorrow. Thirty years later, and the word of love at dusk. He made it. There is no explaining the tragedy. Yet we can acclaim the salvation known in the love of God. Love lifted. A dad's love, in the boat. A family's love, Christmas to Christmas. A community's memory and love, graduation to graduation. And at every dusk, and through every howling cry, still, by mystery, a divine love, a love that outlasts death.

It is this primal word, this hymn to love, that is sung out in the benediction, and valediction of 1 John. We can all together confess how hard it is, day to day, to let love be our aim, to love and to what we will, to let love be genuine, to love one another, to love our enemies, to watch over one another in love, to let God's love be completed in us…

All of us are…

8. Dusk

Four summers ago my sons and I sat, toward dusk, in Yankee stadium. New York and Los Angeles were playing, slow motion, moving toward a dull game end. We were driving home that night, to the cottage, and then on the next day to Rochester to participate in Berta Holden's funeral. Her exemplary Christian life of worship, of education and of care, was very much on our minds. In a way, a life like hers is the goal. Discipleship in worship, education and care? Here is an example…

What we are all driving toward, you could say. A game at dusk, a drive at dusk, toward worship at dusk. About 9pm, in the middle of the sixth inning, we headed for the car, the game having apparently gotten about as interesting as it was going to get. We crossed the George Washington bridge at 9:30, and, expecting the game was about over, tuned in to the radio for the final score.

What a different experience we were given that evening! To our astonishment, the game really began in the eighth inning. We had road and dark and each other and a voice to tell the story. And that was all. A voice at dusk. The game went 16 innings. Four hours after we had crossed the bridge, and just as we arrived at Bradley Brook, the game at last ended. But all through that late evening, over Pennsylvania Mountain, Susquehanna River, Binghamton valley, and that glorious drive up route 26—the prettiest in the state—we heard the word. Oddly, it was the perfect way to follow the game.

It is the word, the word of God, that sustains us on the journey at dusk. *Steel Magnolia* said, "accessorize—it's the only thing that separates us from the animal kingdom". We say, "speak—speech alone makes us human." More, we say, "preach—it is the word at dusk that carries us forward—the word of blessing, valediction, promise, hope". If this is not worth doing, what is? One does not live by bread alone, but by the word—the word of God.

Now we Hill's are leaving the great stadium, Asbury First. It would be a mistake to think that things are about as far along as they can get. The seventh inning stretch is a long way from home. Who knows what God has in store for this extra inning game? Who knows what sacrifice bunt you may provide, what strike out you may throw, what late night homer you may crunch, what double play you may execute? I tell you, this is going to be more than a nine inning game! You have extra innings in store! You have the thrill of an open future! And as Hebrews reminds, you have a heavenly cloud of witnesses, hanging on every call, cheering every hit, hearts dropping with every out and soaring with every run! You have a new pitcher on the mound, that noted southpaw Susan Shafer! You have Lubba at bat, and Olson on deck—and Duane Prill in the hole! And out there in midfield, there is somebody—who is it? It's too dark to see right now---somebody warming up in the bullpen!

And out there, in Red Sox land, you have some fellow travelers, who left the game early, thinking it was time to go, and listening in by radio (and by internet and newsletter and telephone), as dusk falls. The night, and the road, and each other, and voice and word--this is all we have. But believe me, those of us listening in are with you. When you scrape your leg on a slide, we hurt. When you duck a fast ball, we get angry. When you are called out on strikes, especially that last one, low and outside if I ever saw a pitch, we feel indignant. And when the sweet spot of the bat puts the ball over the fence, we just shout and sing and soar!

All of us are better when we are loved…

All of us are better…

All of us…

All…

Asbury First United Methodist Church

1050 EAST AVENUE . . . ROCHESTER, NEW YORK 14607-2293

Phone 271-1050   Fax 271-3743

Pastors

ROBERT A. HILL, Ph.D.   MARGIE J. MAYSON, M.Div.
                                     SUSAN S. SHAFER, M.Div.

Director of Music
DAVID A. KLEMENT, M.M.

Dear New Member:

Welcome to Asbury First United Methodist Church. On behalf of the congregation, we extend to you the right hand of Christian fellowship and rejoice that you have come to be with us.

This booklet is meant to help you find your way into the heart of our church life. May we ask that during your time here you keep one fact clearly in mind: we are eager to be your pastors, to be helpful in times of difficulty, and to be present in times of celebration. Nothing else we do here is more important than this pastoral role, so please do not hesitate to call on us.

We sincerely and warmly welcome you to this congregation.

Bob   Susan   Margie

Asbury First Pastors (l to r): Rev. Robert Hill, Rev. Susan Shafer, Rev. Margie Mayson

Meeting As New Members

Your new member class will meet several times before you are received into the church. If you have any questions, your class facilitator or the pastors will be glad to try and answer them.

At the time of your new member class, or as soon as possible before your reception into the church, you will be having your picture taken. It will go on the bulletin board in the cloister on New Member Sunday. Please fill out and return the information sheet that begins on page 23.

An outline for the discussion in your new member class begins on page 19. You may want to make notes on each point.

✠ Welcome new member

Becoming a Member

Why should I join a church?

Christians believe the church is the body of Christ. The church was set up for believers to let them worship God together, to help them grow in faith and knowledge, and to combine their efforts to serve the world and teach salvation through Jesus Christ. This universal church includes anyone who has accepted Jesus Christ as Savior and worships him as Lord: It is his "body" in the world.

How does a person join a United Methodist Church?

Some are *baptized* into the church. United Methodists consider baptism a rite of initiation. That is why we baptize people of all ages, including babies. United Methodists also recognize all Christian baptisms, so a person baptized in another faith is not baptized again when coming to the United Methodist Church. Baptism at any age implies that the person is beginning to grow in Christian faith. The other members of the church claim the new member for the church and promise to help in that person's growth.

Children who grow up into church membership are *confirmed*. Confirmation is a young person's official welcome into full church membership. Each year, a confirmation class is formed for young people, usually of junior high or senior high school age. The class reviews the meaning of the Christian life and of church membership.

Some new members are received as adults. These people are received in a variety of ways, each involving a *confession* of faith by the new member. A person might respond to an invitation to Christian discipleship during a worship service or at a service of communion, baptism, or new member reception. Or a person might turn to the church and decide to become a member during a time of crisis or decision, seeking God's guidance in life's choices. A person might also be new to the community and seeking the fellowship of a new church.

The United Methodist Church has several classifications of membership. Baptized children are *preparatory* members, people in preparation for full membership. A person who is a full member of a United Methodist Church and temporarily living far away from home can join a local church as an *affiliate* member. A member of another denomination can join a local United Methodist Church as an *associate* member under the same conditions. **At Asbury First, students often make use of these options.**

There is also a category called *constituent*s. This consists of people under the care and teaching of the church who are not members. Unbaptized and dedicated children and preparatory members who reach age 19 without being confirmed as full members are constituents. So are non-member adults. However, individual churches or pastors may classify members under different groupings than these.

How do I join Asbury First United Methodist Church?

Young people and adults considering joining Asbury First meet in a new members' class. The purpose of the class is to explain life in the Christian faith in general, and in the United Methodist Church in particular. The class session is also a time to welcome new members.

The ritual for receiving new members—the "Order for Reception into the Church"—is number 829 at the back of the *Hymnal*. There are five questions:

1. "Do you here, in the presence of God, and of this congregation, renew the solemn promise and vow that you made, or that was made in your name, at your baptism?"

The vows of baptism imply that the person will learn to be a mature Christian. Whether you are baptized as a child or an adult, you are renewing those promises now.

2. "Do you confess Jesus Christ as your Lord and Savior and pledge your allegiance to his kingdom?"

You are asked if you accept Christ's offer of God's forgiveness and assurance of eternal life, and if you follow him as your guide in this life.

3. "Do you receive and profess the Christian faith as contained in the Scriptures of the Old and New Testaments?"

You are asked if you believe that the *Bible* is the Word of God, sufficient for faith and practice of the Christian life, a sure foundation for all things pertaining to salvation. This is the heart of the Protestant reformation and the basis of United Methodist belief.

4. "Do you promise according to the grace given you to live a Christian life and always remain a faithful member of Christ's holy church?"

> You don't have to keep these promises without help. The "grace given you" comes from God himself. You are promising to remain a member of "Christ's holy church," which may some day mean another denomination. You can't predict that. You are acknowledging that you will need the continuing care and support of Christ's people.

5. "Will you be loyal to the United Methodist Church, and uphold it by your prayers, your presence, your gifts, and your service?"

> You are asked to support this church as long as you belong to it in four important ways:
>
> a) By praying for its people and its leaders.
> b) By being here for worship services and other activities when possible.
> c) By giving to the church. Many United Methodists tithe (give 10% of their resources) to the church and to other agencies doing the work of the church. When you become a member, you will receive a pledge card and offering envelopes. In addition, during each year, the church announces offerings for special events and mission endeavors. (Of course, pledging and giving are voluntary.)
> d) By serving it with your time and abilities. Certainly the church needs your help, but you will also find that the more you put into it, the more you will get out of it.

During the new member reception service, you will be given a certificate of church membership to keep.

The Methodists' History

Methodists' roots are in the Church of England. John Wesley founded the Methodist Church, although it was not his intention to do so. He was a clergyman loyal to the Church of England. As a young man, he had carefully followed the teachings and ordinances of his church. He said that he found little satisfaction or assurance in them. He said the turning point in his life came on May 24, 1738, when he realized that only faith in God's mercy through Jesus Christ could lead to joy and peace. After he discovered that for himself, he began to teach it to others.

Wesley's methods differed from those of the Church of England in two essential ways. First, he preached to the poor—the people the affluent church often overlooked. Second, he took care of those who responded to his message by organizing them into societies for Bible study and mutual Christian support.

Wesley and his friends took their teachings to Ireland, then to America. Their methods were especially suited to the American frontier. They organized circuits, and worship services were held whenever a traveling circuit rider encountered a few people to gather around. Wesley encouraged converts to take part in the worship and sacraments of the Church of the England whenever possible. It wasn't until after the American Revolution, when ties to England were forcibly cut, that the Methodist Church formed in America.

The church had two big divisions in the 1800s, one over the issue of lay leadership in the church, and a second over the issue of slavery. The church ended those divisions in 1939. In 1968, the Methodist Church joined with the Evangelical United Brethren Church to form the United Methodist Church. The Evangelical United Brethren had a history similar to that of Methodists, with the exception that they traced their roots to the German Reformed Church rather than to the Church of England.

Much more about the history of the church and of Wesley's ministry is in *The Book of Discipline*, parts I, II, and III. This book contains the history, policies and laws of the United Methodist Church. Despite its title, it provides interesting reading.

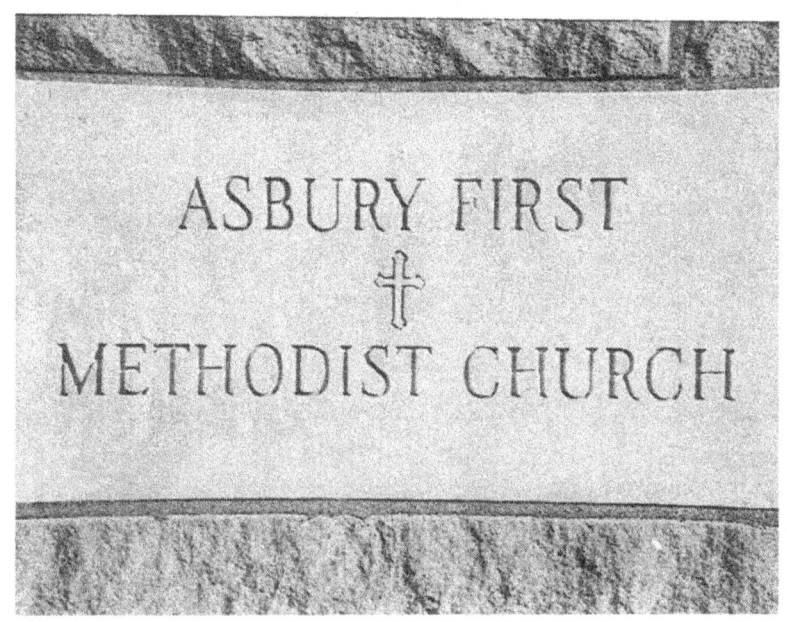

Where Do We Fit In?

Asbury First United Methodist Church is part of:
...The Rochester District. Our campus includes the offices of the Bishop and the Rochester District Superintendent.
...The Western New York Annual Conference.
...The New York West Episcopal Area: all the United Methodist Churches from Western New York.
...The Northeastern Jurisdiction, which includes New York, New England, New Jersey, Pennsylvania, Delaware, Maryland, West Virginia, Puerto Rico, and the District of Columbia.
...The United Methodist Church: five geographical jurisdictions within the United States and a Central Jurisdiction of seven overseas conferences.

DIAGRAM OF THE CHURCH

The church is cruciform in shape (the shape of the cross), the traditional shape of Gothic architecture.

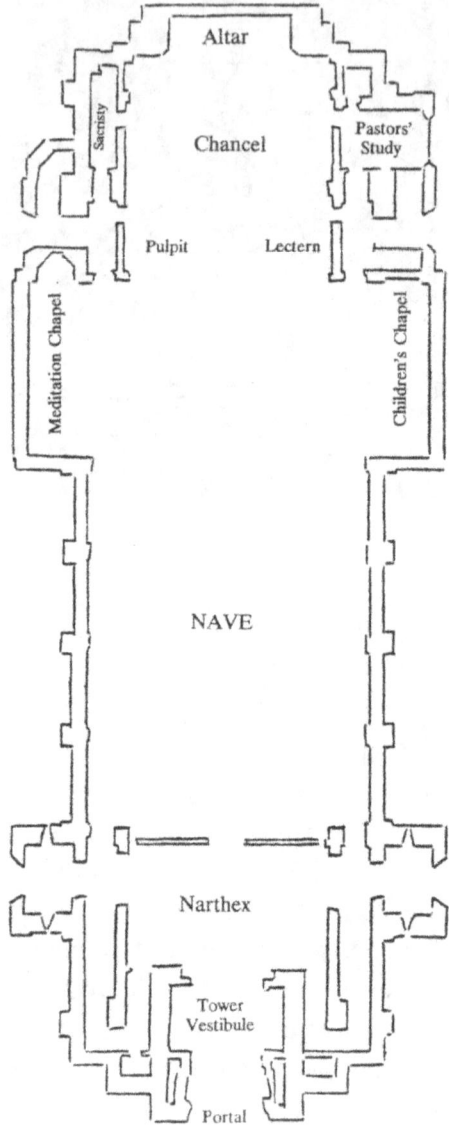

To find our Education Wing, exit the Sanctuary through the door to the right of the altar in front of the church. Turn right, then proceed straight through the wide hallway with doors (Cloister) and into the corridor of our Education Wing. The Childcare rooms for Infants thru 3 year olds are located in this first floor corridor, as shown on the map below.

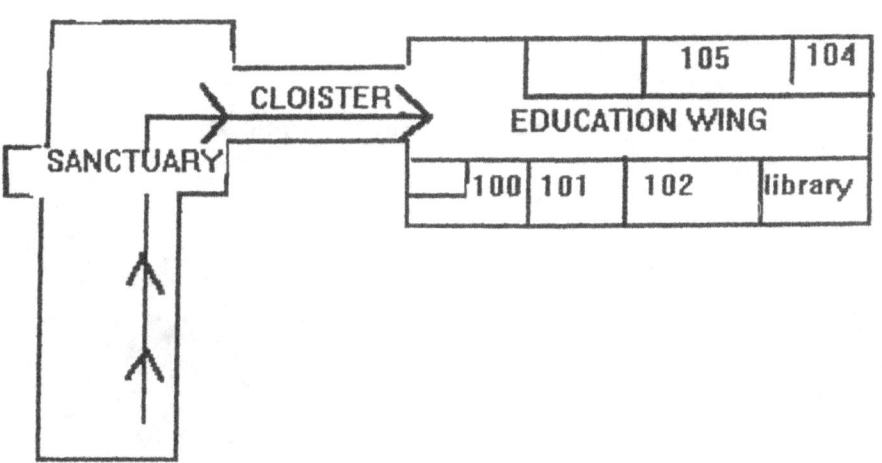

Asbury First under construction, September, 1953

Asbury First, circa 1960

Asbury First: 150 Years

Our somewhat unwieldy name comes about as the result of the union of two churches and five denominations. The First Wesleyan Methodist Episcopal Church of the village of Rochester was formed in 1821. Its first location was on South Avenue, near Broad Street, but it soon moved to Fitzhugh and Main, and later to Fitzhugh and Church Streets. Asbury M.E. Church was formed in 1836 by Methodists who lived on the east side of the river. Its first permanent home was at Main and Clinton, where the Rochester Savings Bank now stands. In 1885 it moved to East Avenue and Anson Place.

Both First and Asbury churches survived hard depressions in the 1840s and 1850s to remain strong influences in the city. They were instrumental in the forming of new churches in the developing areas, and they were served by dedicated lay people and by outstanding ministers of the Genesee Conference. A strong Sunday School was developed early, and has continually been a feature of Asbury, First, and Asbury First churches.

The building housing First Church burned in 1933, and some months later the First and Asbury congregations united. The name change to "United Methodists" arises from the union of three Methodist denominations in 1939, and further union with the Evangelical United Brethren in 1968. The EUB Church was itself a union of churches with Methodist-like theology and organization which had arisen among German-speaking Americans in the 19th century.

The regional formalizing of both the 1939 and 1968 unions took place at Asbury First.

Our present church building was constructed in 1953-55, with the Education Building added in 1961. It is in American Gothic style and its construction owes much to the dedication of Dr. Weldon Crossland, minister for 28 years.

The two mansions completing our campus are historically important. The Wilson Soule House (building 1050, containing our church office and District Superintendent's office) is considered one of the most important 19th-century houses surviving in Rochester. It was built in 1890 in the Richardson style with fine interiors; cost was not considered. George Eastman, founder of Eastman Kodak Company, owned the house for a time in the mid-1890s. Building 1010 (containing the Bishop's office and church meeting rooms) was built around 1907 in a comfortably elegant Tudor style.

Richard Henn, 1981

Building 1050, once home to Eastman Kodak Co. founder, George Eastman, now houses the Asbury First church office, including pastors' offices and meeting rooms, as well as the Rochester District Superintendent's office.

How Do We Run Our Church?

The Charge Conference oversees the organization and program of a United Methodist Church. Our Charge Conference is the link between Asbury First and the general church. The Conference meets each January to review and evaluate our total mission and ministry. This annual business meeting of the church is open to all members.

The Charge Conference oversees the Administrative Cabinet (Ad Cab), its executive agency. Ad Cab speaks for the church on all matters not specifically reserved to the pastors. Ad Cab meets every other month, alternating with meetings of the committees and work areas that report to it. A partial list of committees, work areas, and other groups reporting to Ad Cab is on page 21. All meetings are open and your attendance is encouraged.

For over 25 years, Asbury First has operated a 3-morning-a-week Nursery School for 3- and 4-year-old children. The Nursery School is located on the second floor of the Education Wing.

New Member Worksheet

A. What does it mean to be a Christian?
   1. Believe (see Romans 10)
   2. Belong (see Ephesians 3)
   3. Behave (see 1 Thessalonians 5)

B. What are the four basic books of Methodism?
   1. *The Bible*
   2. *The Hymnal*
   3. *The Book of Discipline*
   4. *The Book of Worship*

C. To what do I commit myself when I join Asbury First?
   1. Prayers
   2. Presence
   3. Gifts
   4. Service

D. In what ways can I serve this church?
   1. By participating in worship. (Possibilities: sanctuary choir, bell choir, lay reader, soloist, accompanist, acolyte, usher, greeter.)
   2. By joining a fellowship group. (Possibilities: Disciple Bible study, United Methodist Men, United Methodist Women circles, youth group, adult Sunday School.)
   3. By serving on a committee. (Possibilities: see next page.)
   4. By helping with the children's education program. (Possibilities: Sunday School teacher, Sunday morning child care—Rocker & Hugger, Vacation Bible School.)
   5. By helping with some of the many volunteer jobs the church needs to have done. (Possibilities: Dining/Caring Center, Storehouse, Monday Morning Crew.)

Members of all ages volunteer at the annual Asbury First Vacation Bible School, held at the church each August.

Beginning on page 23, we ask for information about you. We would like this page turned in at the end of your new member class. We will talk about it and allow time to complete the information during the class.

New members not only make us a bigger church, they also make us a better church. Your ideas and efforts will help us grow. Have you already seen an improvement you think we should make? If so, what is it? How could you help us improve?

COMMITTEES
(provided for in *The Book of Discipline*)

Nominations & Personnel	Memorials
Staff-Parish Relations	Board of Trustees
Altar Guild	Finance
Archives & History	Lay Personnel

PROGRAM AREAS
(carry out work assigned by the Ad Cab)

Christian Education
Membership
Outreach
Music & Worship

OTHER GROUPS reporting to Ad Cab

Church Directions
Communicator
Advisory Council
Stewardship

New members also give us new energy. You can help all of us dare to dream of what our church could be. Do you have a dream for Asbury First? Here's one: To become a congregation of people who are idealistic, irenic, informed, and inviting.

Idealistic: Expecting the best from all of us.

Irenic: Peace-loving; tolerant of individual differences.

Informed: Aware enough of events and trends to avoid prejudice; open to new ideas, new people, new things.

Inviting: Attractive to others looking for a church home to belong to and a church family to love.

Members of the Asbury First family enjoy various opportunities for fellowship, including the Strawberry Festival, Antique Show, Church Picnic, Family Life Retreat, and Summer Fest.

Information About You

Please give us some information about yourself. It will help make our church records accurate and help us to know you better. Please return this page at the end of your new member class, or bring or send it to the church office as soon as possible before New Member Sunday.

1. Name _____
2. Address _____
3. Zip Code _____ 4. Telephone _____
5. Employer and/or school _____
6. What kind of work do you do? _____
_____
7. Your birthday _____
8. Your family: Who else lives in your household? Please include ages of children, if any: _____
_____
9. What drew you to Asbury First? _____
_____
10. Did you belong to a church before you came here? _____
If yes, what church and where? _____
11. Do you want us to request a formal letter of transfer from your former church to Asbury First? _____

12. What information would you like included about yourself on our New Member Fact Sheet?
_____
_____
_____

13. What other organizations, community boards, etc., do you belong to in our area? _____
_____

14. Can you give us the names of other persons who might be interested in a program or service of Asbury First? _____
_____

15. You have read about our church in this book and in the Annual Report and have heard more at the new member class. If you could pick a committee or group to serve on, which one would it be? (see page 21 for a partial listing) _____
_____

16. Do you have a special talent you want to share with us? ____
_____

17. Are there volunteer jobs you are interested in doing? _____
_____

18. Is there something you hope we can do for you or help you with?
_____
_____

www.ingramcontent.com/pod-product-compliance
Lightning Source LLC
Chambersburg PA
CBHW050841230426
43667CB00012B/2089